A
Z
A

Volume
Three

L

E

A

Journal of Korean Literature
& Culture

Korea Institute Harvard University

2010

AZALEA

Journal of Korean Literature & Culture

Volume Three ~ 2010
Publisher: Korea Institute, Harvard University
Editor: David R. McCann
Editor-in-Chief: Young-Jun Lee
Editorial Board: Bruce Fulton, Brother Anthony, Hwang Jong-yŏn,
Kwon Youngmin, Heinz Insu Fenkl
Copy Editor: K.E. Duffin
Design: Wayne de Fremery
Proofreader: Beyond Words Proofreading

AZALEA (ISSN 1939-6120 ISBN 978-0-9795800-4-8) is published yearly
by the Korea Institute, Harvard University, with generous funding by the
International Communication Foundation, Seoul. Translations from the
Korean original were supported by the Korean Literature Translation
Institute.

Subscriptions: $30 (one year); $55 (two years); $80 (three years).
Overseas subscriptions: $45 (one year, air mail only).

Inquiries to: *AZALEA*, Korea Institute, Harvard University, Center for
Government and International Studies, South Building Room S228,
1730 Cambridge Street, Cambridge, MA 02138
Phone: (617) 496-2141   Fax: (617) 496-2141   Email: korea@fas.harvard.edu
Submissions are welcome. Submitted manuscripts and books sent for
review become the property of *AZALEA*.

Printed on acid-free paper, in Seoul, Korea, by Haingraph Co., Ltd.

ISSN 1939-6120
ISBN-13: 978-0-9795800-4-8
ISBN-10: 0-9795800-4-8

CONTENTS

David R. McCann
Editor's Note 5

WRITER IN FOCUS: HAÏLJI

Haïlji
Exerpt from The Statement 9

Haïlji
Exerpt from The Užupis Republic 35

Minsoo Kang and Bruce and Ju-Chan Fulton
Interview with Haïlji 55

FICTION

Pyun Hye-Young
The First Anniversary 97

Han Kang
Exerpt from The Vegetarian 117

Gong Sun Ok
The Cheerful Night Road 171

Yun Young-su
Secret Lover 191

SPECIAL FEATURE: POEMS BY KI HYŎNG-DO

Family on the Brink, 1969; White Night; The Black Leaf in My Mouth;
Sleet; Sounds 1; Blue Paper Covered with Dust; Grass; Flower; The
Wind Leads Me in Your Direction; Put Badly; Fog; Dead Cloud   79

ANOTHER PERSPECTIVE

Peter H. Lee
The Road to Ch'unhyang: A Reading of the *Song
of the Chaste Wife Ch'unhyang*   257

ON CINEMA

Kyung Hyun Kim
Death, Eroticism, and Virtual Nationalism in
the Films of Hong Sangsoo   135

POETRY

Kim Hyesoon
The Horizon; Flu; Starfish; Seoul, Kora; Sand Woman; In the
Oxymoronic World (essay)   241

KOREA FROM THE OUTSIDE

Jean-Marie Gustave Le Clézio
Extreme east, Extreme west (an historico-dream poem); Unjusa,
Autumn Rain   69

Image Index   377
Notes on Contributors   379

Editor's Note

Welcome to the third volume of *Azalea*. Our readers will
find the fine translations of contemporary literary works you have
come to expect in our project, and the artwork as well, in Kim Atta's
resonant photographic compositions.

Three features of the current issue seem especially noteworthy.
After some years, the novelist Haïlji's writing has now come to be
more broadly recognized as part of a world literature that Korean
writing has hopes of engaging. His observations regarding the
initially hostile reception of his work bring an important figure, the
reader, and especially the contemporary Korean literary critic, back
into view as part of the defining matrix in which Korean writing is
situated.

Peter Lee makes the *p'ansori* narrative *Ch'unhyang* an equal
participant in the contemporary world of Korean literature by
reminding us again of the work's performance dimensions, while
showing us that characteristic, performative aspect of all premodern
Korean poetry as song. His point takes on a particular resonance
when we note Haïlji's comments about Korean literary influences
on his work, where he acknowledges the Korean folksong poet Kim
Sowŏl's major impact. And Ch'unhyang's likeness on the covers of
kososŏl (old novels) published early in Korean literature's modern
period, so generously provided by Adan mungo from their 2007
exhibition catalog, animate how Ch'unhyang was performed in the
dime novels of Sowŏl's day. That performance dimension of today's

popular music, TV, and film successes known as the *Korean Wave* phenomenon suggests a route for Korean literature's movement into the world.

A writer who passed away at the age of just twenty-nine, only a few weeks before the publication of his first book of poems in 1989, Ki Hyŏng-do had a voice, view, and secure accomplishment in his poetry that would have surely carried his work to readers outside of Korea. He enjoys great popularity among Korean readers today, and it is a pleasure to have Gabe Sylvian's translations of twelve of Ki's poems in this issue.

My thanks to all the writers, artists, and translators for the work they have entrusted to this, the third issue of *Azalea*.

David R. McCann
September 2009

A

Z

A

Volume
Three

L

E

A

Excerpt from The Statement

by Haïlji

Translated by Minsoo Kang and Susanna Lim

1

Arrested and dragged before the police—never in a million years could I have imagined something like this happening to me. I've lived a quiet life, no big quarrels with anyone. I've never been through an ordeal like this, even during the military dictatorship when so many intellectuals and university students were imprisoned and tortured.

Don't get me wrong. There was a time in my youth when I took part in student demonstrations, and I tasted my share of pepper gas. I also submitted several articles on political and social issues to journals. But I've never experienced horrific persecution like many others did. I was lucky—but then again, nothing I ever did or wrote was that radical.

Don't get excited? How am I supposed to be calm in this situation? You charge me with murder out of the blue and tell me not to get excited? By the way, where the hell am I? Why did you bring me here instead of a police station? Are you even allowed to interrogate me in a place like this? Is this legal?

Does my family know I'm here?

That's that then. Nobody knows where I am or what's happening to me. Though I don't have anybody except for my wife . . . .

In any case, could you please take these handcuffs off? As you know, I'm a professor. I teach philosophy at a university. A national university, no less. You think someone with such a respectable position needs to be restrained because he might, what, run away? I wouldn't run even if I could. If I ran, that would be an acknowledgment of guilt. So rest assured, and please take these things off.

Of course this feels awful, handcuffed for the first time in my life. But I'm not asking you to take them off because they are uncomfortable or because I'm embarrassed to have them on. I can deal with that. I just don't want my wife to see me like this. She's very sensitive, you know, and she might faint from the sight. Besides, she's pregnant.

Yes, I came with my wife. She's probably sleeping like a baby right now, unaware that I've been arrested. Not because she doesn't care. How can she possibly imagine this happening to me? And she must be exhausted. She's on the frail side, you see, and she's worn out from these few days of traveling. She was so excited the night before we left. She could hardly sleep, like a schoolgirl before her first field trip. She'd waited so long for this. So she must be sleeping soundly now.

But in the morning, she'll wake up and find me gone. At first, she'll just think I've gone out for a walk. But then, as time goes by, she'll start to worry.

Finally, she'll timidly go downstairs to the hotel lobby, and the manager will tell her what happened. That when I came down to get some fresh air, I was arrested. She'll be shocked and dazed, but eventually she'll calm herself down and run over to see me, and I don't want her to see me in these cuffs. She might faint from seeing me like this. So please take them off. Please. Not for my sake, but for my wife's.

I am begging you but you are not batting an eye. You people have no heart.

What? I may try to kill myself if you take the cuffs off? Ha ha ha! Now that's the craziest thing I've ever heard. Do I look like the kind of weakling who'd kill himself for no good reason? I have a pregnant wife, for God's sake. . . . So you've put these cuffs on to protect me from myself. How grateful I am to know that.

There's nothing I can do. If you really have to do things this way, fine. I'll do it my way too. If you keep treating me like this, I won't give you a statement. That's the only way I can resist you.

Let me make myself perfectly clear, I will not answer any of your questions.

I refuse to answer.

I refuse to answer.

. . .

. . .

I repeat, I refuse to answer.

. . .

Because I have the right not to be subjected to an interrogation conducted in a mentally and physically abusive manner. So I'm exercising my right to remain silent.

It's no use. You probably have a script all thought out already. One that makes me out to be a murderer. I don't care how you try to set me up. I can simply refuse to cooperate with your unjust interrogation.

Why is it unjust? To start with, you arrested me without a warrant. I'm not a criminal or a fugitive but you arrested me without due process and you put me in handcuffs—now that's a clear violation of my basic rights. That's an abuse of authority. You think you can treat a citizen like this in this day and age? I won't let you get away with it.

Do I know the law well? Well, I can't say that I'm an expert. But one's basic rights are common knowledge.

My coming to this town makes me a fugitive? I don't believe that! I don't know how to respond to such an absurdity. If that's your logic, then people won't travel at all for fear of being charged as fugitives. When did this country suspend the right of free travel? Since when did people need official permission to go anywhere?

So the warrant is going to be issued tomorrow morning. In that case, we can talk then. I'm under no obligation to submit to an interrogation after an illegal arrest without a warrant. Just release me for tonight. I can't leave my wife alone in this unfamiliar place.

You think I might run away or destroy evidence? You people really are pigheaded. I just explained to you that I'm not the type to run. And if you've requested a warrant, that means you already have enough evidence. So it doesn't make sense that you won't release me because I might destroy evidence. And how could I do that when I don't even know what happened? I think I'll go crazy from talking to you like this. Maybe it's best if I don't say anything. At least not until I see a lawyer.

I don't have a lawyer. Why would I have a lawyer when I've never imagined that I could find myself in a situation like this? But now that I'm here, I might need one. Although I think it's unfair for me to incur legal costs when I didn't even commit the crime. But judging by what you are telling me and doing to me, I don't think this is the time to be stingy with money.

You might release me if I cooperate? Tell me, then. What must I do to make myself cooperative in your eyes? Should I just tell you that, yes, I killed someone, and beg for forgiveness? I don't even know who died, when, or how.

2

No, thank you.

I used to smoke. But I quit after my wife became pregnant.

No, thank you.

It's not that I don't like it. I just don't feel like drinking coffee with these cuffs on.

What would people say if they saw me eating or drinking in this situation? They'd say I look like a trapped animal stretching its neck out to eat grass even with a noose tightening around it. And if my wife ever saw me like this, the memory would pain her for the rest of her life. I can't drink your coffee, if only to spare her the humiliation.

One has to eat and drink no matter what others may think? Perhaps that's true. But I can't now. Anyway, could you loosen these cuffs a little? They're starting to hurt my wrists.

That's right.

I teach modern philosophy in the philosophy department of K University.

Of course it's the middle of the semester now. But I got some time off because of overlapping holidays, and it's also student festival season. During the festival professors don't need to be on campus unless they were asked to participate in an event. It's all organized by student volunteers, you see.

Why would I run away? I haven't done anything wrong.

How many times do I have to tell you? I came to this seaside town for an ordinary vacation. Well, actually it's not that ordinary. My wife and I have been planning this for a long time. This is the tenth anniversary of our wedding, you see, and ten years ago on this very night, at the very hotel we are staying in, in the very room, we spent our first night together. So I suppose it's not an ordinary trip since it has special meaning for us. And to think that I've been arrested by the police on this very night.

We haven't been back here in the last ten years. We went abroad soon after we were married, you see. We were away for five years. I was studying to get my doctorate. Even after we returned to Korea five years ago, we couldn't get back here until now. We didn't have a lot of time or money. Then about three years ago we managed to start saving, little by little. So we could eventually take this trip. The overlapping holidays came at the right time, so we decided to go. That's how we finally got here, on this trip that means so much to us, so you understand how flabbergasted I am that you think I'm on the run.

Of course we were excited about this trip. My wife was so thrilled the night before we left, she couldn't sleep. Like a newlywed about to go on her honeymoon. I remember her bustling about late into the night, stuffing our suitcase with a suit, shirt, underwear, pajamas, hat, toiletries, makeup, camera, and a long coat in case it rains, preparing a basket of fruit and a bottle of champagne for our night at the resort. I'd never seen her that excited. And so she ended up dozing during the train ride here.

Why take a train instead of a car? There. That shows how wrong you are to think I'm on the run. A fugitive would have taken a car for convenience, and so he could avoid being seen by too many people.

Anyway, the reason we took the train instead of a car is that we wanted to travel exactly the same way we did ten years ago. We first came here by train, you see.

But one thing I don't understand is how you people found out where we were and came all the way down here. We didn't tell anyone about our trip. Because we wanted to spend an intimate and leisurely time together, just the two of us.

No. I haven't noticed any major change in this place from ten years ago. The long breakwater pointing at the sea, with the lighthouse at its tip, the cherry trees hanging thickly over the road from the train station, the enormous fir standing alone in front of the hotel, the ivy-covered walls, the cedar forest below our window, the sea beyond the forest, the small island floating on the ocean. . . . Not a thing has changed. Even the rose vines that come up to our terrace in full bloom, the bees buzzing over them, and the fragrance of the flowers wafting into the room are exactly the same as ten years ago. Well, there's one difference. Back then there were so many seagulls flying above the town, but that's changed now.

We've never forgotten the seagulls of ten years ago. There were many at the pier, of course, but the sky was filled with them even near the hotel. When you opened the window and looked out, you could see their sheer whiteness floating in the blue or resting on the green grass. My wife loved to gaze at that sight.

I remember how on that night, the shadows of the seagulls undulated on the thin curtain. We lay together in bed, staring at the wavelike movements of the shadows, and we decided to name this place the "City of Seagulls."

But now there are hardly any left. We saw a group of gulls at the pier, but that was nothing compared with back then. Yes, so many seagulls have disappeared, that's something different from ten years ago.

And another thing—last time I was here, I spent the happiest night of my life with my wife, but this time you people ruined everything for me, so, yes, that's another difference. Dragged to this place in handcuffs!

Of course we're a happy couple. No, I think what we have transcends mere happiness. That's because ours is more than an ordinary love.

You want to ridicule me. If you want to say something cynical, go right ahead. I know our feeling for each other is something other people can never understand, and I don't need them to. You know the saying, never boast of your happiness to others.

How can I still be so happy after ten years of married life? Ha! That's a really revealing question. It's true that a lot of people don't find much joy in their marriage. Many fight constantly and end up getting divorced. To tell you the truth, I myself went through a failed marriage. But I don't want to dwell on that time in my life. It was awful. But I'm happy now, and I'll never let go of this happiness.

So how I can still be so happy after ten years? How can I explain it?

Hmm, a philosopher once defined love as a protracted state of exaggerated idealization of another. In other words, when a man says he is in love, he is in a state in which he seeks to prolong for as long as possible an overblown idea of his beloved as the prettiest, sweetest, and kindest of all women, even when she is in reality quite ordinary. When those exaggerated feelings calm down to some extent and he is able to see her more objectively, one can say that his love for her has cooled. From that point of view, I suppose ten years is more than enough for this cooling.

It's possible that my feelings toward my wife are only products of such an idealization. But one thing I'm certain of is that nothing has changed in my feelings for her over the years. No, even after all this time, everything I feel about her seems brand new. I don't care if you believe me, but even now there are times when I look at my wife and I feel my heart race and my breath quicken, like I'm a youth in the throes of first love. And she seems to feel the same way about me. When I hold her, she pants and shivers with such

16

delicate excitement. Like a tiny, exquisite bird. She whispers to me in a dreamy voice as she buries herself into my body, and I am always moved by the fragility of her shoulders. I smother my face in her hair, on her forehead, her nose and her ear, and I inhale her fragrance, which overwhelms me every time. How can I describe her smell, perhaps that of a singular, mysterious flower growing secretly in the ruins of an ancient temple. Anyway, each time I breathe in her scent, I am filled with an ineffable happiness. Just like ten years ago.

My feelings for her go far beyond mere lust. But don't draw any hasty conclusions from that. We enjoy a physical relationship as passionate and intimate as any loving couple, probably more so than is ordinary, since we enjoy it every single night. But what is at the heart of our connection is not mere lust. It's like a clear and wondrous breeze that blows within us, making us one. Ours is not a greedy love, but we never tire of each other.

I don't know about other couples, but for the last ten years she and I have been getting up every morning filled with a sense of having been reborn. When I open my eyes in the morning, I feel a terrific current of happiness flowing from my head to my feet. In that moment, she flashes me a shy smile, her cheeks all flushed, like a newlywed waking up after the wondrous experience of her first night with her husband.

I swear that I would choose a single day with her over ten years of life without her. So leaving her alone and being dragged here on this very night is a real nightmare that I'll never get over. All I want is to go back to her before she wakes up. And be with her as if nothing happened.

How many children do we have? None, except for the one about to be born.

There's no reason to think that's strange. We were in no position to raise a child during the first five years of our marriage when we were living abroad. We were very poor and we both had to work. There was nothing I could do about that, but it pains me whenever I think about all the hardships she had to go through because of me. After we came back, I got the job at the university and our finances improved enough so we could finally afford to have a child. But for some reason my wife couldn't get pregnant for a long time. Then she finally did. She began to experience morning sickness two months ago. And that was when I quit smoking. For the sake of our child and my pregnant wife.

I am forty this year, she is twenty-eight. But she still seems like a sixteen-year-old girl to me.

Yes, that's a bit of an age gap. But so what? That's no problem for us. We get along as well as cousins of the same age.

3

May thirteenth was four days ago. And that was the day before we set off on our trip. So the murder you're talking about happened then.

That morning I went to school to give a lecture. A two-hour lecture, from nine to eleven.

Afterwards, I spent some time talking to students who followed me up to my office. Some come to ask questions they weren't able to during the lecture. Those tend to be the best students.

The students who came that day were . . . oh yes, Kang Minsoo and Yu Hyeonsik. And one more . . . I don't remember who. Anyway, all three are third-year philosophy majors and they asked me about a book I had recently published. They were there for at least an hour. So if you ask them they'll confirm my whereabouts for that time.

After they left? I went to the faculty club for lunch. Probably around noon.

There I met Professor Park Haejin from the Art Department and Professor Lee Sihyeong from English. We ate lunch and drank some beer. The menu that day . . . it was sushi with fried shrimp. You can verify that too. Ask the chef.

The lunch lasted longer than usual. About forty minutes, no, almost an hour. Because we got into a rather serious discussion.

Well, we talked about the "IMF" economic crisis. Professor Park began by criticizing the current state of politics, the former presidents, the *chaebols*, and American foreign policy.

Our master painter Park gets excited very easily, a typical artist. A real hot-blooded fellow. But after listening to him, Professor Lee said, "Master Park, why are you getting so worked up? Perhaps it was all for the better, now that things are going well." To which Park replied, "What do you mean? We have rampant unemployment and people are killing themselves because of financial hardship. You're liable to be cursed for uttering such ignorant nonsense." The atmosphere suddenly became tense. "People kill themselves when the economy is fine too," Professor Lee countered. "Do you remember way back, that one incident when this family couldn't keep up with the rent on their place so they committed suicide by breathing in coal gas, leaving a note that said that they want to live in a heaven where there was no rent to pay? At least now people don't kill themselves because they can't keep up with the rent." Professor Park seemed at a loss for words, so Professor Lee went on with his argument. So it became inevitable that the discussion would be a long one.

Well, maybe you're right. We might have been discussing something altogether different that day. Come to think of it, I'm sure that's not what we talked about. People are saying the IMF crisis is pretty much over, so it's unlikely we would have had such a passionate argument about it then . . . . So, you're right. The topic was what happened on the way to the racetrack.

What do I mean? Just what I said—what happened on the way to the racetrack. If you listen you'll understand what I mean. The argument began with Professor Park's criticism of K. He claimed that K, by not standing up to the doctor who called him up every day to give him injections, was surrendering to the injustice of the world. As I've said, Park is a real hot-blooded fellow, a typical artist.

But after listening to Professor Park, Professor Lee said, "Master Park, why are you getting so worked up? Perhaps it was all for the better, now that things are going well." To which Park replied, "What do you mean? How can you say such a thing when so many people are dying from taking drugs? You're liable to be cursed for uttering such ignorant nonsense." "People killed themselves even before the racetrack existed," Professor Lee countered. "Those who headed east, believing the rumors about the tracks, what did they end up doing? Didn't they kill themselves by slashing their wrists with razors? At least now there aren't people who take their lives in such a horrible way—it's all for the better." Professor Park seemed at a loss for words at that. He could only mutter, as if excusing himself, "That's because of the alder tree at the racetrack." But Lee ignored Park's words and continued his argument. The discussion went on for quite a while.

You don't understand what I'm talking about? But is that so important? Whatever we talked about, what's certain is that there was an argument between Professor Lee and Master Park.

Well then, check it with them.

Why don't I remember a discussion that happened only a few days ago?

Because . . . because I wasn't listening that carefully to what they were saying. Because . . . .

Because just then I suddenly recalled the sound of insects on an autumn evening, when we were living abroad, and my wife's expression on that occasion. No one but the two of us will ever understand the sad and beautiful story of what happened at the racetrack.

To be precise, it was our first autumn living abroad, only five months after our marriage.

At the time we were often so short of money we didn't even have enough to eat. We were in a foreign country with no friend to help us. We spent days wandering in search of menial jobs but our efforts were always in vain. When I considered what my wife was going through because of me, I felt like giving up philosophy and all my ambitions, and just settling down to make a living as a dry cleaner. One night, my wife suggested we go out for a walk, and as we were going out, I noticed she was taking along some plastic bags. I wondered what she was planning as she led me down a moonlit road, to the fence of a nearby house.

A big pear tree loomed, its branches drooping heavily with luscious, ripe pears, some branches stretching over the fence. White pears were scattered on the ground below. She'd been thinking of those pears for our dinner.

But they had all been crushed. They'd fallen on the cement, and had been stepped on by passersby or run over by cars.

"It's okay for us to pick up the ones that dropped over the fence, right? Didn't the Buddha say it was all right to eat fruit that had fallen outside fences? Isn't that right, my teacher?" she asked, looking up at my pained expression. She meant it as a joke, to soften the embarrassment of our poverty.

"But this is . . . ." I could barely reply, before she went on. "Of course they're a bit old. But they still taste good." A moment later she continued with her justifications. "I ate a bit earlier today to see how they were. Just one." She then furtively opened the plastic bags and began to pick up the fallen, damaged pears. At that moment, I heard the chirping of insects that sounded strangely loud in the late autumn evening, as if the buzzing was coming from inside my ears. Then I suddenly realized that my wife had filled her stomach with those pears earlier that day. Imagine that, an eighteen-year-old bride relieving her hunger by gobbling crushed pears beneath a stranger's fence.

As I stood in the moonlight, listening to the loud insects, I finally said to her, "Should we just go back to Korea?" But she remained silent as she continued picking up the pears. Like she was pretending she couldn't hear me. So I asked again, "Should we go back to Korea right now?" At this she straightened and turned to me.

"What are you thinking, my teacher? How humiliating it is to see me picking up pears outside a stranger's fence? You want to give up everything and go back to Korea just because of an insignificant woman like me? What'll you do when you go back? Become a tutor? So you can make enough to build a five-story building in Seocho District and live on the rent?"

I didn't know what to say.

"My teacher, don't you know who you are? You are soon going to be another Heidegger, another Merleau-Ponty. How can a man like you even think of giving up on your studies and going back to Korea, all because of a pint-sized woman like me?" She had me cornered, and I was at a loss for words. I was miffed and grumbled, as if to myself, "But why do you keep calling me teacher? We've been married for five months."

At this my wife burst out laughing. "What else can I call you? My teacher, that's what you are." With those words she went back to picking up crushed pears in the moonlight. When I think of her bent shape, her girlish laughter, the sound of insects buzzing in my ears, I feel this terrific pain in my heart. And it was because I was haunted by those memories that I couldn't participate in that heated argument between Lee and Park, or remember what exactly was said.

I didn't leave them. I didn't take part in the discussion, but I was there until the end of the meal. Yes, I'm quite sure I was present the whole time. Because the discussion between Professor Lee and Master Park finally came to an end when Professor Choi Seongryong, the library supervisor, appeared.

As soon as he came to our table, Professor Choi began to tell us about the monkey labor strike that happened in a mountain village in Gangwon province. This was such a great story that Professor Lee and Master Park forgot all about their argument.

The incident occurred in a mountain village, Professor Choi's hometown in Gangwon province, a region rich in pine-nut trees. But there were not enough laborers to harvest all the nuts. So the villagers pondered this problem and came up with a brilliant idea: get monkeys to pick them. So they bought a pair of monkeys at an exorbitant price, and the story was about the astonishing event that followed.

After lunch I went back to my office and then went home presently after I got a call from my wife.

She rarely calls me at the office. She has a rather conservative side, and thinks it inappropriate to call one's spouse at work unless there's an emergency. Anyway, this is what she said:

"Do you remember, my teacher, that ten years ago today, on May thirteenth, we spent the whole afternoon buying things for our honeymoon?"

She still calls me "teacher," just as she did ten years ago. She was a student of mine back when I taught at her high school.

"Of course I remember! I was just on my way out," I told her, and then I went to meet her, to spend the entire afternoon walking through the city, buying things for the trip.

But why are you asking me all this? What exactly happened on the thirteenth?

4

Kim Sunam? You mean the psychiatrist Kim Sunam? Of course I know him. He's my brother-in-law, my wife's oldest brother. We went to high school together, though he was senior to me. But why are you asking me this? Has something happened to him?

Who told you such a lie? My wife and I see him at least once a month. No, maybe more often than that. To say that we hardly see him is complete nonsense.

It's true, we have become a little distant lately. Last time I saw him was . . . three months . . . no, two months ago. I called him a few days after my wife began to have food cravings. I wanted to let him know that she was pregnant. If my father-in-law were alive, he would have come running, fat belly and all. But he had passed away, so my brother-in-law was the only one left to tell.

I called . . . and he said we should get together for a drink. He loves to drink. So we met, and my wife came along too. She didn't stay long though, because she couldn't stand the smell of all the food at the place. But has something happened to him, something bad?

His hospital is only a ten-minute walk from the university, and twenty minutes from our house. So I guess it's pretty close. I can see how you might think that we're not on good terms because we haven't seen each other for two months despite being in such close proximity. But that's life these days, isn't it? Everyone's so busy they barely have time to see their neighbors.

Of course not! I told you, we went to school together and he's my wife's oldest brother. Why would I resent him? If we'd become a bit distant recently, it's because of my wife's pregnancy. And I've also been busier than usual.

I recently published a book called *Illusion and Reality*. It took up all of my time—completing the initial draft, editing it, checking the index, writing the preface, sending it out to colleagues . . . not that it's the kind of book likely to sell well.

Publishing a book isn't as simple as people think. So obviously I didn't have time to get together with my brother-in-law very often, no matter how close we were.

24

How much can one make from publishing such a book? Ha! Do I need to make a statement about that too? It all depends on the book and the author.

In my case, especially with this book, there's no money in it at all. Even if it's in print for twenty years, I'll probably make enough money to buy a pair of shoes each year. Young people these days prefer wasting their time on the Internet to reading a book like mine.

So why do I still write books? Ha! Well, what can I say? I just do, because that's my life. Well, to be more honest, I write to make my wife happy.

Every time I publish a book she's happier about it than anyone else. If it weren't for her, I wouldn't write nearly as much.

Once when we were abroad, I woke up in the middle of the night to find that she wasn't next to me in bed. I wondered where she'd gone off to at such a late hour, but then thought that she must be in the bathroom and went back to sleep. But when I woke up again after feeling a chill, I was surprised to see my wife slipping back under the covers, her body freezing, with the day dawning outside. She had a blissful smile on her face. And she kept smiling, even though she was hiccupping from the cold. I had never seen a woman look so happy.

As I enfolded her frigid body in my arms I asked, "Where did you go with only your nightgown on?" But she wouldn't answer, and just kept smiling with her nostrils quivering. "What are you so happy about? Your body's so cold." She caressed my cheeks with her small cold hands and said in a rapturous voice, "Oh, it's amazing, my teacher! I feel like I'm in a daze. How can you write so much? And in a foreign language too!"

I finally caught on and said, "So you were in the igloo all night?" That's what we called my study because it was never heated. So while I was sleeping, she was in the igloo, spending the whole night reading my manuscript.

"At first I only meant to read a few chapters. But I couldn't stop. Line after line, I just had to go on. Come here, my teacher, let me hold you," she said and held me very tight, as if she couldn't stand how proud she was of me. And she was hiccupping all the while. "You read the whole manuscript, in that cold room?" I asked with concern. But she kept holding me and caressing my cheeks, brimming with happiness. Imagine my satisfaction at seeing her so happy. But I pretended to be nonchalant. "You're really something, going to that freezing room to investigate me. You should work for the National Security Agency when we go back to Korea."

She broke into laughter. The sound of her girlish merriment made me so happy my eyes filled with tears.

Ever since, when one of my books is about to come out, she works more fervently than I do—organizing the manuscript, editing, meticulously checking the index . . . . Sometimes she falls asleep with a new book held tight in her arms. So how can I stop writing?

What's my latest book about? Are you checking to see if it has political content?

You needn't worry. It's only a dull theoretical work of philosophy.

By the way, could you please turn that light away? It's been pointed at me all this time, so my eyes hurt and I can't concentrate. I can't even see your faces.

I don't need to know what you look like. All I have to do is answer your questions. But even so, if you want an honest statement from me, can't you show me some good will? I need to know what you look like, whether you even exist at all. I'm the only one exposed under this blinding light while you're hidden in the dark. All this stress makes it difficult for me to give you a proper statement.

It's no use. You want to stick to your rules. And you are doing just that by leaving these cuffs on me and having this light on my face.

What's my book about? Why is that important?

If you really want to know, I'll tell you. The new book is, as the title indicates, about the difference between fantasy and reality. Whether it is possible to distinguish between the two, what fantasy is and how it is created, whether what we think of as reality truly exists, and whether we can actually prove the existence of reality etc., etc. Does that help your investigation?

Anyway, I don't think you arrested me and put me in cuffs so we can have a leisurely discussion about my book. And why did you bring up my brother-in-law? What's happened to him? Please tell me exactly what happened.

Murdered? Oh, how . . . how's that possible? It's true? Oh, this is terrible! If my wife finds out . . . . Please don't tell her, I'm begging you. At least for a while. Who would do such a terrible thing? He was never the type to have problems with anyone . . . .

Well, it could have been one of the patients at the hospital. Most of them are crazy. Yes. He himself told me once that a psychiatrist should never trust his patients.

5

Why did I kill him? Are you saying I'm a suspect?

If that's true, then . . . . I see now! So you mistakenly think I'm the murderer. And that's why you arrested me. I feel such a chill. But why do you think I did it?

For the money? Ha! So that's why you asked how much I make from my books. You people are scary. And I was naïve enough to answer all your questions honestly without suspecting a thing.

I'm not rich. But my wife and I don't need much money. We're quite happy the way we are. Besides, we live comfortably enough from my income. So please stop harassing me with your ridiculous implications. I'm so shocked about brother-in-law's murder. This is unbearable.

I can't bear even to listen to such questions. And I don't think I'm under any obligation to answer them either. But if you really think it might help you catch his murderer, then I'll tell you just so you know that I want to cooperate.

Yes, I knew that when my father-in-law passed away a few years ago he must have left behind a great deal of wealth. But I've never been interested in that. I've always been so grateful to him that he let me have his precious only daughter that I've never wanted anything else from him. Besides, I don't know how much he left behind and I don't care. Honestly, it offends me that I have to even tell you these things. So don't you dare ask if I killed my brother-in-law for his money.

How many times do I have to tell you? What kind of twisted world do we live in that you think I could murder my beloved wife's brother just to get my hands on some money? That a respected professor could do such a thing.

You people are really irritating me with your word games. Yes, I've heard of that case where a professor killed his own father for his money. So? What's that supposed to mean? That I must have killed my brother-in-law because I'm also a professor?

Yes, when my wife and I wanted to get married, my future father-in-law and brother-in-law were both against it. But if you think about it, that was perfectly understandable. There's the significant age difference between my wife and me, and also, I wasn't even divorced from my ex-wife at the time, though we had been separated for three years. If I were in my in-laws' shoes I would have been against the marriage too.

28

But their opposition wasn't as absolute as it seemed. You see, they soon realized that it was impossible to separate us. And then they had to realize that far from being a base villain, I was a sincere and promising person.

How exactly did my brother-in-law show his opposition to our marriage? But all this happened ten years ago. Why are events so far in the past so important now?

Actually, he was even more opposed to our union than his father. He refused to acknowledge our relationship until the day we went shopping for our honeymoon trip.

What happened then? But that was ten years ago. Why must I make a statement about things that happened way back then? You already requested an arrest warrant, but since you're asking me about events that occurred so long ago, your case must not be that solid.

If it's for a contextual purpose, then I'll tell you. But I want you to know how difficult and distressing it is for me to talk about this after all this time.

Ten years ago, my brother-in-law called me and said he wanted to see both of us together. We were on our way out to shop for our honeymoon trip, so we decided to stop by his hospital first. But we didn't go through the front door. We took the back way to the director's office, as he instructed us to do. I think he didn't want the hospital staff to see us coming in together as a couple. Even then he was embarrassed by the very sight of the person who wanted to marry his young sister.

How did I feel about that? Do you have to ask? I don't know about my wife, but I was miserable. To take my mind off my anxiety I counted the number of steps as we climbed up the narrow staircase at the back of the hospital. One, two, three, four, five, six, seven, eight . . . twenty-one stairs. At the top was the door that led into the director's office.

How could I remember the date?

I see what you mean. If it was on the same day that my wife and I went downtown to shop for our honeymoon trip, then it must have been May thirteenth. Yes. It was May thirteenth, ten years ago. But, so what ?

When we opened the back door and entered, we were surprised to see my brother-in-law working out with weights. He was lifting huge dumbbells, perhaps ten kilograms each. It seemed like he was doing that purposefully to calm himself down. He continued lifting even after we came in, without so much as looking in our direction. So we just stood in a corner, our heads bowed as if we had done something wrong.

After a long while, he looked at me and spoke in a firm voice. How could I, an educator, do this to a student of mine? If I really loved Yuri, that's my wife's name, I should give her up for her own sake. He went to say a great deal more, attacking my character. I finally fell to my knees and told him that I had committed an unforgivable sin. That I knew I shouldn't love Yuri, that I should give her up for her own sake, but this was no longer something I could do. My feelings for her were no longer under my control. At this point he couldn't hold back his anger and rushed toward me with a dumbbell in one hand. He looked as though he was going to crush my head with it at any moment. My wife let out a piercing scream and rushed over to stand between us.

That's how it was. As brother-in-law stood there huffing, my wife held my head in her arms and cried out, "Oh, my teacher, forgive me! Please forgive me! Because of such an insignificant girl like me . . . you have to go through all this because of a little thing like me . . . ."

And then she turned to her brother and protested. "Even father gave us permission to be together, so why are you doing this?"

At this point I quickly covered her mouth and said, "Please don't talk in such a disrespectful tone to your older brother! You have to understand his position. He's doing this for your sake, because he loves you."

While we were huddled on the floor, holding each other and saying these things, my brother-in-law sat down on the sofa and started smoking. After he had gone through an entire pack, he told us to come close. His expression and voice softened considerably, as if he had a change of mind.

When we approached him, he told us to sit down across from him, which we did. He then unexpectedly pulled out a pair of million-*won* checks and handed them to his sister, saying, "So you're going shopping for the honeymoon trip? Here, use this money too. But don't buy too many useless things. You'll make things difficult for your husband."

My wife, her face wet with tears, looked up, dumbstruck, at her brother. He then turned to me and said, "I'm sorry. I guess I was being too rigid. I was only thinking of the age difference between you and Yuri. I'd lost sight of who you are. You're a genius, the kind that our high school produces maybe once every ten years. My little sister is still immature, so be patient with her and teach her. Be happy together."

When my brother-in-law was saying this I was truly close to tears. He's a little quick-tempered but he can also be a warm person. And he also gets over things quickly. That's what happened ten years ago.

After that, we never once had an argument about anything. He treated me like a brother. When I received my degree and returned home, when I became a professor at the university, and every time I published a book, he was the one who was the happiest and most proud of me. So for the last ten years I have trusted and relied on him as my own older brother.

What's so strange?

Well, I guess it is a little odd that this terrible thing happened to him on May thirteenth exactly ten years after that day. But that's just a coincidence. There's no reason to think there's a connection just because the two incidents happened on the same date.

Similarity? You people are really something. You make me tell you about some minor incident between us, and then you try to find some link between that and something that happened ten years later. So, what's this similarity you're talking about? Was he killed by being hit on the head with a dumbbell, or some such thing?

How did I know that? What, he really was killed by being hit on the head with a dumbbell?

How's that possible? On May thirteenth, in the same place, and by the very same dumbbell he threatened me with? If this is a coincidence, then it's a really terrifying one. But I'm begging you not to tell my wife about this. At least for a while. If she finds out what a horrible end her brother came to, I know she'll faint from the shock. She loved him like a father. Now that she has lost him too, she's a true orphan.

Wait, you aren't considering some ludicrous theory about all this, are you? That I killed him with the dumbbell to avenge myself for what he did to me ten years ago? Any reasonable person would find it laughable if that's your solution to this case.

There's another similarity between the two incidents?

The murderer came into the office through the back door? That's really awful to think about. The criminal sneaking in through that door. But what proof do you have of that?

Oh. If it was left open, then I guess he did that.

But why do you keep trying to draw parallels between this case and what happened ten years ago? You think there was some significance to the criminal using that door?

Well, that's true. There aren't many people who know about the door. So it must have been an employee who is familiar with the interior of the hospital, or someone who is close to my brother-in-law. Also, he usually keeps that door locked, so if the door was open then he must have been waiting for someone. Considering that, the criminal was probably someone close to him.

But what if this is just a simple case of burglary? Because there's a road at the back of the hospital, and the staircase at the back is near that road.

If nothing was stolen, then . . . then I guess it wasn't robbery. But wait, the murder could have been committed by a patient being treated at the hospital. The patients there are mostly crazy and capable of doing such things for no good reason. Ah! Speaking of that, I remember something that might help you. There's a patient there named Choi Taewon, and he's said to be very dangerous. He once broke into the office with a knife in his hand.

Choi Taewon is dead? I guess it couldn't have been him then.

Exerpt from The Užupis Republic

by Haïlji
Translated by Bruce and Ju-Chan Fulton

Y onas the Taxi Driver

When the Asian man appeared at immigration control,
the official, a young woman in an olive-colored uniform, was
startled. It seemed that Asians were not a common sight in this
country.

With an amiable smile the Asian man presented his passport.
As the young woman flipped through it, a concerned expression
came to her face. She spoke briefly into a telephone, a note of
urgency in her voice. Then she turned back to the man.

"Mr. Hal, someone will be with you shortly."

And soon two other officials arrived, border control agents.
Like the young woman they wore olive-colored uniforms; they were
also armed. One of the men was gigantic, six and a half feet tall. The
first thing they did was size up this Asian man named Hal. What
they saw was a clean-shaven, neatly dressed gentleman in his mid-
forties at the most. His expression was calm and thoughtful, his
demeanor refined.

"Your boarding pass, please," said the big agent.

Hal's only response was an uncomprehending look. Granted,
it wasn't easy to understand the big man's accented English, but
who expects to be asked for a boarding pass at the immigration
booth? Besides, the other arriving passengers were going through

immigration without a hitch—why the absurd request only for his boarding pass?

"Boarding pass," said the other agent, also in English, extending his hand. "Boarding pass."

Finally Hal responded, his voice polite but firm. He had presented his boarding pass to the airline agent upon boarding in Amsterdam. Why were they demanding it now? He didn't understand.

The two agents seemed taken aback. Was their command of English so weak that they could not understood Hal?

At this point the young woman stepped in: "You are 'no visa,'" she explained to Hal. "Which means your stay in this country is limited to fifteen days. But before we can admit you, we need proof that you will leave the country within that time. That's why we're asking for your return ticket to Amsterdam."

Hal shrugged. "But I'm not returning to Amsterdam, I'm going somewhere else, and so I didn't purchase a round-trip ticket. You're not saying you're denying me entry because I don't have a round-trip ticket, are you?"

The young woman interpreted for the two agents, who then conferred with each other, their expressions serious, before giving the woman instructions.

The woman turned back to Hal: "When do you plan to leave the country?"

"As soon as I can. By the end of the day if possible."

The woman looked dubious but interpreted for the agents. The two men instructed the woman further.

"And where is your final destination?"

"The Užupis Republic."

When this response was relayed to them, the two agents once again conferred, this time at some length, and then appeared to reach a decision. After one last directive to the woman they left.

The young woman produced a form and asked Hal to sign it, and when this was done she stamped his passport. "We are admitting you for forty-eight hours. If you are unable to exit the country in that time, it's your responsibility to report to the Ministry of Foreign Affairs authorities who deal with foreign nationals; the address is here," said the woman as she returned Hal's passport along with the form.

After thanking her, Hal was proceeding toward the arrival area when she asked him one last question.

"The Užupis Republic?"

"That's right."

"Where is that, anyway?"

Hal looked dubiously at the woman without answering.

After changing money Hal left the terminal with his overcoat draped over his arm. It was snowing and there was a sodden chill to the air. Hal quickly donned the coat. It was stylish and of high quality but looked too lightweight for the severe winters of this country. Evidently Hal didn't realize what winter was like here.

The plaza outside the terminal was nondescript and there wasn't much activity. It reminded Hal of a train station you might find in a small city in the countryside. A file of yellow taxis, a dozen or so, waited for fares, and a short distance off, a blue metro bus sat idling; there were no other vehicles. The plaza had turned into a sheet of ice, and beyond it spread a grove of birches. Hal looked as if he didn't know what to make of it all, as if he had never seen such a small, unprepossessing international airport.

"Where are you going?"

One of the taxi drivers had approached Hal, a man who looked to be in his mid-forties at most but whose hair had already turned white. His English was passable.

"Užupis," said Hal.

"Užupis?" said the taxi driver, as if he had never heard the name before.

"Yes, the Užupis Republic."

"Užupis Republic?" The taxi driver looked even more puzzled.

Hal produced a postcard and offered it to the driver. "Here's the address. I think maybe it's not so far from here. Because the postmark is Vilnius, Lithuania."

The taxi driver put on his reading glasses and inspected the postcard for a while, then approached his fellow drivers, who were huddled nearby, and inquired of them, displaying the postcard. Stamping their feet against the cold, the drivers looked at the postcard and conferred among themselves, occasionally glancing in Hal's direction. Finally, Hal set down his suitcase on the ice-covered plaza. Turning up the collar of his coat and putting on a pair of gloves, he took in his surroundings.

Shrouded by the falling snow and the advancing dusk, the birches at the far end of the plaza seemed to be floating on air. The blue bus took on one last passenger and set off toward the birches—beyond which the city must have been located—and before long it too was floating through the falling snow. The plaza lapsed into desolate silence.

And then a voice cried out: "Yorŭgit'a!"

It was an imploring voice, and it startled Hal. He turned to see a beautiful young blond-haired woman with a doleful expression. Floundering toward her was a large man in his mid-fifties, a farmer by the look of him, clutching to his chest a huge goose. It was he who had called out the soulful "Yorŭgit'a!" which must have been the name of the beautiful young woman. The melodramatic meeting of this graceful young woman and comical-looking farmer was like something out of a play. Impervious to it all, the snow continued to fall.

"Okay, let's go!"

The taxi driver was back, returning Hal's postcard and loading his suitcase into the trunk of the taxi. Hal continued to gaze at the meeting of Yorŭgit'a and the farmer. Whereas the farmer appeared to be overcome with emotion and about to burst into tears, Yorŭgit'a stood where she was, her expression as doleful as before. It was as if she were a princess returning home after a long exile, to be welcomed by a former palace servant whose station had fallen to that of a farmer.

"Please," said the driver, gesturing toward the taxi. After one last look at Yorŭgit'a, Hal climbed in.

The taxi was of ancient vintage and with the weather as cold as it was, the engine did not start up immediately. After it had turned over in vain several times the driver opened his door, planted his left foot on the icy dirt road and managed to push the taxi several yards forward, at which point he released the clutch and the engine finally engaged. Back in went the driver's foot, the door shut, and off they went.

The first image to pass by the window was the sight of the other taxi drivers, large, well-built men stamping their feet to keep them warm, shoulders hunched up against the cold. They gazed vacantly at Hal as the taxi passed them by.

The next image was that of Yorŭgit'a and the farmer. While Yorŭgit'a stood there, still looking doleful, the farmer deposited the goose on the icy ground and hefted her bags. Hal looked back as the image retreated, as if drawn by the intensity of her beauty. He felt as if she might have been looking his way, but he couldn't be sure. Presently she vanished from sight. The taxi continued toward the birches.

As they passed the birches the driver turned on the radio and Hal heard a broadcast in Lithuanian, not a word of which he understood. He wondered if it was the news.

Once past the birches, Hal could see the outlines of the city. Gray buildings occasionally came into view, dismal-looking structures that might have been factories or apartments. He felt no warmth from this scenery, though these buildings too, owing to the fall of snow and night, seemed to be floating in the distance. And yet his expression was buoyant as he gazed out the window, anticipating imminent arrival at his destination.

Some ten minutes later the taxi abruptly slowed and turned onto a through street. There wasn't much traffic and the snow had accumulated on the road, which was flanked by empty snow-covered lots; beyond them were somber, dirty-looking apartment buildings.

Hal watched with an uncomprehending expression as the taxi went in this new direction. And the taxi driver too, so sure of himself when they had left the airport, now wore a different expression. As if he had suddenly lost his way, he looked left and right, examining each sign they passed. The strange thing was, the road itself was not difficult to follow, not the sort of road on which one would get lost.

Finally, on an empty stretch on the outskirts of the city, the driver came to a stop. "Would you please show me that address once more?"

Hal produced the postcard and handed it to the man, who once again put on his glasses to examine it. Then he pocketed the glasses and started cruising slowly along, reading road signs left and right as if expecting that before they went much farther, Hal's destination would appear. Hal wore an expression of disbelief: Did the taxi driver really think he was going to find the Užupis Republic in the outskirts of this dreary city? And all the while the meter was running.

And then the driver stopped again, on the side of the road, set the hand brake, and got out. "I'll be right back." So saying, he set off through the snow across an empty lot toward a run-down apartment building visible in the distance. The man was definitely milking his passenger for all he was worth, thought Hal.

The driver approached three residents who were standing outside the building and spoke to them. Inside the taxi Hal smiled, as if he knew what the driver was up to: *Let's see how much you try to squeeze me for,* he seemed to be thinking. The unintelligible broadcast was still issuing from the radio, the meter still clicking, the fare working its way up. Above the meter was a clock that read 4:47. Hal removed his watch and adjusted the time accordingly. When he coughed suddenly, he realized how damp and chilly it was inside the old taxi. So much for the heater.

40

Just then Hal noticed a large man who appeared to be in his mid-fifties plodding through the snow with a huge grandfather clock balanced across his shoulders. He wore shabby clothing and appeared exhausted, as if he had borne his heavy burden a long distance. It was a curious sight, the man's leaden steps dislodging snow and the clock that rested on his shoulders looking rather like a coffin. Hal watched, fascinated.

The taxi driver was on his way back and he and the man with the clock crossed paths. But neither seemed aware of the other. Each walked on in silence.

"I'm sorry," said the driver once he was back inside. Just as the taxi was pulling away, a second taxi approached from the opposite direction. Hal's driver quickly brought the taxi to a halt again, set the brake, rolled down the window, and beckoned the other driver. The second taxi stopped beside Hal's, down came the driver's side window, and out popped the head of a man who looked to be in his mid-twenties—very young for a taxi driver. The two drivers began a conversation, none of which was intelligible to Hal. Hal's driver produced the postcard Hal had given him and passed it to the other driver, who inspected it for a time and then, looking exasperated, got out of his taxi. Hal's driver got out as well, and the two men continued their conversation, at one point the young man fishing out a cell phone and punching in a number. It seemed as if the conversation would never end. The fare kept climbing. Waiting patiently, Hal suddenly felt drowsy and began to nod off. Shaking his head to dispel the drowsiness, he gave a big yawn. It must have been the jet lag.

"Okay," said Hal's driver when he finally returned to the taxi. The sky was distinctly darker by now.

"All right, you've had your fun, yes?" said Hal, his tone indicating that he had finally lost patience. "The game's over—let's be on our way."

The driver's embarrassment was almost palpable. But he didn't respond; it was almost as if he hadn't understood. Instead he whirled the taxi about and set off in the direction from which they had come. Once again the dreary, dismal scenery passed by outside the window. Hal watched the still unfamiliar sight, with no sign of interest. Night had fallen.

They drove through the darkness for some time. Along the way they had to stop at a railroad crossing to wait for a dark freight train to pass. It seemed as if the train would never end. Hal fell asleep in the back seat.

And then he lurched awake, wondering how far they had come. Outside was a lit-up city street. But with the snow accumulating everywhere, it didn't look much like a city street—it was practically lifeless.

The taxi was turning in a circle in front of an ancient white building. What building was this? Hal asked. City Hall, replied the driver in a gruff tone, perhaps upset that he wouldn't be able to string Hal along any longer.

The taxi left the City Hall plaza, turned down a dark, narrow alley, and crossed a bridge. Along the way Hal noticed a sign— "Airport 6 km." So, an hour to travel six kilometers.

Across the bridge the taxi came to a stop. They seemed to have finally arrived. The driver got out and opened the trunk to retrieve Hal's suitcase. Hal got out as well.

Before him Hal saw a side street faintly lit by a traffic light that couldn't have been more forlorn. Beneath the light the snow continued to accumulate.

"That will be eighty-five *lit'a*," said the driver after he had set down Hal's suitcase. "But let's call it sixty, since I got us a little lost back there."

Hal looked about with a dazed expression.

"Don't get me wrong," said the driver as if he felt the need to explain. "I'm actually a professor. I only do this on the side—that's why I don't know the roads so well."

The part about not knowing the roads was presumably a bald-faced lie, but there seemed to be an element of truth to the claim that he was a professor: not many taxi drivers could be expected to have such a good command of English.

"But this isn't Užupis," said Hal in a restrained voice.

"No, this is the right place—no doubt about it," said the driver with a tone of assurance as he indicated an old three-story building beside the street. On the front of the building a small neon sign reading Hotel Užupis blinked on and off.

Hal clapped a hand to his forehead in dismay. "I said Užupis Republic, not Hotel Užupis!"

The driver was visibly agitated; he seemed to realize he was in a fix.

"Well, no matter," said Hal as he produced a hundred-*lit'a* note from his wallet and offered it to the driver. "It's dark already—I guess it'll be all right if I spend the night at this hotel and head out tomorrow."

At this the driver's expression relaxed. He put a hand in his pocket to find change.

Hal made a dismissive gesture with his hand. "Forget it— consider it a tip—nice job with that little game you played."

At first the driver couldn't believe it. But when the realization set in, he became ecstatic: "Oh, thank you, thank you! You are so generous, sir! A true gentleman, sir!" And then he bowed to Hal.

Hal, though, looked as if he could not have been more dissatisfied.

"I tell you what—if you wish to go to the Užupis Republic, then I will be your guide—I will take you there tomorrow. You see, I have no classes tomorrow morning."

So saying, the driver produced a business card and gave it to Hal.

"My name is Yonas. May I ask yours, sir?

"Hal."

"Aha! Mr. Hal, you are my true friend now." And with that he climbed into his taxi and made his getaway.

Hal remained in the empty street, gazing at his surroundings. The darkness and the impassive accumulation of snow made everything look the same; nothing distinctive caught his eye. Still, Hal continued to stand where he was, looking about vacantly. Finally he hefted his suitcase and opened the door to Hotel Užupis.

The People of Hotel Užupis

Hotel Užupis was an ordinary European inn consisting of a lounge on the ground floor and guest rooms in the two stories above.

The front door opened onto the dimly lit lounge. From it issued a song sung by a voice with an unusual timbre that Hal first thought was a soprano's but then decided definitely was not. Attracted by the singing, Hal glanced around the lounge, curious.

It was full of people, a cloud of cigarette smoke hovering over their heads. Hal hadn't seen many people on the way here from the airport, and appeared taken aback by this sudden encounter with a throng.

At the far end of the lounge was a stage where a bony man was singing, accompanying himself on some sort of medieval European instrument. At the center of the lounge was a space where several couples were dancing slowly to the music.

The peculiar thing was, this place where so many people were gathered was virtually soundless except for the music. And so at first, Hal assumed he had come across some kind of solo recital. But the more he looked, the more he felt that the mood was not right for that—most of the people wore gloomy expressions, gazed vacantly at those who were dancing, and silently sipped their drinks and smoked their cigarettes. After he had looked around the lounge, Hal spotted a vacant table and settled himself there.

No sooner was he seated than the people in his vicinity all turned to gaze at him, seeing his large suitcase, rare Asian features, and the still unmelted snow coating his hair and shoulders. Especially curious were the five men and women drinking at the nearest table. One of them, a woman who looked to be in her early thirties, seemed startled at the sight of him. She had a pale face, huge eyes, and hair so black that it intensified the whiteness of her skin.

A young waiter appeared, and the first thing Hal did was ask if a room was available. Fortunately, one was. Then he ordered a glass of *pálinka*. Not that he was familiar with this beverage. Rather, as he was glancing nervously about the lounge, wondering what to drink, a large man with a dark red beard displayed for Hal a glass containing a bright red liquid, then gave a thumbs-up gesture. Taken with the man's playful expression, his beaming smile, his manner, Hal asked the waiter what the beverage was.

"*Pálinka.*"

"I'll have a glass."

As soon as he had placed the order, the men and women at the next table erupted with laughter, the man with the dark red beard giving the okay sign with thumb and forefinger and nodding in satisfaction. Hal offered the man a slight nod, grinning, thinking that this *pálinka* was simply the local name for wine.

No one at the next table had yet spoken to Hal. They didn't appear open-minded enough to readily begin talking with a foreigner who looked different from themselves. Yet the way they kept stealing glances at him and whispering to each other suggested they were very curious about him. To Hal the one who stood out the most was the startled woman with the pale face and huge eyes. She alone remained silent, smoking her cigarette in a deliberate manner. No doubt she was aware of Hal, her huge eyes coming to rest on him from time to time.

A short time later the waiter arrived with a room key and Hal's *pálinka*. Should he take Hal's suitcase upstairs? he asked. "No," said Hal, his hand clutching the handle of the suitcase as if it contained something valuable. "I can do it." "As you wish," said the waiter. As he turned to leave, Hal detained him with a question.

"How did this hotel ever get its name?"

The waiter merely shrugged, as if he hadn't expected such a query.

Hal tried again: "How long ago was it built?"

The waiter shrugged again. "I don't know anything about it. You'd have to ask the owner."

So saying, the waiter left for the bar, where he began speaking with a heavy-set middle-aged man, gesturing a couple of times toward Hal. The middle-aged man said something to the waiter, stealing glances at Hal as he did so. Hal assumed from this that the heavy-set, middle-aged man was probably the owner. The waiter returned to Hal.

"Why it's called Užupis? And how old it is? He doesn't know either. The ownership has changed several times. But I do know it's been here at least two hundred years. Because Napoleon came through back when he was invading Russia. He housed his cavalry officers here. You can look it up."

One of the women at the adjoining table overheard and started to giggle, as if this were absurd. She appeared to be in her early thirties and wore glasses with angular black rims. And it was perhaps those glasses that made her look formidable and intelligent, like the kind of person who might teach mathematics in a high school. In any event, the way she laughed gave the impression that there was nothing credible in what the waiter had said. Even so, Hal thanked him. "You're welcome," the waiter said with a sheepish grin before scurrying off. As soon as he was gone, the schoolmarmish woman leaned toward Hal and addressed him.

"What he told you is a lie. This hotel wasn't built until after Lithuania became independent. And it was built with money from the Russian mafia, there's no doubt in my mind. When he sees Japanese tourists like you, he likes to cook up extravagant stories."

Hal nodded, as if this made sense. "But I'm not Japanese and I'm not a tourist. I'm on my way to the Užupis Republic, and I'm just on a layover here."

The woman gave Hal a doubtful look. "Where did you say you were going?"

"The Užupis Republic."

At this she burst out cackling is if she could no longer suppress her hysteria. The others at the table stared at her uncomprehendingly, so she offered them an explanation in Lithuanian. And then they too erupted in laughter. The commotion attracted the attention of parties at other tables. Only one person kept a serious expression—the woman with the pale face and huge eyes, smoking her cigarette.

Hal was bewildered—why had he become a laughingstock all of a sudden?

The woman with the black-rimmed glasses now explained to him, "This is Užupis; you're here, at the Užupis Republic." She began to cackle again, while the rest of her group, all except the pale woman with the huge eyes, kept watching Hal to see how he would react, each of them seemingly about to burst into laughter.

Hal shrugged, as if to say he didn't understand why they weren't taking him seriously.

At this point a man with black hair and dark eyes who seemed to be in his late twenties or early thirties joined the gathering. "I hope you'll forgive us if we seem rude. But please don't misunderstand—there's a reason for our laughter."

Maybe it was the dark eyes, but the man seemed to take Hal seriously and he sounded like a sensible person. Also, his English was passable.

"The people of this city call this particular area Užupis—it means 'the other side of the river.' It's supposedly the most run-down area in the city of Vilnius. As a joke, the struggling artists who live here began calling the area the Užupis Republic. They even made a Declaration of Independence and established April Fool's Day as their Independence Day. Every year they celebrate it and by now it's well known throughout Vilnius—the Lithuanian president himself takes part in the festivities. And so we couldn't help laughing when you said you were going to the 'republic.'"

Hal remained silent. Observing the sour expression on his face, the woman in the dark-rimmed glasses began cackling again. Hal waited for her to stop before speaking.

"That's interesting—a fake Užupis Republic. But the place I'm going is not a joke, it's the actual Užupis Republic." With that, Hal produced the postcard from his pocket and displayed it. "This was mailed from the actual Užupis Republic."

The postcard was a black-and-white photograph of a castle from antiquity seemingly rising from a lake. The castle appeared to be built of marble slabs; the workmanship was exquisite and elegant. Flying from a tower was a flag, but of what domain it was impossible to tell. Sprawling in the distance were mountains clad with permanent snowfields, reminiscent of the Alps. The worn corners of the postcard attested to its age.

The man with dark eyes examined the image and finally shrugged, presumably unable to identify the castle.

"That's the castle of the president of the Užupis Republic," Hal pointed out. "It says so there." And indeed, printed in small letters in the corner of the card were the words "President's Castle, Užupis Republic." By now the woman with the black-rimmed glasses, who had been examining the postcard along with the dark-eyed man, was no longer laughing.

The man with dark eyes showed the postcard to his companions, explaining in Lithuanian. The man with the red beard and the bony blond-haired man next to him bent over the postcard and began to inspect it. However, the woman with the huge eyes continued to smoke her cigarette, still looking disinterested.

After staring for quite some time, the man with the red beard finally gave a big shrug, while the bony, blond-haired man looked up and asked, "T'ŭrakke?" The red-bearded man shook his head vigorously. Seeing this, Hal asked the dark-eyed man, who was close beside him, "Where is T'ŭrakke?"

Overhearing this, the red-bearded man slowly wagged his

right index finger in Hal's face, saying, with a heavy accent, "No T'ŭrakke. No T'ŭrakke."

Red Beard's attempt at English drew a hearty laugh from the others at his table.

"There's a castle from the Middle Ages about thirty kilometers from here," the dark-eyed man explained. "It's called T'ŭrakke. But it's not the castle in this photograph. T'ŭrakke is made of red brick, but this one's marble, isn't it? And Lithuania doesn't have any mountains, not like in the photo. And on top of everything else, the flag is different—it's not the Lithuanian flag."

And then it occurred to Hal to turn the postcard over. "You can see the flag better here," he said, indicating the stamp, which showed a bosomy woman from the waist up against the background of the flag, which was still unidentifiable. The woman resembled Yorŭgit'a, from the airport.

The man with the dark eyes examined the stamp, then showed it to his companions. They merely cocked their heads and shrugged—except for Red Beard, who exclaimed in wonder, apparently at the beauty of the woman. This drew a burst of laughter from his companions, who proceeded to chide him.

Finally the man with the dark eyes spoke: "Well, it seems that the Užupis Republic where you're going is different from the Užupis that we know." He didn't appear to be joking.

Hal responded with a concerned expression, like a traveler who has suddenly lost his way.

The man with the dark eyes looked at Hal and said, "Why did you come here anyway? This is Lithuania, not the Užupis Republic."

"Because I've heard that the best way to get to the Užupis Republic is through Vilnius. You take a taxi right across the border and you're there. It's written here on the postcard." Hal indicated the text.

The man with the dark eyes looked closely at the words, then sighed elaborately, seemingly unable to read the unfamiliar writing.

"If you want to take a taxi right across the border, this is the only place," said the woman with the black-rimmed glasses. "So if it's the Užupis Republic you're looking for, this is it." She had a mischievous smile, as if she might burst out cackling again at any moment. But when she saw Hal's furrowed brow, she managed to stifle her laughter.

And with that, the group gathered around the next table stopped talking about Hal for the time being. Sitting there morosely, Hal picked up his glass of *pálinka*. At the next table, the man with the red beard responded by holding his glass high, offering a toast. Hal did likewise, then downed his drink.

He found the *pálinka* stronger than he had expected—powerful in fact. He screwed up his face, drawing another burst of laughter from the adjoining table.

The man with the red beard extended a hand, his face showing his acceptance of Hal. "My name is Rowenas—what is yours?"

Hal told him, and shook hands.

"Hal! Welcome to Lithuania!" said the man.

And then the woman with the black-rimmed glasses, her expression still mischievous, extended her hand as well. "My name is Aisŭtte." And then in English: "Welcome to the Republic of Užupis!"

Hal shook her hand. And then the man with the dark eyes introduced himself as Albidas, and the bony man with the blond hair, who was sitting next to red-bearded Rowenas, introduced himself as Marius. Finally, the woman with the pale face and huge eyes who seemed to be in her late twenties or early thirties, spoke one word—her name, Vilma.

As Hal was shaking hands with each in turn, dark-eyed Albidas suggested he join them. Hal readily agreed, and transferring his suitcase and empty glass, seated himself at their table.

"Where are you from?" said Aisŭtte, who sitting next to him, once he was settled.

"I'm from Han," said Hal, drawing looks of surprise from everyone.

"Hun," murmured bony Marius. "Wow—that's a long way from here."

"Hun," said red-bearded Rowenas. "That's quite a country!" It seemed that in Lithuania, Han was pronounced "Hun."

"Pop'a Tchiang," murmured Aisŭtte. It sounded as if she was referring to the world-famous Han actor Chang Pop'a. In addition to this actor they carried on among themselves about this thing and that, the conversation seeming to be about how large and amazing a country Han was.

"But I'm more fond of Užupis," Hal interjected.

"Why exactly are you going there?" dark-eyed Albidas asked.

"Because I was born there. I'm an Užupis citizen," said Hal. After saying that, he took from his pocket an old black-and-white photo. In it was a middle-aged man in uniform, sitting stiff and immovable, a medal pinned to his chest. Next to him sat a woman whose clothing bespoke refinement. Standing before the man and woman were a boy of six or seven and a girl of five or six. And behind the middle-aged man and the woman was a man in his thirties, tall and with a stylish mustache, striking a pose for the camera. Judging from the attire of the personages and the elegant background, they appeared to be the family of a high-ranking official at the end of the nineteenth century.

"That gentleman is my father," said Hal. "He was the Užupis Republic ambassador to Han. Of course that was a long time ago. And while he was posted in Han, Užupis, my fatherland, was forcibly occupied by the surrounding countries. My father couldn't return there and had to live out his life in Han as an exile. But now Užupis, my fatherland, is independent, and so I am going back there."

By now even Aisŭtte of the black-rimmed glasses had grown serious. "So there really is an Užupis Republic and we didn't know about it?"

Red-bearded Rowenas picked up on her question: "It's true that many countries have become independent recently. Our very own Lithuania, for instance. So maybe there really is a country named Užupis that has become independent."

Hal then proceeded to identify the remaining individuals in the photo, pointing out each in turn: "This lady is my mother, this is my sister, and this is me."

"That cute little boy is you?" said Aisŭtte in wonder, glancing back and forth between Hal and the boy in the photo.

"And this gentleman is my uncle," Hal continued. "He's a poet. He may still be alive, I'm not sure . . . . The photo was taken in Užupis. And afterward the four of us, everyone except my uncle, left for faraway Han."

The man with the dark eyes interpreted this for Rowenas and Marius, whose English was limited.

Rowenas, hearing this, muttered, "Vladimir Shatenovsky can tell us about this."

Albidas nodded, as if this made sense. "That's right! Problems like this, Vladimir Shatenovsky is the only one to ask."

"Ah yes," said Hal. "Now that I think about it, I seem to remember my father mentioning a man by that name. Was that the playwright?" But the next moment he cocked his head skeptically. Maybe the man wasn't a playwright after all. Quickly he corrected himself. "No, he wasn't a playwright. I think he was supposed to be the conductor of the Užupis National Symphony Orchestra."

This time it was Albidas who cocked his head skeptically. No, he probably wasn't the conductor either.

"Well, if he isn't a playwright and if he isn't the conductor," said Hal, "then maybe he's a different person but with the same name. If he's the Shatenovsky that my father mentioned, then I think he had a limp. He had polio as a child."

"That's right!" exclaimed Albidas. "Vladimir had a limp. Whether from polio I don't know. So you know him too. He's a great scholar. I believe there's not a person in Lithuania who doesn't know who he is. If you ask him he'll know. He'll know if there is in fact an Užupis Republic, and if so, where."

While Hal and Albidas were having this conversation, red-bearded Rowenas, sitting somewhere beyond them, faltered in his clumsy English, "Yes, Vladimir knows everything except for one thing—women."

This elicited a burst of laughter from the others. Hal joined in, even though he did not know why they were laughing. In the midst of it all Vilma uttered not a word, and wore a worried expression.

"You should go see Vladimir," Aisŭtte told Hal. Her expression and tone were sufficiently sincere, unlike a short time before.

"But how can I? I'm a foreigner."

Bony Marius responded in Lithuanian. Aisŭtte interpreted for Hal: "He says Vladimir is going to a party tonight at Egus's; you can meet him there."

Albidas chimed in: "We're going there too—that's why we gathered here. You can join us if you want. And then you can meet Vladimir Shatenovsky."

"But how far is it?" said Hal with a worried expression.

"Very close," broke in red-bearded Rowenas with his limited English. "Very close. Only a five-minute walk."

"But I wasn't invited," said Hal, his expression and speech hesitant.

"No problem," said Aisŭtte and Rowenas simultaneously in English. "No problem."

All of a sudden the music changed into something loud and cheerful—dance music. Apparently the weepy solo on the medieval instrument had come to an end. People flocked to the center of the lounge to dance.

Just then the door to the lounge opened and half a dozen men and women entered, swaying to the music. It must have still been snowing, for their heads were covered with white.

The newcomers swarmed toward Albidas and his party, and when they arrived, each made a show of shaking hands and saying hello. Everyone seemed to know everyone else.

Among the new party the most outgoing was a large man with glasses who seemed to be in his late twenties. Extending a huge hand to Hal, he introduced himself enthusiastically as Andrei.

Hal accepted the offered hand. "My name is Hal."

Because of the music the other man seemed not to have understood. Drawing close to Andrei, Albidas practically shouted in his ear, apparently repeating Hal's greeting.

"Oh! Welcome to Lithuania, Hal!" shouted large Andrei as he shook Hal's hand vigorously. Then, producing a flask, he filled Hal's shot glass, now empty of *pálinka*, raised the flask high, and cried out, "*Kampai!*"

Surrounded by unfamiliar people, a puzzled expression on his face, Hal responded with a "*Kampai!*" and drained his drink.

"Good!" shouted Andrei in English as he gave Hal a pat on the back. "Good!"

Albidas again drew close to Andrei and spoke loudly into his ear. Andrei nodded repeatedly and, when Albidas was done, shouted to Hal, "*Amigo!* Let's go, my friend from Hun, we're off to Egus's."

"Now?" said Hal, still puzzled.

"Sure!" cried Andrei. "We're going to have a wild night." And then, addressing the others in English, "Let's go!"

And with that, Albidas and his party rose. Hal did likewise. Then, picking up his suitcase, he followed the others outside.

Minsoo Kang[1] and Bruce and Ju-Chan Fulton

Minsoo Kang: Modern Korean fiction has been dominated by social realism. Even in recent decades there has been a great deal of resistance to the postmodern and experimental narratives associated in Korea with Western culture. This, despite the fact that many of the best and most celebrated postmodern works came out of areas other than Europe and North America: Latin America (Gabriel García Márquez), South Asia (Salman Rushdie), the Middle East (Orhan Parmuk), and Africa (Ben Okri). Yet your works have been consistently experimental and surrealistic, even when you deal directly with contemporary social issues, especially in your celebrated and controversial novel *To the Racetrack* (Kyŏngmajang kanŭn kil). What is your general assessment of the state of contemporary Korean fiction and your place within it?

Haïlji: I am a Korean writer but I have no special interest in contemporary Korean writing trends. I also do not spend much time thinking about my position in Korean literature as a whole. I am indifferent to such issues because, first of all, they are of no assistance in my own literary pursuits, and second, my focus is on world literature, and how I will be received by its readers.

---

1. The author's answers to Minsoo Kang's questions were co-translated with Susanna Lim.

Yet if I had to assess the state of contemporary Korean literature I would say that even during the 1980s, Korean fiction was firmly stuck in the social realist mode and there was strong opposition to works that employed innovative literary techniques. You can see the same situation in modern Chinese literature as well.

I find it rather ironic that the literature of a country as thoroughly capitalistic as Korea should be so dominated by social realism. But I think there is an understandable reason for this development. During the 70s and 80s Korea was under a series of military dictatorships, and writers of the period harbored a deep resistance toward the inhumane and rampant progress of capitalism under those regimes. One can see their social realism as a direct product of that resistance.

Unfortunately this led to a closed-mindedness that rejects the value of any new form of literary experimentation. As a result, in literary culture there is a general feeling of antipathy or suspicion toward even exploring the earnest debates in the West on the nature of postmodernism and new forms of literary narratives.

In the early 1990s I found such intolerance in Korean literary culture rather tragic. I felt that writers and artists were neglecting their duty by allowing literature and art to be sacrificed for the sake of politics. For this reason, in 1990 I attempted to create a new literary form with my first novel, *To the Racetrack*. In a sense one might say that my position in contemporary Korean literature is that of a "traitor."

MK: What is your assessment of the sharp criticism you have received for your *Racetrack* novels, especially from advocates of social realism? And what is your general response?

Haïlji: It's true that when I published my *Racetrack* series in the 1990s, I was attacked mercilessly by Korean literary critics. When I tried to understand the source of their strong objections, it didn't take long for me to realize that my writings were regarded as almost heretical given the politically unified front Korean writers were trying to present at the time. And I also became convinced that such a perspective was wrong for literature. As a result I became involved in a vociferous argument with the critics about the nature of high literature. But that argument turned into a ridiculous farce. One critic, in taking on my literary works, resorted to attacking my personal life to threaten me in some way.

When I think about it now, I find the critics of that time quite pitiful. One can regard them as victims of the terrible political situation in Korea during the 70s and 80s who lost sight of the true meaning of literature and art.

MK: During your graduate studies in France you wrote about the works of Alain Robbe-Grillet. How have his experimental writings and perhaps other examples of the *nouveau roman* influenced your own work?

Haïlji: When I was young I had the opportunity to study modern French literature and surrealist literature. From the *nouveau roman* I learned the aesthetic value of literary discipline. I was extremely impressed by the thoroughly disciplined manner, sometimes bordering on the obsessive, with which the *nouveaux romanciers* constructed their works. And I learned about the unfettered imagination from surrealist poets.

But I do not regard the French *nouveau roman* as the main inspiration for my works. I was of course greatly influenced by Shakespeare, Tolstoy, Kafka, García Márquez, and among Korean writers by Kim Tongin, Kim Yujŏng, and Kim Sowŏl. And the poets of the Tang dynasty of China also had a great impact on me. From their works I learned not only about literary technique but also about humanity's inherent sense of nostalgia.

MK: How did you arrive at the idea of writing your novel *The Statement* (Chinsul), in the form of a single character's monologue? How did you decide to use the device of an "unreliable narrator" and create a psychological novel in the form of a murder mystery?

Haïlji: I got the idea for writing *The Statement* as a long monologue from the "life laments" of mothers and grandmothers in traditional Korean culture. Listening to these endless laments you learn a great deal about the essential joys and pains of living, as well the profound despair that comes with deep insight into the nature of life itself. And the narratives unfolded by these women are sometimes quite *unreliable*. While the *Odyssey* may be read as a *reliable* narrative of a hero on his way to victory, *The Statement* is an *unreliable* account by a pitiful man on his way to defeat.

For a long time I have been fascinated by the structure of Ancient Greek tragedies. If *The Statement* can be described as a psychological novel in the form of a murder mystery, a major influence would be *Oedipus Rex*.

MK: What is the role of Buddhism and Buddhist ideas in *The Statement*? Could it be characterized as a Buddhist novel?

Haïlji: I do not think *The Statement* can be categorized as a Buddhist novel, but I cannot deny that it is greatly informed by Buddhist ideas. It was, after all, written at a mountain temple.

But beyond that, what is Buddhist about this story is the spirit of concerned tolerance with which it observes human relationships. Also, notions derived from the philosophy of Korean high priests— the *Constancy of the Cycle of Life and Death* and the *Spiritual Basis of All Things*—are present in the story as well.

MK: What Korean and Western fiction writers do you most admire and why?

Haïlji: One of my favorite Korean writers is Kim Yujŏng, who succeeds in describing the tragedy of life in a witty and humorous way. Also Kim Sowŏl, who brings us a distinctively Korean brand of the lyrical.

Among international writers, there is Kafka, because he describes the agony of existence with unparalleled precision. And I have been greatly moved by the works of García Márquez, because of his unbounded imagination and deep insight into life.

MK: What can be done to make modern Korean fiction better known to the rest of the world?

Haïlji: I guess a good start would be to translate as many works as possible for a larger readership. But beyond that I think the most important and urgent thing is for many Korean writers to write great works that can move all readers.

Bruce and Ju-Chan Fulton: Judging from the "Author's Note" at the end of your novel *From the Crossroads to the Racetrack*, it seems that the literary establishment (*mundan*) in Korea tends to be very conservative. Has the *mundan* stifled your creativity as a writer? Has it made you feel isolated?

Haïlji: The answer seems simple enough. It could be that my works are valuable only to the extent that they're acknowledged by the *mundan*, or it could be that Korean critics and the *mundan* in general haven't been able to understand my works. I'm not sure which of these possibilities is correct. And I don't really want to know. Instead I'll just continue to do my part as a writer. You ask if it's a lonely road. Well, it's manageable.

BF & JCF: Your published fiction consists entirely of novels (*changp'yŏn sosŏl*). It seems that the majority of established fiction writers begin by publishing short fiction (*tanp'yŏn sosŏl*). Why do you prefer to write novels rather than short fiction?

Haïlji: In Korea there is no distinction between the novel and short fiction; both are referred to as *sosŏl*. People who write novels and people who write short fiction are called *novelists* (*sosŏlga*). The majority of creative writers in Korea are acknowledged as fiction writers by the critics for the short fiction they publish in newspapers or literary journals; short fiction tends to draw critical attention. You can think of this as coming not so much from Korean tradition—strictly speaking there was no such thing as short fiction in premodern Korean literature—but from what we were taught during the colonial period.

In Korea and Japan the novel (*changp'yŏn sosŏl*) is considered a "long story," and a shorter work of fiction (*tanp'yŏn sosŏl*) a "short story." But I don't think these genres should be defined simply in terms of length; instead they are distinguished by their structure. For example, I don't think of Joyce's *Ulysses* or Kafka's *The Castle* as "long stories"; instead they simply have a distinctive literary form because they cannot take fewer pages. I wonder if the tendency in Korea and Japan to think of the novel as a "long story" preceded the birth of the genre of *sosŏl*—that it goes back to the oral recounting of remembered stories. *The Tale of Genji*, from before the advent of literary fiction, is indeed this kind of "long story."

In any event, I believe it's because of this tendency to think of the novel as a "long story" that the novel is not that well developed in either Japan or Korea. And it's because I want to write something that is neither a "long story" nor a "short story" that so far I have written only novels.

BF & JCF: Memory seems to be a very important issue in contemporary Korea, because certain parts of post-1945 Korean history (such as the Communist uprisings in South Korea between 1948 and 1950) and certain authors (for example, the *wŏlbuk* writers) were removed for decades from official history, and therefore from the collective memory of Koreans. Is this why memory seems to play such an important part in *The Užupis Republic* (*Užupis konghwaguk*)?

Haïlji: It's a fact that many Korean writers tend to use events from post-Liberation Korean history as the basis of their works. And in doing so it seems that they feel it necessary to take a political or moral stance. Frankly I don't find this kind of literature all that desirable. And so you could say that memory in *The Užupis Republic* bears no relation to the political or moral issues that engage these writers.

To be sure, the characters in my works have memories of certain political events. But for readers, the political events embedded in those memories have no reality. In *The Užupis Republic* the important thing about memory is that it distinguishes one character from another, and that's because it's bound up with each character's fate. Consider: if I'm different from you, doesn't that mean I have a different store of memories?

BF & JCF: In your opinion, why has Korean literature fallen behind Korean film and many other aspects of Korean culture in gaining recognition abroad?

Haïlji: It's true that Korean literature is not that well known around the world, compared with Korean film, music, dance, art, and so forth—you might even say it lags behind those areas. There seem to be several reasons for this.

The most important reason is that the medium of literature is language, and so the only way for readers outside Korea to approach Korean literature is through translation, and as you are most likely aware, translation involves considerable difficulty.

But the difficulty of introducing Korean literature abroad isn't limited just to the constraints imposed by language. Even if Korean writers are exposed to new currents from overseas, many difficulties remain. For one thing, only a few Korean writers can read the works of authors from abroad in the original language.

But I think we can't continue to use language as an excuse forever. Much of the responsibility for the fact that Korean literature lags behind other areas lies with the literati themselves. As far as their responsibilities are concerned, the first is not to be complacent in seeking new techniques, not to be content to repeat the same form of writing. Otherwise, readers also become complacent and vulnerable to losing the capacity to comprehend works written in new forms. A second factor is that the literati have become this collective authority called the *mundan* that unapologetically wields a dictatorial influence over new writers seeking new literary forms, and it is precisely this influence that has thrown up obstacles to the development of Korean literature.

I have no desire to indict Korean authors, though. My more immediate priority is writing my own works.

BF & JCF: What meaning does *The Užupis Republic* have for you?

Haïlji: I realize my answer makes no sense, but for me the Užupis Republic means the title of my tenth novel.

BF & JCF: *The Užupis Republic* is very different in terms of its demands on the reader and the way in which its message is conveyed—what kind of reader are you aiming for?

Haïlji: When *To the Racetrack* was first published almost twenty years ago, many readers found it difficult. And that's perfectly understandable—its form was utterly unfamiliar in the context of the Korean literature of that time. Happily that form has now secured a place among the Korean literary classics. By the same token, whereas I found it awfully difficult to get a feel for Kawabata Yasunari's *Snow Country* when I first read it forty years ago, today I think I can say I consider it a work of beauty. And I believe that someday many readers will come to love *The Užupis Republic*.

BF & JCF: In *The Užupis Republic* there are several scenes in which a character carries a grandfather clock on his back, and a scene in which a Colonial-period poet wears a watch on his left wrist. Can you help us understand what we're supposed to see by this?

Haïlji: Authors always get themselves into a fix if they try to explain matters like this in detail. I'm hoping that readers can answer these questions themselves through their imagination and affective response to the work. I think I can say that readers have to use these faculties in reading my work, and this is one difference between my works and those of other Korean writers.

BF & JCF: We understand you've published some poetry. Poetry and poetic elements appear throughout *The Užupis Republic*, but we can see in this novel people who are ignorant of poetry, people whose memories have been lost to them, and people who speak English well but not as their first language—all of them have lost their language to some extent. What are your thoughts on that? And second, what are some of the difficulties that poets face when they write fiction?

Haïlji: First of all, I'm not a poet, so I can't answer the second question. The first time I wrote poetry was in 1993 in the United States. But when I was invited to participate in the International Writing Program at the University of Iowa that year, it was not as a poet but as a fiction writer who had already published five novels. At the time, though, I couldn't really get by in English, so I took up writing poetry as a way to pick up the language as well as kill time. These poems were published in the U.S, but only because Kerry Keys, an American poet, discovered them.

I wrote my French poems when I spent a year in Strasbourg in 2002 and decided to write in French so I wouldn't forget all the French I had previously learned. And that's the only reason I have a volume of French-language poetry; it was published the following year in Paris.

I don't know either Russian or Persian, but if I were to spend any length of time in Russia or Iran, there's a good possibility that I'd end up writing poetry in Russian or Persian.

Interview
with
Haïlji

Here you have my second novel, *From the Crossroads to the Racetrack*. Six months earlier, with the publication of my first novel, *To the Racetrack*, I entered the so-called literary world. No sooner had I set foot on those grounds than I drew fierce attacks from certain critics. One individual, having attacked the novel, didn't hesitate to follow up with a downright personal attack . . . .

Listening to those who attacked *To the Racetrack*, I came to realize that they were criticizing this work because they felt I wasn't being truthful about my feelings toward others, but also because I wasn't sensitive enough to conventional, customary values. Their argument, in a word, was that I was guilty. Characters in a novel, especially intellectuals, are supposed to act in a certain way. But my characters didn't. Therefore my novel and I were found guilty. At first I was perplexed by these arguments. Only later did I realize that it was unavoidable, psychologically and situationally, that the critics would develop such arguments.

The first thing these critics talked about was morals, but the morals they preached were beyond my grasp. According to the critics, an intellectual should not have sexual desires; should not be employed, no matter how poverty-stricken or starving; should not complain about having to put up at seedy inns; should not express anger openly; should never seek a divorce; should not make insulting remarks about Korea or Koreans; and should not think about the contradictions that exist in Korea . . . .

. . . Reading what these critics said about my work, I had to conclude that the precepts they spoke of were on the same level as what you might find in an elementary school primer, precepts that the critics themselves didn't even follow. Of course I understand the cultural and educational background that led these critics to preach elementary school precepts. Even so, it came as a shock to me that they hadn't advanced beyond that level.

. . . I do not endow the characters of my novels with moral absolutes. I have that to thank for the fierce attack I came under from several righteous critics, who like to refer to themselves in the plural, *uri*. Why did I allow myself to be attacked this way in the first place? The answer is simple: in this day and age you cannot discuss the human condition in terms of moral absolutes. When I see fictional characters endowed with these absolutes, they strike me as being ghosts of the legendary Good Brother and Bad Brother, Hŭngbu and Nolbu . . . .

Let's be honest: The reason certain critics took such offense at *To the Racetrack* is clearly the amorality of the characters. I'm sure there are still critics who believe my works are amoral. Granting this, we could categorize such critics as follows: first, those for whom literary conventions are so narrow that their understanding of human beings is simplistic—they are either black or white; second, those who still don't understand my works; third, those who are forever under the illusion that they are capable of making absolute moral distinctions, which is characteristic of those educated for any length of time in a dictatorial regime. If none of these categories applies, then I can only conclude that those who took offense from my novel simply lack intelligence. By now, no critic with any common sense should be saying that my works are amoral.

. . . What is the issue, then? I'm convinced that the real reason this group of critics can't address my work on its own merits is because they have a peculiar psychological reaction to it. They judge me, in other words, because my work makes them feel insecure and uncomfortable. That is the real issue.

. . . I have realized that the more these critics stoop to uncivil discourse, the more you'll see them indulging in the curious phenomenon of relying on the words *our* and *Korean* in their criticism; I realize that for this group of critics, *our* and *Korean* form a singular smoke screen behind which they can hide. They insult others, while uttering *our* and *Korean* to protect themselves. Armed with these words, they can always feel complacent while regarding others as guilty. Sure, this may be the only option for a person who wishes to make a living as a critic, but what must it feel like, this pathetic and oh-so-feeble logic? What these critics must remember is that their constant use of *our* and *Korean* prostitutes those very words, and in the end serves no other purpose than to reveal their own inner selves. The deeper a society's morality complex, the more obsessed it is with "noble" precepts, and by the same token, the more psychologically disturbed people are, the more they tend to crow about the culture or group to which they belong.

. . . Why are certain intellectuals so insecure, so psychologically weak? Why do they consider *To the Racetrack* a foreign import, merchandise from abroad? Why do they insist that it isn't even fiction? What are they so attached to? What do they see in my novel that makes them so anxious? Why do they have no confidence in themselves?

. . . Has there ever been a time in our history that has left the intellectual in such a wretched state? As a particularly acute critic has pointed out, *To the Racetrack* is a gloomy portrait of these very intellectuals. And he is right. Perhaps that is why certain intellectuals are so exasperated by my works.

. . . In times past, you could become an intellectual by preaching the same old textbook precepts—but not today. Today there is only one willing audience for that sort of gibberish, and that is unmarried women in their early to mid-twenties. Intellectuals will need a broader audience than this if they are to occupy a preeminent position in our society. In *To the Racetrack* I have tried to present one final opportunity, one last hope for the intellectuals.

Author's
Note:
Haïlji

Two Poems by Jean-Marie Gustave Le Clézio

Translated by K.E. Duffin

Korea
from the
Outside

EXTREME EAST, EXTREME WEST
(AN HISTORICO-DREAM POEM)

At an altitude of 12,000 meters
at 870 miles an hour
with a headwind of 40 km/h
in four hours' time
I pass over the ice bridge,
the white lakes, the forests
the tundra
there
where they crossed
for thousands of years
around twenty-six million years ago
(during the Würm glaciation)
men
women
small children
old women, old men
who discovered the new world

In spring

when the buttercups were blooming

and when the shrubs were filling with berries

they would resume their trek in the direction of the rising sun

Each morning, folding sorghum stalks

securing provisions of smoked beef in baskets of dry leaves,

carrying the eternal ember enclosed in its nest of willow

and flints strapped to the backs of old men

Infants were whimpering in their cradles of reindeer skin

Mist was stretching its cottony expanses through the valleys

A cold wind was blowing across the grasslands

Water was streaming over mossy rocks

Dogs were yapping, eager to greet the dawn

or grieving one of their own torn apart by wolves in the night

Women, women

armed with lances and atlatl, with axes,

running through forests of quaking aspen

all the way to the deer bedded down on the riverbank awaiting

death

Men armed with spears chasing the bear

and the stag Elaphus with antlers in the shape of a fan

In the evening, they would find a clearing, a hill

they would sleep huddled together under their tents sewn with

sinews

Perhaps they would sing

A grandmother would tell the children stories so they would sleep

A woman would dance, turning, her long robe shaped like a hut,

her hair plaited with shells spilling over her shoulders.

Her piercing voice would summon the spirits of the dead,

or open the way for infants to come into this world

Women would give birth by the riverbank,

holding the hands of midwives

then get up and begin walking again

With them they were carrying the past

Yon the dragon who changed names

who was called Mixcoatl, the serpent of clouds,

Kukulcan, the bird-serpent

With them, the four colors, the white of the north, the yellow of the

south, the black of the west, the red of the east, and at the centre,

OK, the color of jade

Today, the bridge is forgotten

The plane flies over the path of exile at 12,000 meters

America is another continent

Those who come up with east and west

do not know they have confused the direction of the journey

Perhaps they do not know how to read the tranquillity of faces

Over there, in New Mexico,

before leaving, the day before my plane trip,

in the parking lot of K-Mart

I saw the car of a Navaho Indian

and above the license plate

was written

"I remember Korea"

Unjusa, Autumn Rain

Lying beneath a fine mist of fresh water

meditative sleepers with dreamy eyes

turned toward the sky

They say there used to be three, and one of them got up

walked to the edge of the cliff

The two Buddhas still have their backs joined to the stone

one day they will rise in turn

and a new world will be born

On the streets of Seoul,

young men, young women

disrupt time, grasping at seconds

Buying, selling

Creating, inventing, seeking

Who still thinks of the two Buddhas

dreaming on the mountain

at Unjusa

Pillar of clouds

rising in the midst of red autumn leaves?

Seeking, running

Seizing, carrying off

The stone Buddhas

with the faces of Loas

with the vision of shamans

do they sometimes dream in their sleeplessness

of the great stores of the Dongdaemun market

of neon letters as numerous

as the branches of the forest?

On the other side of the world

on the other side of the sea

a shattered country

a blind country

clawed by fear

Buying, selling

seeing

foretelling

zigzagging the night

when Seoul is lit up like a ship

And the mornings are so calm

gentle at Insadong

on Gwangju's Rue des Artistes

sweepers are picking up cardboard cartons

in a café still open two lovers are holding hands.

Living, moving

Tasting, letting the senses glide

the aroma of frying silkworms

kimchi

soup with noodles, seaweed

ferns

peppery filaments of jellyfish

this land sprung from the depths of the sea

tasting of the ether

Wanting to dream, living

writing

On the other side of the world

at the end of the desert

phosphorus bombs light up the night that has just begun

Desiring, careening

overreaching

the letters lighting up

like broken branches in the forest

I think of the wind that writhes

of the wind that lays children grayed by death

on the bitter coffin of the desert

Waiting, laughing, hoping

Loving, loving

in the palace garden in Seoul

children are plump like gods

their eyes painted with the tips of brushes

Waiting, watching, pouring

under the rain which falls gently at Unjusa

slipping over the red leaves of autumn

its fingers merging into arms reaching toward the sea

returning to its native depths

The faces of the two reclining Buddhas are eroded by this rain

their eyes see the sky

each century that passes is a passing cloud

they are dreaming of another time, another place

they are sleeping with their eyes open

the world has begun to tremble.

Seoul—Paris

Monday, 22 October, 2001

* long faces with straight noses and prominently arched eyebrows which traveled over time from Africa to Haiti, and that I saw again in Korea, in the peace of Buddhism.

Twelve Poems by Ki Hyŏng-do

Translated by Gabriel Sylvian

FAMILY ON THE BRINK, 1969

In late spring that year, Dad collapsed feebly like pills spilling from a glass bottle. The long summer, he ate nothing but rice soup. Under the lamplight, Mom put on a towel headband. We can do with storing fewer pickles this winter. . . . Don't say that, Mom . . . . Leaning against a pile of quilts, my big sister shouted at the top of her throat. The radishes are no good this year, nothing but holes! . . . . Closing my notebook, I looked at Mom. I need a new jacket, a bunch of the foam lining's gone . . . . That jacket will do you another winter! Your dad will be back on his feet in the spring! . . . My little sister, who had been shelling the garlic, rubbed her eyes and groaned. We already tried all the medicine for his palsy. . . . But Mom didn't say a word, she just quietly caught the towel slipping down her forehead and re-tied it tighter.

2

Dad, those chickens aren't ours. Why do you have to take care of them?. . . . ossing a handful of poultry feed, I complained, my lips smeared a deep blue from the eggplant I'd eaten. Dad answered as he jumped over the farm's wooden fence, To get feed for you! . . . A ripe yellow moon over the poultry farm gleamed like an egg yolk.

Each time Dad's long, thin shadow darted back and forth in the moonlight, I clutched at his arm and made a whistling sound. Let's plant our flower seedlings by the pump tomorrow. Which flowers would be nicest?... Flowers die really fast, Dad.... You'll be ten come spring, Mom said, ladling up noodles and broth from a brass bowl. I know. I'm not a baby chick anymore. Hey, Mom, why did you add so much red pepper to the noodles?...

3

I waited a long time by the riverbank before my big sister, spindly as a pickpurse blossom, came tottering through the autumn dusk. I got paid overtime this month for working night shifts. I'm buying a green sweat jacket with the money. All my friends have been wearing them to work.... Squid's what I want, 'cause you can chew it forever and it tastes good!... It was a long way home. The spoon in my sister's lunch bag kept jingling like music. You're worried about a sweat jacket? You'll have to take night classes at the high school from next spring!... Mom! Did you water all the bean sprouts?... Don't worry about the bean sprouts! You kids need to do the growing!... I was reading with my head down and blew my nose, and soot came out... Trim the wick. Burning an untrimmed wick just makes soot .... My little sister grumbled. Look at Dad. None of the medicines worked. Dad never did much before he took sick. Mom slapped Sis on the cheek. We can't cut down the medicine bills! .... The potato Sis was peeling dropped with a thud. After your father's business failed he fished for three years, but he kept you from starving! Then he went to the neighbor's farm and kept chickens, and saved the money to buy a field!... In the end, Sis burst out in tears. Her red underwear peeped out from her sweater like a withered cockscomb. But Dad was only nursing pills then, not vegetable seeds ....

4

Don't think about days in the past. They're mostly rotten anyway. Would you pick up old potatoes from last year's field?...

80

Dad stopped shoveling and lit a short cigarette, his ankles still stained with soil from the green garden. What'll you plant this year? . . . I intend to plant anything with tough roots, and with fruit you can eat . . . . Stars had already popped up in the sky like puffed rice. Mom's calling everybody to get washed up . . . . What do the morning glories think they're going to show the next day, sleeping puckered up like that? . . . Dad slowly walked out from the dirt. Look. It doesn't take much to pull me out of the ground . . . But Dad, you should try moving and planting yourself in better soil . . . .

5

Don't visit our home, sir. Our house is too far . . . But you're the class president . . . There's nobody at home. Dad's there by himself during the day . . . After school let out, I walked beside the long bank, thinking about the certificate for high test scores in my book bag. Along the bank an endless sea of pinks were in bloom. To think each one has its own seed! How do tiny seeds get to be big flowers? . . . I planted myself in a grass field and fell asleep. That night my little sister returned home late. How's Dad feeling? . . . She smelled like kerosene. Well, how will you deliver newspapers without a bicycle, and carrying your book bag? . . . When I opened the window, I saw in the darkness a few poplar trees blowing in the wind, puffing out like huge loaves of bread. That day, I didn't tell anyone I'd folded my certificate into a paper boat and let it sail downstream.

6

That winter, it snowed a lot. Dad still couldn't talk, all his speech was gone. How much snow had to melt before the words would start flowing again? Mom was winding yarn into a ball. Your dad will be back on his feet in the spring . . . . When will that be? Is spring the day when everybody gets well? . . . But when sledding, I saw blue water flowing under the ice. And above the ice, I set fire to some paper and the flame burned a perfect square, burning the whole way up until the paper was gone. On really cold nights, I slept with my body curled up like a sunflower seed under the covers. Mom, do you want to see a really big flower? I learned how to clip off some of the leaves to help the flower grow bigger. Mom, I'm talking about Dad's seeds! Think how bright our family tree will be after the longest night is over! Look, it's jumping, like a wire spring! See it there, in the dead of winter? The light, the light, the light!

WHITE NIGHT

The snow stops.
The lights are out at the wintry windows of Incheon houses
and the sky hangs like hard planks
between the low-hanging roofs.
In dimensions defying imagination
the winds easily encase the dirty walls
as snow pellets shriek and ricochet through the air.
Among the scarified black and white screen titles,
a man is walking slowly.
With fingers bent like farm tools,
he parts with his last cigarette
in front of a shuttered store, recalling warm memories
of bottles he'd drunk somewhere, then forgot.
The empty alleyway lies forlorn, like an outspread blanket
A few of the man's long, shaky coughs echo
above the low-watt light and sleet. Passing under a shadowy frozen
    signboard
he staggers off, to where?
On this night when black and white are twin,
on this frightful evening shining like bright ice,
he makes a snowy path that grows harder with every step,
carrying his whimpering young son on his back, beneath his army
    coat.

The taxi driver pokes his head out the dark window
bellowing now and then at the top of his lungs, chasing the birds off
I've never passed this field or this sunset before
My thoughts go to him, a man I never met

The day it happened, I was far away in the countryside
in a dusty room, my nose in a book
When I looked outside, fog had rolled over the fields
The ground was dragging off the books and black leaves that
 summer
White smoke sprang from clothes when you unfolded them
"Silence is for servants," he'd written
I'd seen his face once
in the paper, his head bowed slightly
Then it happened, and after that he died.

The whole funeral glistened in lashing rain and fierce wind
The car with his dead body moved slowly, unbearably so
The people clung stubbornly to the funeral procession
The black leaves fluttered as they crowded against the white hearse
I slowly lost all voice to speak, his young son
could not bear the blizzard of leaves and burst out crying

The names of the missing piled up that year
Then, before the silence of the shocked, they began turning up one
 by one
The tongues of the dead spilled over onto the road
The taxi driver keeps looking back at me now
I don't trust him, seized with terror
I stammer, That man is dead
How many funerals kept under wraps because of him?

Who is he? Where am I going?
I'm not waiting around for answers anymore. No one knows
where an incident will take place, it can happen anywhere
I have to get away to someplace, nearby, in the country

I've never passed by this field or this sunset before
I fear the stubborn black leaf stuck in my mouth

SLEET

Just in time, the sleet whirls and scatters

My hands stiff in my coat pockets

Soon the snow will soon be tramping over streets I don't know

and roaming among men and buildings I've never seen before

A square business envelope falls onto the snowy path, I start to lean
down

Then I stop and think, how graduating from college

I'd been so ready to take on the world

Now the sleet, it's falling, no surprise really, you legs, you never stay
on course

I read about such a route home in a novel once

Memories relished so often, now crushed under my shoe soles

On a dark alley road, an empty truck is stopped with its lights
turned off

Some men fall down drunk, I recall days of sleet sprinkling down

My boyhood when I used to ride the bus all day long

People flocked by an old white wall are brushing off the snow

The sleet's pouring harder now, suddenly tears fall, I am unhappy

It wasn't supposed to be this way, I've experienced enough for one
life, sleet

I thought I heard a noise though it was barely audible. When I
pulled back the curtain, I saw a window open in the three-story
building across from me. A pale wrist popped out and flung
several bunches of withered flowers onto the street. The petals
of the flowers fluttered for a while as though they might stay
afloat in mid-air, but then they dropped downward toward the
ground, slowly, each at a different speed. I returned to the table
and glanced through an old newspaper. In the spot where he stood
until a moment ago, a touch of faint, indistinct color had collected
and settled. I was going to turn off the light when I looked at my
wristwatch and saw that the hands were no longer moving. In a
futile gesture, I turned the hands back to the day before. When I'd
asked him, "Where are you going?" in a tone that said no answer
was necessary, he'd roared with laughter and said, "Just out to the
street"—Then the sound of something falling on the stairs near the
entryway. On the table, I saw that a name-card holder, fountain pen,
ashtray, each object with a shape, had its own faint shadow close
by. Without thinking, I turned my head to look behind the chair.
Once again I heard the sound, barely audible. When I went to the
window a second time, it was the same cold, damp wind I'd felt a
hundred times before. It filled every empty crevice on the street as
it rolled past. "Where are things without cracks in them supposed
to go?"—Then I saw a long, dirty pink curtain streaming out from a
second-story window of a building next to the one opposite. It was
moving softly and sadly, as though no one cared what happened to
it. "Just let it go," he'd said. "Isn't the most beautiful part of anything
the beginning?" As though he'd suddenly remembered, he took his
gloves from the locker and added, "No, it's the moving around, I
mean." A piece of hard, half-eaten bread looked at me silently with a
solemn expression as though to say there was no getting around the
fact. I'd always looked at the darkness and at roads. I slowly stood

up and said quietly to the ceiling, "I'm stuck like a thumbtack." In the spot where he had stood until a moment ago, a touch of faint, indistinct color had collected and settled. "When no one is around, footsteps always seem louder." I heard a sound as I turned off the light. In some unknowable place in my heart, there was a thud, like something breaking. That sound that I knew so well, ringing clear as a bell.

I own an old musical instrument. All of the guitar's six strings are broken, so I haven't played it for a long time (it once put my sadness and passions to music paper, turning them into soft notes). The strangest thing happens. Every now and then, when I am alone in the dark empty room, beautiful sounds flow from the guitar. It stuns me. But my senses carry powerful memories. When the music stops, I fumble around for a candle. Yes, I have an old musical instrument. Yes. Every now and then I walk into a dark, empty hope. I listen to the strange performance and sometimes my whole body vibrates lightly in the darkness.

Blue paper covered with dust is still blue.
No dust can change its color.

GRASS

I have an appendix but
I don't like eating grass
I am
a poor excuse for an animal

I live as a spirit pitched to and fro
roaming clouds streaming with sleep
baring the veins on my wrists
a long sorrow

When I take my body, empty, and stand before you
your waving gestures
are signals so green it makes me sad
Ah,
but the love you retched up while guarding the night!
Was that your beautiful soul
that sustained the darkness, erected the blades?

Now I shall take root!
Better to be grass, having to cry smiles
Let's suffer life's afflictions
Let's bind our feet together and sob

When the winds blow on clear days
and lightly caress my bruised sides
my song, which delves into my heart, springs up, and becomes you,
will form groups, crisp and fresh,
and float in the air.

FLOWER

On days
when my soul bursts into flame
I will stand as a flower
in the garden of your sick heart,
and become the blood you hotly spit up throughout the night

I don't care if I'm snipped in my middle
if it's by your hand

With my deep breaths
I will stitch up your chest

If I can place my head where the winds blow
I won't care, even if I fall asleep standing up.

I can no longer hide in the dark and shake the tree branches.
Readying my one and only soul and hushing the sound of my
footsteps, I move nearer to your window. Light from the cattle's
gentle gazes gives me a dim path, while above, nervous leaves
just parted from their branches seek out empty places in the air.
I am lonely. My friend, when the soft sound of my cough slips
into the sketches of your sleep, light a small lamp and place it at
the windowsill. The distance of my desire is too great, and silence
always has me in its grip. You must open the window only when it
is very late. The flame's light is too faint and will not reach the field.
You, with your head tilted to one side—how I have longed to enter
into your sighs! Ah, soon you will extinguish the leaf of flame with
a stream of your breath. I break the smallest branch without making
a sound. I will hide my body behind the branches and quietly gaze
at the remote area of existence where I can never go—until that
dim hour when you rub the globe of your weary lamp, until some
movements stop in the misty darkness, and the wind, wearied,
finishes its brief repose.

PUT BADLY

A few shadows hung around in the dark
Some stayed by the pitch-black wall
Sensing trouble, vehicles killed their lights
In an instant, each building bolted its door
and waited in fear. An explosion of kerosene fumes
a thin, slinky sound of dragging metal
black leaves leered as they tumbled by
hands and feet moved quickly
the flicker of cigarettes, somebody who walked into the alley
uttered a cry of shock

Those guys, why do they gather in the dark every night?
Where do the desires of those young men go?
Why are human pleasures all the same?

FOG

1

Fog cloaks the inlet each morning and evening.

2

Everyone coming to this town for the first time
must pass through the great fog river.
Like lonesome cattle they must stand at the long riverbank
until the party ahead of them slowly clears the way.
Until they suddenly realize with a shock that they are all alone,
trapped in an empty hole in the fog.

Some days, the mist battalion will not budge an inch from the inlet
until the hard, yellow sun hangs on the thick paper sheet of sky.
Giggling factory girls pass by, late for work,
and children, released from the long darkness,
seep out slowly from between gruff black trees.

Those unaccustomed to the fog employ caution when walking,
but before long they are cutting their way through the fog
and wandering around in it like the others. Habit
really makes it very easy. They soon make kin with the fog
and flow around inside it as though insane
until the transmission tower reveals its faint body in the distance.

On fogless days,
those walking on the bank don't recognize each other's faces.
Leery of one another, they pass by hurriedly,
but clear, gloomy mornings are very rare,
because this is the fog's holy precinct.

When dusk falls, the fog casts off its speedy clothes above the inlet
one layer at a time. The air instantly swells with a hard, white liquid.

The vegetation and factories are sucked into it
and half of the man walking several paces ahead
is cut off by the whiteness.

There were just a few minor incidents.
A factory girl was raped in the dead of night.
It happened near the workers' dorm, but they put a gag on her
    mouth, and
that was that. Last winter, a drunkard froze to death on the
    riverbank.
A three-wheel vehicle passed right by him,
thinking he was a pile of garbage.
But those were only individual misfortunes, and not the fog's fault.

As the fog retreats and noon approaches,
the factory's black smokestacks aim their barrels in unison at the
    sky.
A few men were injured and left the sewage habitat,
cursing it roundly, but it was quickly pushed out of everyone's
    memory
because none of the men ever returned to the town.

3
Fog cloaks the inlet each morning and evening.
The fog is now the town's special attraction.
Everyone holds at least some stock in the fog.
The faces of the factory girls are bright and beautiful.
The children grow like weeds and all go to the factory.

DEAD CLOUD

Below the dirty window filled with clouds,
a man has collapsed,
his hand upturned on the floor like a toy
He'd waited for this chance, it seems,
for death gaping like the mouth of a plastic bag
those unfeeling foods tormenting his hunger until the very end
Now a dog stares at his dish, having lost its strength, its fur,
I saw the dead man several times while he was alive,
People called him crazy, threw silver coins
at his outspread coat blotched with wine and spit
No one knew his private thoughts,
the sexual desires and sorrows he hid to the last,
his shoulder muscles clearly once had a function
His pitiful, vile bare feet
were gifts for tender-hearted women
but no matter, clouds must be observed with great caution
Now this fool, this dead man, even the raindrops do not fear him
The old dog, becoming bolder, knocks over the dish
and while villainous stains spread like human hands across the floor
two police officers enter and converse idly,
"All towns have one or two of these empty houses
A crazy fool like this—how did he know to come here and die?"
The old dog, having lost interest, seems sad
But no one knows, for the cloud that vanished alone
had no part in the window from the start

The First Anniversary

by Pyun Hye-Young
Translated by Cindy Chen

Clutching the oppressively large box to his chest, he made his way into the apartment building. It was as dark as during the monthly air-raid blackout drills: all the lights were out except for the elevator display, its red flicker reflecting on the bank of mailboxes. A flood of brochures, unclaimed mail, and empty cans foretold the building's imminent demolition.

The man steered himself toward the stairway. It was best to avoid the elevator, given the increasingly capricious state of the power supply. He had once been trapped inside it during a power outage. He had jabbed at the emergency call button hoping the custodian would come to his rescue. No such luck. He had begun to wonder if the demolition crew would get to him first. Eventually he had fallen asleep even as he willed the elevator not to plunge to the bottom of the shaft. It was not until the next morning that power was restored and he was liberated along with his parcels.

He felt spellbound as he climbed the stairs, his upper and lower body seemingly disconnected. While his eyes searched for the outlines of the stairs, his legs bore him upward with synchronized strides. He knew by heart the number of steps between each floor, the rise between each step and the next, and the location of each bicycle-obstructed emergency exit. What he didn't know was that mounds of trash and garbage had been accumulating each day in front of the emergency exits, and one such mound now caused him to trip.

It was just as dark in the fifth-floor stairwell as elsewhere in the building, and he crouched down to gather up the parcels that had gone flying. He found the last parcel, returned it to the delivery box, and gave the box a shake. No unusual noises or smells. No signs of leakage. There were times when kimchi juice had leaked out, leaving a trail of red splatters on the stairs behind him as well as pungent blotches on his khaki pants. The splatters on the concrete were a bit more faded each time he returned to this unlit flight of stairs—which meant several times a week and always with a delivery for the same woman. Sometimes it was kimchi he delivered, at others it was crab pickled in soy sauce. Sometimes it was hot pepper paste, and sometimes instant noodles that the woman could have purchased at any supermarket. He had delivered sandals, Western-style leather boots, and platform sneakers, as well as breathable underwear, a polka-dot dress, an upright steam cleaner—the list went on. His employer offered the only home delivery service in the region, and so when the woman ordered something through home shopping channels or online shopping malls, he delivered it. He was getting to know her pretty well—at least this was how he felt when he pictured her wearing the bra and underwear he had delivered, eating rice topped with the pickled crab he had delivered, and going out afterward in the polka-dot dress he had also delivered.

He felt a puff of air, and breathed in its burden of concrete dust. Dust-laden air had been circulating stubbornly through the city ever since construction of the new amusement park had gotten under way four years earlier. The park grounds and the building where the woman lived were separated only by the river bisecting the city. From a distance, the amusement park was a jumbled mess, resembling demolition as much as construction. But closer up, the array of construction cranes announced the arrival of the new park. A temporary office trailer sat in a secluded corner of

98

the construction site. Workers in yellow hardhats streamed in and out of the site while debris-loaded trucks barreled up and down adjoining streets.

Construction was the obvious source of the city's unabating noise and dust, but the amusement park project was not the sole culprit. In fact, the entire city was being rebuilt. For every new building that took a month to erect, an old one was torn down in mere hours. Hodgepodges of residential areas were gradually being replaced by apartment jungles. The noise, the temporary perimeter walls, the truckloads of debris and the yellow hardhats—these sights and sounds of construction were as familiar to the residents as their daily shortcuts through the alleys. But the more the city changed, the more it remained the same. Buildings would age and when their time had come, their owners would have them razed and rebuilt on the same spot.

He inadvertently kicked something made of glass and heard fragments ricochet off the floor. The sharp *crack* sent a cat darting out from an apartment and scurrying down to the far end of the hallway. The hallway was heaped with garbage where stray cats foraged. He plunked down the delivery box and tried to catch his breath. The numbers outside the apartment units had peeled off— was this number 4 or number 5? He peeked through an open door and saw only a dusty gloom mottled with trash and abandoned furniture.

The building was going to be renovated. The man assumed, correctly, that renovation in this case meant more than just replastering the exterior walls and repainting the building. Only the structural skeleton and the number of units would remain the same; everything else was to be replaced. When it had been completed, this building where the woman lived, along with its utility poles, was one of the tallest structures in the area. But that was nineteen years before, and with construction on surrounding apartment blocks soon to be finished, this building might end up looking no grander than the smokestack of a garbage incinerator. His deliveries to the woman's apartment had given him firsthand knowledge of the mass eviction of the residents, who had been rushed into signing off on the renovation. After putting up with three years of bare-bones accommodations elsewhere, they would finally be allowed back into their face-lifted apartments.

He tried the doorbell for number 607—dead. He was certain the elevator display had been flickering down in the lobby. The power to the building must have gone out while he was trudging up to the sixth floor. After thanking God that he hadn't taken the elevator he banged on the steel door to the apartment. Nothing stirred. He pressed his face to the door and shouted, "Hello! Anyone home?" Not once during the past year or so that he had been making deliveries to the woman had she failed to answer. He fished out his cell phone and punched in the number on the packing list. He heard a faint ringing inside. He let it continue, then checked the packing list by the glow of the cell phone. The list included a potted rubber tree, whose pot had probably been smashed as a result of his recent pratfall. He had once refunded the woman the cost of a jar of makeup that had arrived broken. Even though the manufacturer was entirely at fault for the inadequate packaging, he had to take the blame, and the refund was taken out of his paycheck.

It wouldn't be a problem leaving the woman's parcels in the hallway, given that she was the sole remaining resident on the sixth floor. How likely were the remaining occupants of the building to steal things from her hallway? The only thing ever left out was trash. And no one would be able to distinguish the delivery box if he camouflaged it beneath a pile of garbage. The very idea brought life back to his sore arms. The woman would be expecting more items. He would return, and then deliver everything together. If the rubber tree died in the meantime, well, too bad. Back down the stairs he went. The gloomy recesses of the stairwell had the musty stink of a garbage incinerator's ash pit.

Instead of going home, the man drove to the photo shop. A stop at the company warehouse earlier in the day had pushed him further behind schedule than usual. He had been determined to get to the woman's neighborhood by afternoon, but his day hadn't gone as planned. Her building was the only occupied one left in the neighborhood, the others having already been vacated to clear the way for apartment complexes that would constitute a new, full-fledged residential suburb. So he could have avoided the neighborhood altogether if he hadn't needed to deliver her parcels. Her neighborhood was isolated, remote from others on his delivery route. The distance involved meant a lot of energy wasted driving the same miserable circuitous loop, particularly when he needed to return to the warehouse to re-load. Several attempts at rearranging his route had proved futile. His delivery zone extended over nine localities and his schedule was complicated by detours to the warehouse and the sorting center—no wonder he often found himself still working at ten o'clock at night.

At the sound of the small door chime, the photographer emerged from the back room of the shop. He greeted the man with a nod and headed directly to the camera. The two men had gone to the same elementary school and had been rooted in the city's outskirts since the day they were born, even after the majority of their schoolmates had moved away. A handful that couldn't leave made peace with their lives, and either sought employment or opened their own businesses. But all of them, including the photographer, had high hopes for the new suburb. And to a certain extent, the deliveryman did too. Once people began to settle there, the demand for deliveries would soar—and that would be a good thing, he figured. But it also meant that his daily workload would increase, a thought that made his heart sink. He saw himself driving for eternity a truckful of mysterious boxes as burdensome as his future. If only he could retrieve the bonding and insurance deposit he had paid the company when he was hired, he would quit the delivery job on the spot. But he knew the deposit would never be returned to him. He was trapped. All his hopes rested with the new suburb—how else could someone be lured to this urban fringe and pay the necessary deposit for becoming a home deliveryman?

"Are you up? Sorry if I woke you." The man retrieved a stool from the recesses of the shop and perched on it. His question was just a formality, for he knew that a photographer who couldn't get through a day without complaining about how bad business was would always welcome a customer. "Don't worry, it happens all the time." The photographer gently shook his head and bent down to look through the eyepiece of his imported camera.

The man looked into the camera and as though he was using the lens as a mirror, he adjusted his shirt, slid his glasses to the very tip of his nose and squared his shoulders. It was pointed out to him at the previous headshot session that he tended to slouch toward the left.

"Relax your shoulders a little."

The man let his squared shoulders drop. He wondered if his sagging shoulders implied cowardice.

"The usual?"

"Yes," the man answered, afraid of nodding in case his glasses slid off his nose. The photographer faced him and counted to three. Off went the flash.

The man flipped through a weekly tabloid magazine while waiting for his headshots to be developed. He could hear a little child fussing in the living quarters in the back of the shop.

The photographer craned his head toward the sound, then asked, "How's it going with your job?"

The question was unexpected. Though the two had gone to the same elementary school, their acquaintance was only skin-deep and they had never talked much. It was routine for the deliveryman to leaf through the weekly tabloids while the photographer busied himself with the developing.

"Good enough to keep myself fed," the man answered with a snort. The words sounded pitiful even to him. He forced out a louder laugh to disguise his despair.

"I'm afraid I might need to find another job. That's why I'm asking. Thought I'd leave the shop with my wife. So little needs doing, she shouldn't have any trouble."

"Do you have anything in mind?"

"Well, I'm looking."

The man was silent for a while. "How about home delivery?"

"Do they need someone? I wouldn't mind doing that."

"There aren't any openings at the moment. . . ," and here the man paused for effect, "*but,* if you're interested, I can look into it for you."

"Would you? That'd be great!"

The man returned to his magazine. *I could use him to get back my deposit! Hey, calm down. Not so fast with the promises. And don't count your chickens before they're hatched. Talk up the job too much and you'll lose your credibility.* He feigned nonchalance as he flipped through the magazine.

"What are all these headshots for?" the photographer asked as he handed over the prints. A fair question considering that the man had been coming in for a sitting every week or so.

"Well, they're anniversary souvenirs."

"Souvenirs?"

The man nodded emphatically.

"You have that many anniversaries?" the photographer chuckled as the man paid.

Jotting down the date on the back of each print, he replied philosophically, "Every day is an anniversary." He sounded as though he had given some thought to his answer. But the words jerked him back to reality—his life was, in fact, devoid of any meaningful anniversaries. The day his parents died came closest. They had passed away only hours apart in a freak accident, struck by another vehicle as they were looking underneath the bumper of their broken-down car on the shoulder of the highway. He was barely out of his teens. He didn't care to remember their deaths. He had no close relatives to take his parents' place in celebrating his birthday. Nor did he have a girlfriend with whom he could count down to their hundredth-day anniversary or relive their first kiss. No past employers or jobs seemed worthy of commemorating. And he despised national holidays and Christmas, because deliveries always mushroomed on such days.

"Anniversary," he repeated under his breath. His voice was weary.

The truth was, he needed the headshots for the dozen or so résumés that he liked to busy himself with on his days off. With black ink, he would tediously fill in the blank spaces with the details of his high school–level education and the odd jobs he had worked, all the while asking himself, *How the hell have I managed to lead such a shitty life?* The question was cast like a fishing line into the deepest corner of his soul, and what he reeled back in was self-pity. Rolling a glue stick over the backs of the photos, he pasted one onto each résumé. All the headshots had turned out horribly comical. He didn't look pathetic—he looked downright ridiculous. He sent his completed résumés to big companies around the city.

Whether it was his lack of qualifications or his photo, none of these companies ever contacted him. Perhaps handwritten résumés were too primitive by current standards to be taken seriously. Nevertheless, he faithfully filled out these résumés as if writing a journal. Some days he would neatly record weekly lists of items he'd delivered, or the names of the localities he'd delivered to. Other days he would record the names of apartment buildings that had sprouted up in the new suburb, and he would list and group, based on their manufacturers, all the instant noodles that he had bought from supermarkets near those apartment buildings. By now, he could even include in the résumés his dual certifications in English- and Korean-language typing, and his abacus-mathematics certification, though they added little substance. On the day of his typing tests, he was so nervous his fingers slipped off the keys, and yet he passed with flying colors. He enjoyed the clicking and tapping made by the keyboard. The sounds reminded him of the drumming of raindrops. And on the day of his abacus-mathematics test he was stumped by a mental arithmetic problem involving one two-digit number and one three-digit number. He copied the problem down and returned to it to fill in the right answer during the part of the exam when the test takers were allowed to use an abacus. He had taken both tests long ago, and neither certification was of any use now. He was fully aware that his qualifications alone would never land him a job with a company in the city, and that sending out more résumés wasn't a quick-fix solution to the problem. He was doomed to remain a marginal applicant. There were times when he found solace in the potential of a new suburb to transform the housing project where he lived into something recognizably metropolitan. But he also found it humiliating that no amount of new construction could rescue him from his nomadic lifestyle of skipping from one rented basement jail cell to another. Whether it was humiliation or solace, he realized that nothing could improve his life at this point.

In the hallway he located the large delivery box holding the woman's potted rubber tree, and placed a smaller box on top. His view was obstructed as he piled up the boxes, but it made no difference because it was so dark inside the building. Tonight, dust was stealing away in gentle sighs from the aging walls lining the stairway.

"Hello! Anyone home?" he called to the woman's closed door, his voice echoing along the empty hallway. He tried the woman on his cell phone. No answer. He peered through the door crack into the pitch-dark apartment. Maybe she had moved. He recalled the renovation notice in the building lobby, which mentioned the date when interior demolition would begin. That day was approaching, and the residents had been taking leave of the decrepit building.

Puzzled, he looked down at the two boxes in his arms. *If the building's going down, what's she buying a rubber tree for? Is she planning to hang around for a while?* Inside the smaller box was a bottle of grapeseed oil. He tried to imagine the woman tidying up the living room with its new rubber tree, and cooking with the grapeseed oil. He could picture how the woman's clothes, the oil, and the potted plant might look though he had never actually seen them. Her face, however, remained obscure. He pounded on the door. From the far end of the hallway he heard, in the sombre hush of the building, the wind rustling among some plastic bags.

He considered leaving, but instead gave the doorknob a twist. The door swung open silently. He stepped inside and called cautiously into the darkness, "Hello?"

Nothing in the inky blackness suggested that the woman was there. Boxes in his arms, he scanned the apartment. Everything looked to be in its proper place, as though the woman had left only moments ago. Was she coming right back, or was she gone for good? He couldn't tell.

Just as he was about to leave, light spilled into the apartment through the balcony off the living room. Like a searchlight, it brought every detail into glaring view—a grease-stained frying pan on the kitchen stove, a pair of woman's sandals in the doorway. He glanced at the sandals. *Did I deliver those?* His guess was that the woman probably wouldn't be back any time soon, but this was only a vague hunch—after all, he knew nothing of the woman aside from the items he had delivered to her. Drawn by the light, he drifted toward the balcony, and through the window he traced the light to a huge wheel that was radiating a symphony of primary colors. The wheel slowly turned, gazing all the while into the woman's apartment. Its light illuminated the river, the water glimmering in a spinning kaleidoscope of colors. The wheel, he saw, was sitting on the other side of the river, in the amusement park that was still awaiting its grand opening.

He stared blankly. It was a while before it dawned on him that the lights were coming from a Ferris wheel and that the maintenance crew was probably testing the ride. He had never been on a Ferris wheel. When his parents were alive, they were always overextended, trying to make ends meet. Even if they had had the wherewithal, there was no Ferris wheel where they lived on the outskirts of the city. And his was not the happy family that would have gone on a Sunday outing to an amusement park miles away. Not until he was older did he discover the pleasures of these parks, visiting them on occasion with his friends. He had ridden roller coasters at seventy miles an hour and faster. He had zipped along upside down on rides. In comparison, the Ferris wheel was a bore. It wasn't a ride that attracted droves of boys. It offered no speed, no adrenaline rush from watching the world go topsy-turvy. It left people with no trembles and no thrills. The Ferris wheel moved as sluggishly as his life, and only high enough to offer a bird's-eye view of the city's fringes with their clusters of low apartment blocks. He knew that couples sought the close confines of the Ferris wheel gondola to make out, or engage in steamier activities. If only he had known a woman intimately enough to do that . . . .

He brought home the two delivery boxes and opened them. Company regulations required him to return all undelivered parcels to the sender, but he chose to ignore that. The more he looked at the woman's name on the packing list, the more it became his own. The woman still wasn't answering the phone. A few days earlier he had attempted another delivery, but it seemed that demolition was already under way. Not only was the building littered with debris, he was prevented from approaching by the construction crew. He flattered himself by thinking that the woman had disappeared so she could leave him with these packages to make up for all the presents he had been deprived of by his life. And it was with the curious anticipation of opening presents that he now opened the woman's packages. On a wall calendar he itemized every parcel—the potted rubber tree, the grapeseed oil, a lace nightgown, a kitchenware set won in a lottery commemorating his company's ten-millionth customer, a seven-piece knife set complete with wooden block, a bamboo sleeping mat, and a pillow embroidered with chrysanthemums.

He enjoyed guessing the function of an object, so he delighted in unexpected gifts more than thoughtful ones tailor-made for his needs and tastes. He put the rubber tree outside where it wouldn't be knocked over and where it would shield his window. After showering, he rubbed grapeseed oil all over himself before oiling a frying pan for a meal of eggs and stir-fried potatoes. He wondered why the woman preferred such bland oil, and decided she was either health-conscious or susceptible to trends. Even a culinary ignoramus like himself understood that cooking had its own fashions. From the kitchenware set he picked out the vessel with the widest base; he would use it as a washbasin. Coincidentally, his own plastic washbasin had cracked and he had been considering buying a new one anyway. He spread out the bamboo sleeping mat on the floor and added a layer of bedding—the weather was getting chilly. He wondered why the woman had bought a bamboo sleeping mat now that summer was all but over. Perhaps she was hot-blooded. He remembered a school classmate nicknamed Hotpants because he wore his summer uniform longer than anybody else. Maybe the woman had a similar nickname. He felt as though the parcels were full of clues that would allow him to piece together the puzzle that was this woman.

There were times when he delivered identical items to the woman. The wide-brimmed hat was one such item. A few days after he had attempted delivery of a pink hat, he was given the exact same hat to deliver, except this one was blue. *It's the same hat! Is she that vain?* He ended up giving the hats to his landlady. "Where am I supposed to wear these?" the landlady had complained, only to find herself so enamored with the way they looked on her that the hats quickly became an extension of herself. He had beamed with pride, as if he were the one who had gone to the trouble of finding them. The landlady always wore one of the hats while supervising the changes being made to the housing project where he was living. The plan was to turn the original two-story house into a four-story building, as well as repair the exterior wall. The construction forced him to permanently shut the window in his basement room to keep out the clouds of dust mixed with cement and sand. Even then, an immaculate white veil of dust managed to steal into the room and settle on his black television. The house trembled with the drilling. Whenever he was in bed, the shriek and rumble from the construction nauseated him. When he couldn't stand it any longer he would hurl his pillow at the ceiling, rattling the fluorescent light fixture. And then he would retch, a long thread of saliva hanging from his chin. The clamor would bombard him until late at night.

He kept the seven-piece knife set in its original packaging. It would be a gift for the photographer's wife. For the last few days the photographer had been shadowing him at the sorting center. The idea was to give the photographer a taste of the home-delivery job. So long as the photographer was with him, the man would pretend to be through with work by seven. This pleased the photographer, who would ask if work always ended so early. He equivocated, saying not always. He left out the part about how he would wait till the photographer had left for home before delivering his remaining parcels. He didn't tell the whole truth, but he didn't feel guilty. Once the photographer had taken the job and the man had quit, the photographer would learn that he had been deceived, and that the job was nothing more than a ploy to get back the bonding and insurance deposit. But of course, the photographer would also come to the realization that things had worked out perfectly for everyone.

From his drawer the man produced all the headshots he had had taken for his résumés. Aside from subtle differences in the length of his hair and the style of his clothes, his comical face had remained unchanged. He tried to arrange the pictures chronologically on the floor without looking at the dates written on their backs. The oldest and the most recent of the bunch could be easily distinguished; not so with the rest. He pored over his many inscrutable faces from the past. They betrayed no thoughts, no emotions.

He selected a headshot taken last winter. In it he wore a black turtleneck and looked emaciated, though in reality he was just tired. He was always tired and exhausted. And whenever he was out on the road making deliveries, he would struggle with migraine the entire time. His hair was longer then—out went the hair; he cropped it from the picture with scissors. Next, he cut his eyes out of a headshot taken the previous summer. They were guilty of being bloodshot. He remembered the day that photo was taken—he had caught conjunctivitis from a worker at the sorting center. Tears were oozing from his festering eyes. Mucus was gelling into pools of pus. Through those eyes he saw a world that was blurred by the pus and fragmented by the stinging pain. The photographer had asked him if he still wanted a picture taken with his eyes in such a state. Instead of answering, he had reached out toward the photographer to shoo a fly off his shirt, but the startled photographer had pulled out of his reach. In a dejected voice he tried to explain himself, "There was a fly on your shirt."

And then there was that photo from two years ago. His short hair exaggerated his sagging, nearly lobeless ears—out went the ears. The cropped hair, the cut-out eyes, and the excised ears looked grossly misshapen because the photos were small to begin with and his scissoring was clumsy. He pasted these cropped features onto his most recent photo, in which he had slid his glasses down to the tip of his nose. And suddenly the hair grew lush, the bloodshot eyes looked ghoulish, and the elfin ears protruded from the unkempt hair like a pair of devil's horns. He glued the mutilated photo onto a résumé. Beneath the name of his high school, he listed every last item that he had received by way of the woman.

The woman suggested that they meet at the amusement park. Until she mentioned her name the man hadn't recognized her voice on the phone. Her name had come to be synonymous with his own. While the woman retold the ordeal she had had to go through to track him down, he scanned every corner of his room for her items. The rubber tree was wilting under dense construction dust, its shriveled, yellowing leaves fluttering to the floor like the dust. To revive its barren roots would take a miracle. The pink and blue wide-brimmed hats had lost their colors to gray layers of dust and were now virtually indistinguishable, but the landlady continued to wear them when supervising construction. The seasons had come and gone, yet the construction was still dragging on with no end in sight. The cookpot was badly scratched from being kicked around the tiled bathroom floor. More than half the bottle of grapeseed oil had been used on his body and for making side dishes. The bamboo sleeping mat was plastered to the floor like oiled floor paper under his heavy bedding. He liked to eat instant noodles and to cut his nails on the naked mat, leaving filth to saturate its every slit. And when he masturbated to mental images of the woman's lace-clad body and her indiscernible face, his scattershot ejaculate left the mat dirty with yellow stains. At night he slept on the woman's chrysanthemum-embroidered pillow. His head had left a depression in its center. They were never her presents to him, these items, and it was his mistake to have thought otherwise. He would need to apologize to the woman and refund her money if he wanted to avoid legal problems.

The amusement park rides were undergoing safety tests. A blazing red roller coaster was tearing up and down its track alongside the river, following a choreographed sequence of loops and dives. Traveling over seventy miles an hour, it could induce vertigo in mere onlookers. The chance of derailment was slim to none, but the man's heart remained in his throat until the roller coaster finally pulled into the station. Adjacent to it a pirate ship was oscillating like a pendulum, each upward swing higher than the previous one.

The Ferris wheel sat in a far corner of the park. The woman was waiting at the entrance to the ride. "There's no place to sit here—let's go for a ride."

Moving tentatively, as though in tandem with the sluggish Ferris wheel, he followed the woman into a gondola that had just arrived. As soon as the woman had taken her seat she started a stopwatch.

"I'm timing the ride," she explained, adding that she was in charge of the safety inspection for the Ferris wheel. "The wheel revolves at the same speed, but for some reason each ride times out a little differently."

He looked out the gondola window and saw teetering on the end of each bicycle-spoke-like steel arm another gondola. Instead of being frightened, he relished the gondola's subtle sway in the breeze. They were ascending at an undetectable speed.

"I just want to say I'm sorry." He hung his head.

"What's done is done, yes?" Her tone was mild. No haughty demands to have the packages returned to her at once. He offered to refund their entire cost. The woman nodded with a matter-of-fact expression, and resumed staring at her stopwatch.

"You seem to like hats," he ventured.

"I do?" The woman looked puzzled.

He reminded her of how she had bought two of the same designer hats, in different colors.

"Did I really?" The woman chuckled, her smile exposing her discolored front teeth. They looked black. He countered with a fleeting smile, for lack of anything to say. He wondered if his front teeth were black too. The woman's bland countenance offered no answer. He studied her. He had forgotten what she looked like. Her face was unfamiliar, as though he was meeting her for the very first time when in fact he had made deliveries to her almost weekly. He had only seen her face through the crack in her apartment door, and its impassiveness had blinded him to the harmony of her features, leaving him with only an impression of unfriendliness. "Where are you staying these days?"

"Here." She didn't bother to look up from the stopwatch. He wasn't sure if she was referring to the gondola, the amusement park, or the city itself. He began to feel uneasy and his hand kept reaching for the résumé in his breast pocket. That résumé was urging him to work up his nerve. But for what he didn't know.

He sighed and swept his eyes across the panoramic view

outside the gondola window. He was rising high above the
construction zones down below. He could see the empty frames
of the park's mammoth rides spinning and spiraling tirelessly,
could hear their motors moaning. A little bit higher and he saw the
woman's apartment building across the river. It was gleaming, most
likely from night-time construction. The lights made it hard to see
that the building had been disemboweled and was now an empty
shell. The overwhelming grayness of the cement in the surrounding
buildings accentuated their resemblance to a forest of half-buried,
decaying trees. Yet higher now, and there was the housing project
where he lived. Its sprawl was encircled by apartment blocks,
making it look from above like the sunken pit of a trap. He wanted
to see even farther—if possible, out to the scar-like chaos of roads
that led into other cities. He stood up but in doing so banged his
head against the ceiling. Defeated, he sat back down and leaned
forward.

The woman was across from him. Their knees sometimes
brushed when he shifted in his seat. He felt tempted to steal glances
at her. Her face remained blank. He wanted to ask her what else she
liked besides hats, whether she was sensitive to heat, if she hated
being petite enough to need platform sneakers. He wanted to tell
her that she actually didn't look very small at all. He wanted to
tease her—"You can't seem to cook!"—and he wanted her to laugh
with him afterwards. He was curious why she had left behind her
sandals—they were still new—and indeed why she had abandoned
everything in her apartment. Did she know that the Ferris wheel
lights illuminated her apartment every night? But he clamped his
mouth shut as his mind mulled over the restless deluge of questions
that he was afraid he might unwittingly blurt out.

The ground was a dazzling orb of light. In it he saw himself
driving a truck, taking packages to an endless list of strangers, his
face hard like cardboard from hauling boxes all day. He saw the
photographer taking headshots for customers who, if not stoic,
had an elusive curl to the corners of their mouths. The stiff prints

of their headshots were being cut to standard size. He saw his landlady in her designer hat, dozing off in a chair overlooking the construction work. Then there was the woman, latching a gondola door shut and staring absentmindedly at her stopwatch. He waved at them all.

Cheerful staccato music entered the gondola, as though acknowledging his wave. A mellifluous prerecorded voice announced that at 500 feet off the ground, they had reached the apex of the Ferris wheel ride. He had never expected the ground to look so fantastical from this height. It would have been a romantic spot for a kiss, and knowingly the mischievous music lingered. He suddenly felt embarrassed and pretended to be oblivious to the music. The woman was unmoved. Was she even listening? He tapped stupidly at his parched lips.

"I gave your hats to my landlady," he blurted as the woman stared out the window.

"I see." After a brief pause, she asked, her face still and unreadable, "What did they look like?"

"They have a wide brim with a little ripple in front, and a small bow in back." Her eyes followed his fingers as they outlined the shape of the hat in the air. He thought there was a hint of a smile on the woman's face, then decided he was mistaken.

The day had passed when the photographer should have paid his bonding and insurance deposit for the delivery job, but he had yet to hear anything. He was getting anxious, but resisted calling. The more desperate he seemed, the more suspicious the photographer might become. For the time being, he would skip the weekly headshot session. He might have to haul the photographer to the sorting center himself, and beg him to pay the deposit. The longer he waited, the harder it would be for him to get his deposit back, which meant he would have to keep roaming the refurbished city making his deliveries. Unnerved by the thought, he pulled the résumé out of his breast pocket.

"What do you think of this photo?"

"The red eyes look weird."

He ran his hand over his bloodshot eyes and his elfin ears. He had an idea. He offered the woman his résumé.

"Would you like to have it?"

The woman stared incredulously at him and shook her head. Of course—whatever would she want with it? So, what now? In the end he slid it through a tiny slit in the seat, leaving one corner of the paper to stick out of the gondola like a white flag. Submitted thus to the outside world, his résumé would ride the Ferris wheel in a perpetual circle. On a cloudless day his bloodshot eyes might be able to see into the distance, commanding panoramas of other cities being rebuilt.

The Ferris wheel continued to revolve after they had touched down. The feeling of solid ground beneath his feet was dizzying. He steadied himself enough for a polite bow to the woman and bade her good-bye. She handed him a piece of paper with a list of the packages she hadn't received, and the cost of each. He slid the paper into his pocket and asked, "How long did it take?"

The woman glanced at her stopwatch. "Less time than usual."

He left the woman and walked toward the amusement park entrance. In his car were some parcels he was supposed to deliver to the woman tonight. He hadn't mentioned them to her. He didn't know their contents, because he hadn't had a chance to look over the packing list. Perhaps it wasn't even the woman herself who had placed those orders. He wanted to keep those parcels for later—they were his excuse to continue delivering to her after he reimbursed her for the packages he had kept for himself and opened. As long as there were parcels to be delivered to the woman, he could continue to visit her at the amusement park and ride with her on the Ferris wheel. He toyed with the thought of ordering something under the woman's name.

Outside the park, he looked back at the Ferris wheel and its empty gondolas, the wheel's glistening lights cascading onto the night-cloaked fringes of the city. The wheel dawdled on its axis, as if to say the world would come to a grinding halt if it stopped. His eyes searched for his résumé-waving gondola but it was nearly impossible to pick out in the neon glow. As he climbed into his car he thought he heard the parcels pushing and shoving one another in the crowded trunk. He drove off into the night toward the city. Those parcels needed delivering.

Excerpt from The Vegetarian

by Han Kang
Translated by Janet Hong

Until the day my wife turned vegetarian, I didn't think there was anything special about her. To be honest, I wasn't even attracted to her the first time we met. She wasn't short, but neither was she tall. Her bob cut wasn't short, but neither was it long. She had chapped sallow skin, Asian eyes with no double eyelids, and protruding cheekbones. She wore neutral colors, as if she were afraid of standing out. She walked up to the table where I was waiting for her in black shoes of the plainest design. She walked in a way that was neither fast nor slow, firm nor dainty.

I married her in the end because I didn't find anything wrong with her, just as I didn't find anything special about her. I was comfortable with her ordinary personality that wasn't refreshing, witty, or polished. There was no need to impress her by pretending to be extremely knowledgeable, no need to panic when I was late, and no need to feel intimidated by the male models who appeared in fashion catalogues. I didn't have to worry about my belly that started bulging in my mid-twenties, my skinny arms and legs that wouldn't get bigger no matter how much I worked out, or even my small penis that was the secret source of my insecurity.

I've never liked feeling inferior. When I was young, I preferred hanging out with those who were two or three years younger than me so that I could boss them around, and when I got older,

I applied to lesser-known universities that would give me enough funding. I was happy to routinely collect my small paycheck that was hardly worth bragging about from the small company that valued my insignificant skills. Considering all this, it was only natural for me to marry a woman who appeared to be the most ordinary woman in the whole world. I simply wasn't comfortable around women who were beautiful, clever, sexy, or rich.

Just as I expected, my wife performed the duties of an ordinary wife with ease. She woke up at six every morning to prepare my breakfast of rice, soup, and a chunk of grilled fish. She even contributed a little to our finances by working part time as a teacher's assistant at a computer graphics institute, a job she'd started before we got married, and she also worked from home on contract, inserting words into speech balloons for a comic book publisher.

She was on the quiet side. She rarely demanded anything of me, and she didn't care how late I came home. On the weekends we happened to be together, she didn't ask if we could go somewhere. She shut herself up in her room while I stayed on the couch in front of the TV all afternoon with the remote control in hand. She was probably working or reading. Reading was just about the only hobby she had, but most of the books she read looked so dull I didn't even want to crack them open. She only came out of her room when it was time to eat, and she prepared the meal without a word. To be honest, there was nothing exciting about living with a wife like her. But I was just glad she wasn't like my colleagues' wives who called their husbands all day long or those wives who nagged constantly and set off earsplitting fights.

If there were one thing that was different about my wife from other women, it was the fact that she didn't like bras. During our brief and rather dull courtship, I once got a little aroused when I put my hand on her back and realized I couldn't feel her bra straps underneath her sweater. For a moment, I saw her in a whole new light. I watched her carefully to see if she was sending me some sort of silent message. The conclusion I came to was that she was doing no such thing. Was she just lazy then? Did she not care? I couldn't understand. It was ridiculous that she'd even go without a bra on that shapeless chest of hers. If anything, she should have worn thickly padded bras. Then maybe my friends would have been more impressed when I introduced her to them.

After we got married, she never wore bras at home. In the summertime when she had to step out, she reluctantly put one on in case her nipples showed, but even then, she'd undo the clasp right away. If she wore a shirt that was fitted, thin or light in color, the unhooked bra was clearly visible, but she didn't care. When I said something, she put on a vest in the sweltering heat rather than redo the clasp. She said she could hardly breathe, the way the bra crushed her chest and ribcage. Since I've never worn a bra, I didn't know how suffocating it could be. But I could certainly see how other women did not seem to mind as much, and so, I didn't take her complaints seriously.

Besides that, everything was fine. We were entering our fifth year of marriage, but since there hadn't been any passion in our relationship to start with, there wasn't any passion to be missed. I started thinking maybe it was time I became a father, for we'd been putting off having a baby until we bought this condo last fall. But I never imagined for a second that our lives would change until late one night this past February when I discovered my wife standing in the kitchen in her nightgown.

≈

"What are you doing over there?" I asked as I was about to flick on the bathroom light. It was around four in the morning. I'd just woken up, thirsty and needing to take a piss, thanks to the bottle and a half of soju I'd had with colleagues after work.

"What are you doing?" I looked in her direction and felt a chill run down my spine. I was wide awake in an instant. My wife stood perfectly still, staring at the refrigerator. Since it was too dark, I couldn't make out her expression from her profile, but something was eerie. Her thick, naturally black hair was disheveled. Her white nightgown that came down to her ankles was curled up a little from the hem, as usual.

It was chilly in the kitchen. My wife got cold very easily, so she would normally throw on a cardigan and look for her fur slippers. How long has she been standing there like that? She stood frozen like a stone statue in her thin nightgown and bare feet, as if she didn't hear me at all. As if something I couldn't see—maybe even a ghost—was standing where the fridge was. Was she sleepwalking?

I walked toward her. "What's wrong? What's going on?"

When I put my hand on her shoulder, she didn't flinch. So she had been aware of everything—me coming out of the bedroom, the questions, walking toward her. She was just ignoring me. Like the times she'd been so wrapped up in watching late-night TV that she'd pretended she didn't hear me come home. But there was nothing fascinating about the white refrigerator door, especially in the dark kitchen at four in the morning.

"Hey!" I stared at her face. Her eyes had a look I'd never seen before. They glittered coldly and her jaw was clenched.

". . . I had a dream." Her voice was surprisingly clear.

"A dream? What are you talking about? Do you know what time it is?"

She turned and slowly walked toward the bedroom. When she crossed the doorsill, she stuck her arm out behind her and quietly shut the door. Left alone in the dark kitchen, I stared at the closed bedroom door.

I turned on the bathroom light and stepped in. For the last few days, the temperature has been hovering around -10 degrees Celsius. The plastic bathroom slippers were still cold and wet, splattered with water from the shower I'd taken a few hours earlier. From the black vents above the bathtub to the white tiles on the floor and walls, I felt the harshness of the season.

When I went back into the bedroom, I didn't hear anything from my wife's side of the bed where she lay curled up. It was almost as if I were alone in the room. When I listened carefully, I could hear very soft breathing. It didn't sound like it was coming from someone who was asleep. If I stretched out my hand, I could have touched her warm skin. But for some reason, I couldn't touch her. And there was nothing I wanted to say.

∼

I lay under the blanket, staring vacantly at the winter sunlight that penetrated the white curtains and filled the room. When I half raised my head to look at the clock on the wall, I sprang out of bed and kicked open the bedroom door. My wife was in the kitchen in front of the refrigerator.

"Are you crazy? Why didn't you wake me? Do you know what time—" I stopped when I stepped on something mushy. I couldn't believe my eyes.

My wife was crouched down, still dressed in her white nightgown, her tangled hair hanging down her back. Scattered all around her on the kitchen floor were containers and black and white plastic bags. There was absolutely no room to set my foot. On every inch of the floor were sliced beef for shabu-shabu, pork belly strips, two beef hocks, squid in vacuum-sealed packages, the pre-prepared eel that my wife's mother in the country had sent us, dried yellow corvinas tied up in yellow string, unopened bags of frozen dumplings, and countless other bundles. One by one, my wife was dumping everything into a large garbage bag.

"What do you think you're doing?" I yelled, losing my temper momentarily. Like the night before, she continued to ignore me and kept stuffing each bundle into the garbage bag. Beef and pork, chicken cutlets, a sea eel worth at least two hundred thousand *won*.

"Are you nuts? Why are you throwing all this out?"

I waded through the plastic bags and grabbed her wrist. She was surprisingly strong. Stubbornly, she gripped the bag of meat. My face started to heat up from squeezing her wrist. She finally let go. Then she spoke in her usual calm tone as she massaged her reddened wrist with her left hand.

"I had a dream."

There it was again. She gazed at me steadily. Just then, my cell phone rang.

"Shit!"

I started searching the pockets of the coat I'd tossed on the couch the night before. My hand finally found the shrieking phone in the inside pocket.

"I'm so sorry, there's been a family emergency. . . . I'm really sorry, sir. I'll do my best to get there as soon as possible. No, no, I'll be there right away. Can I ask you to be patient for just. . . . No, please, there's no need for that. I'm so sorry. I really don't know what to say . . . ."

I hung up and ran to the bathroom. In a rush to shave, I cut myself in two places.

"Did you iron my shirt?"

No answer. Cursing, I rummaged through the laundry for the shirt I'd thrown in last night. Thankfully, it wasn't too wrinkled. I threw on my necktie like a scarf and pulled on my socks, but even while I was getting my wallet and planner, my wife didn't come out of the kitchen. For the first time in five years, my wife was not seeing me out. "She's lost her mind. She's completely lost it."

I stuffed my feet into the dress shoes I'd bought recently. Because they were new, my feet still felt cramped. I kicked open the front door and after seeing that the elevator was stuck on the top floor, I flew down three flights of stairs. After I managed to get on the subway car just a second before the doors closed, I looked at my reflection in the dark window. I finger-combed my hair, did my tie, and smoothed out the wrinkles in my shirt with my palm. It was only then I thought about my wife's hard voice and her serene face that made my blood run cold.

Two times, she had said she had a dream. Her face slipped past beyond the racing window, above the darkness of the tunnel, unfamiliar as if I were seeing it for the first time. But there was no time to think about my wife's strange behavior, since I had a mere thirty minutes to come up with an excuse for why I was late and to go over my presentation for today's clients. "You should go home early tonight," I told myself. "Ever since you changed departments, not once have you gone home before midnight." All I could do was to say these words to myself over and over again.

～

It was a dark forest. I was alone. Scratches appeared on my face and arms as I pushed aside branches with prickly leaves. I'm sure I'd been with others, but I must have gotten lost. I was scared. It was cold. I crossed a frozen valley and found a brightly painted building that looked like a barn. I stepped on the straw mats to get inside, and that's when I saw them. Large, red hunks of meat, hundreds of them, hanging from long wooden racks. Blood that hadn't dried was still dripping from some of the meat. I pushed aside one carcass after another, but I couldn't see the end. Blood soaked my white clothes.

I don't know how I managed to get out. I ran upstream through a valley. I ran and ran. Suddenly, the forest became bright and densely green with spring trees. There were sounds of children and I could smell something delicious. So many families were out having a picnic. It was blinding. A stream flowed past, and people sat on the banks on mats. They were eating kimbap and others nearby were grilling meat. The sounds of singing and laughter rang out.

But I was scared. My clothes were still stained with blood. No one saw me crouch behind a tree. There was blood on my hands. There was blood on my mouth. In that barn, I had picked up a piece of meat that had fallen on the ground. I had eaten it, smearing blood from the mushy raw meat on my gums, on the roof of my mouth. My eyes had glittered, reflected in the puddle of blood on the barn floor.

It was so real. That texture of the raw meat, the way it felt between my teeth. It was as though I were seeing my face, my eyes, for the first time, but it was definitely my face. No, it was the other way around. As though I'd seen that face countless times, but it wasn't my face. I can't describe it. Familiar yet unfamiliar, vivid yet strange . . . that terribly strange feeling.

≈

The dinner my wife prepared consisted entirely of kimchi, lettuce with soybean paste, and a thin seaweed soup made without beef or clams. That was it.

"So you threw away all the meat because of that stupid dream? Do you have any idea how much that was worth?"

I stood up from the kitchen table and opened the freezer. It was empty, all except for some roasted grain powder, red pepper powder, a few frozen unripe red peppers, and a bag of minced garlic.

"At least fry me up an egg. I'm exhausted. I didn't even have a proper lunch today."

"I threw out the eggs, too."

"What?"

"I asked them to stop the milk delivery."

"I don't believe this. Are you saying even *I* shouldn't eat meat now?"

"I couldn't keep those things in the fridge. I just couldn't."

I stared at her. How could this woman think only of herself? She sat with her eyes cast down, looking more serene than usual. This was a surprise. Who would have known she could be this selfish? So unreasonable?

"So you're telling me from now on, we're not having any meat in this house?"

"You only eat breakfast here anyway. And you probably eat a lot of meat for lunch and dinner . . . you won't die if you don't have meat for one meal." She replied calmly as if she were being perfectly reasonable.

"Okay, fine, but how about you? You're not eating any meat from now on?"

She nodded.

"You're sure? Forever?"

". . . Forever."

I was speechless. There were things I've seen and heard, so I was aware of the latest vegetables craze. People became vegetarians because they wanted to be healthy and to live longer, to get rid of allergies and dermatitis, or even to protect the environment. Of course, Buddhist monks who enter the monastery must vow not to take life, and she wasn't an adolescent girl on a diet, so what was going on? She wasn't trying to lose weight, she wasn't trying to cure an illness, she wasn't possessed by the devil. It was ridiculous that she would change her entire diet because of one nightmare. I couldn't believe she could be so stubborn, so pigheaded that she wouldn't even listen to her husband.

If she'd been the type to find meat nauseating from the beginning, I might have understood. But she's always had a good appetite, and it was that quality I especially liked about her. She flipped short ribs on the grill with an expert hand, and there was something comforting about the way she held the tongs in one hand and the large scissors with which she snipped through the meat in the other. And after marriage, the dishes she made on Sundays were hard to beat. Pork belly strips marinated with minced ginger and starch syrup that smelled fragrant and sweet when fried. And her specialty—thinly sliced shabu-shabu beef she seasoned with salt, black pepper, and sesame oil, covered with sweet rice powder and then fried up; it tasted just as if you were biting into a hot rice cake or a juicy patty. Then there was her bean sprout *bibimbap*. She would take rice that had been soaking in water, stir-fry it with ground beef in sesame oil, and then steam this with bean sprouts on top. And what about the thick potato chunks she put into her spicy chicken stew? The spicy broth that simmered at level with the chicken and potatoes would seep inside the meat and I would often have three helpings in one sitting.

But look at this meal now. Sitting on the edge of her chair, my wife spooned seaweed soup into her mouth. I didn't need to taste it to know it wasn't any good. She wrapped some rice and soybean paste in lettuce and put it in her mouth, making her cheeks bulge out. She chewed.

I realized I didn't know anything, not a thing, about this woman.

"Aren't you going to eat?"

She asked me in the dispassionate tone that would better suit a middle-aged woman who had given birth to and raised four children. Ignoring the fact that I stood simply watching her, she crunched on a kimchi stalk for a long time.

≈

My wife didn't change, even when spring came. Although I ate only vegetables every morning, I didn't complain anymore. When a person undergoes a complete transformation, the other person has no choice but to follow.

She became thinner and thinner each day. Her protruding cheekbones became even sharper. When she didn't wear makeup, she looked like she was ill. If people were to lose weight like my wife just because they gave up meat, there wouldn't be all this fuss about dieting. But the reason she was just skin and bones wasn't only because she had become a vegetarian. It was because of her dreams. In fact, she barely slept.

She was never someone who required little sleep. Many nights she would already be asleep when I got in late. But now when I came home after midnight, I'd wash up, crawl into bed, and still she wouldn't come into the bedroom. She wasn't reading, chatting on the Internet, or watching TV. And there was no way she had that much contract work, inserting words into speech balloons.

She'd finally lie down around five o'clock in the morning. She would toss and turn for about an hour then utter a small groan and get up. And with tangled hair, a haggard face, and bloodshot eyes, she would sit at the kitchen table with my breakfast, without having eaten a single bite herself.

But what bothered me most of all was that she didn't try to have sex with me anymore. My wife, for the most part, met my needs without a word, and sometimes, she was the one to initiate. But now, if my hand so much as brushed her shoulder, she would quietly shift her body away. Once I asked her why.

"What's the matter?"

"I'm tired."

"Then eat some meat. That's why you don't have any strength. You weren't like this before."

"Actually, it's. . . ."

"It's what?"

". . . it's the smell."

"The smell?"

"The way you smell. You smell like meat."

I burst into laughter. "Didn't you see me take a shower just now? So where could the smell possibly be coming from?"

". . . From every single pore." She was perfectly serious.

Sometimes my thoughts turned grim. What if this was just the beginning of something serious? What if this led to paranoia, delusional disorder, or a nervous breakdown?

But it was hard to think she was actually crazy. As always, she didn't talk much and she kept the house tidy. On the weekends, she'd marinate a few different sprouts, and she'd use mushrooms instead of beef to make *japchae* noodles. If you considered the fact that it was now trendy to eat vegetables, there was nothing strange about this kind of behavior. Nothing strange at all, except that she couldn't sleep, her face looked more vacant than usual, and she always replied the same way—"I had a dream"—when I asked her in the morning why she looked so troubled. I didn't ask her what the dream had been about. I didn't want to hear anything about barns in dark forests, her reflection in a puddle of blood, ever again.

She continued to waste away, lost inside her private pain and nightmares I had no way or desire to understand. It seemed as though she was going to get thin like a dancer, but in the end, she was as gaunt as an invalid. Every time my thoughts turned dark, I thought about my wife's family: her parents who ran a small sawmill and a corner store out in the country, her older sister, her younger brother and his wife. It seemed very unlikely that mental illness ran in the family.

Whenever I thought about them, I naturally thought of a thick cloud of smoke and the smell of frying garlic. As the grease from the meat burned on the grill and we poured each other one soju shot after another, the women talked noisily in the kitchen. The whole family, particularly my father-in-law, enjoyed a good dish of minced raw beef, and my mother-in-law could filet live fish. My wife and her sister were women who could brandish a butcher's knife and chop up a whole chicken. I admired my wife's resourcefulness that could slap down a few cockroaches with her bare hand. Hadn't she been that most ordinary woman I'd searched the whole world for?

Even if I'd considered her condition to be serious, I wouldn't have been comfortable with counseling or treatment. "A mental illness is merely a type of illness. It doesn't reflect badly on a person," I'd always said. But I'd been able to say that only because it didn't concern me. Honestly, I wasn't prepared for anything like this.

~

The day before I had that dream, I was slicing a chunk of frozen meat in the morning. You got angry and told me to hurry up.

Damn it, are you just going to stand around like that?

You know how I can't think straight when you rush me. I get all flustered like I've become someone else, and I end up floundering even more. Faster, faster. My hand that held the knife moved so fast that my neck heated up. Suddenly, the cutting board slipped away from me. It was then I cut my finger, then that a small piece of the blade broke off.

When I held up my index finger, blood started to bloom. It grew fatter and fatter. As soon as I stuck the finger in my mouth, I became calm, as if that scarlet color, that sweet metallic taste was calming me down.

You picked up the second piece of meat and started chewing when you suddenly spat it out. You plucked out something that glittered and yelled.

What, a shard? This is a piece of the blade!

I just stood there. You jumped up and down with rage, face twisted with fury. All I could do was stare.

What if I swallowed it? I could have died!

Why wasn't I shocked? I was actually calmer than ever. As if someone had laid a cool hand on my forehead. Suddenly like the tide washing out, everything that surrounded me slid out. The table, you, everything in the kitchen. As if I and the chair I sat in were the only things left in that vast void.

It was the next night. The puddle of blood inside the barn, the first time I saw the face reflected there.

⁓

"What's wrong with your lips? Why aren't you wearing makeup?"

I took off my shoes. My wife stood in a stupor, dressed in a black trench coat. I grabbed her arm and dragged her into the bedroom.

"You were going to go out like *that*?" I saw our reflections in the dresser mirror. "Do your makeup again."

Silently, she shook off my hand. She opened her compact and patted the puff over her face. Caked white with powder, her face looked like a cloth doll that was covered in dust. When she put her dark coral lipstick on her ashen lips the sickly pallor left her face, though the result was far from perfect. I was relieved.

"We're late. Hurry up."

I went ahead and opened the front door. With a finger pressed down on the elevator button, I watched impatiently as my wife took forever slipping into her navy blue sneakers. Trench coats didn't go with sneakers, but there was nothing I could do. She didn't have any dress shoes. She'd thrown out all her leather belongings.

As soon as I got in the car that I'd left running, I tuned the radio to the traffic station. I strained my ears in order to check traffic conditions around the traditional Korean restaurant where my company president had made reservations. I put on my seatbelt and released the handbrake. My wife got in, bringing with her the cold outside air. She fidgeted in the passenger's seat and put on her seatbelt.

"I have to do well today. I'm the first out of all section leaders that the president has invited to a couples' dinner. It means I've gotten on his good side."

By hurrying and taking side roads, we were able to arrive just in time. It was a two-story building with a spacious parking lot; it looked high-class at a single glance.

The lingering cold spell was worse than usual. My wife, who stood at the edge of the parking lot in her thin spring coat, looked cold. She didn't say anything on the way to the restaurant, but I wasn't very concerned; she was always quiet. I got rid of my anxious feelings by telling myself it was good to be quiet, that older folks liked women who were quiet like her.

The president, the vice president, the executive director, and their wives were already there. The department head and his wife came in right behind us. After greeting each other with nods and smiles, my wife and I hung up our coats on the coat rack. The president's wife, with eyebrows plucked to thin lines and a large jade necklace wrapped around her neck, directed us to a spot in front of the long banquet table. Everyone seemed comfortable, as if they'd been there many times. I gazed at the ridged roof and at the goldfish that swam in the aquarium made out of stone. I sat down. The moment I turned to look at my wife, I saw her chest.

She was wearing a black blouse that was a little fitted and the outline of her nipples showed clearly through the material. She wasn't wearing a bra again. When I turned to check if anyone else had noticed, I made eye contact with the vice president's wife. I instantly recognized curiosity, astonishment, and contempt that lurked under her calm gaze.

I felt my cheeks go red. My wife sat dumbly, not participating in the sociable conversation between the other women. I tried to compose myself, while perceiving the glances that were directed at my wife. The best thing I could do at this point was to act natural.

"Did you have any trouble finding your way here?" the president's wife asked me.

"Not at all, I've driven past it several times. I really liked the garden and I've wanted to step inside ever since."

"The garden is pretty, isn't it? It's nicer during the day, because you can see the flowerbed through that window."

But when the food began to come out, the control I'd been straining to maintain finally snapped. The first dish was *tangpeongchae*, thin strips of white jelly mixed with shiitake mushrooms and beef. My wife, who hadn't said a single word until now, spoke softly when the server tried to ladle some of it onto her plate.

"No thank you." She spoke very softly, but everyone stopped moving. Now the focus of attention, she spoke a bit louder. "I don't eat meat."

"Oh, you're a vegetarian?" the president asked heartily. "In other countries, there are many vegetarians, and strict ones at that, but in Korea, it seems that vegetarianism is just catching on.

Especially nowadays, since they're saying it isn't healthy to eat too much meat. If you want to live long, I guess it might be perfectly natural to consider avoiding meat."

"But still, can you really avoid meat altogether?" The president's wife smiled.

While the white plate before my wife remained empty, the server filled our plates and disappeared. The conversation naturally turned to the subject of vegetarianism.

"You've heard of the human mummies they discovered recently from about half a million years ago? Well, they've found evidence of hunting on them. I tell you, it's a natural instinct for humans to eat meat. Eating only vegetables is going against your instincts. It's not natural."

"Well, some people are switching to vegetables these days because of the Sasang Constitution.[1] . . . I actually went to a few places myself to see which constitution I was, but every person I spoke with said something different. Even though I changed my diet every time, I always felt uneasy. . . . Now I think it's best not to be so fussy and to just eat everything."

"Someone who can eat anything and everything, now isn't that a healthy person? It's proof that the person is physically and mentally sound."

The vice president's wife, who had kept eyeing my wife's chest, spoke. This time, the words were aimed directly at my wife. "What were your reasons for becoming a vegetarian? Was it because of health . . . or for religious reasons?"

"No." My wife spoke quietly with perfect composure as if she had absolutely no idea what kind of situation this was. A chill ran down my spine. I immediately knew what she was going to say. ". . . I had a dream."

I rushed to cut her off. "She's been having stomach problems for a long time now. She's even had trouble sleeping because of

---

1. Sasang Constitution is a traditional Korean medical typology, which was systematically theorized by Lee Jae-ma. Basic Sasang Theory divides humanity into four distinct types.

them. But she's gotten a lot better after we took the advice of a Chinese medicine doctor who suggested that she stop eating meat."

It was only then that everyone nodded.

"Oh, you must have been relieved. Actually, I've never dined with a real vegetarian before. I'd always thought it'd be awful to eat with someone who might be disgusted by watching me eat meat. I guess if people become vegetarians for psychological reasons, that means they're disgusted by meat?"

"It's probably the same thing as when you're enjoying a live octopus that's squirming on your chopsticks and the woman sitting across from you glares at you like she's watching an animal."

Everyone laughed. While I laughed along, I noticed that my wife wasn't laughing. She wasn't paying any attention to the conversation that drifted back and forth. Instead, she was staring at the sesame oil from the *tangpeongchae* that glistened on everyone's lips. And I could tell that this was making everyone feel uncomfortable.

The next dish was sweet-and-sour chicken and the dish after that was tuna sashimi. While everyone ate, my wife didn't touch a thing. With her small acorn nipples jutting plainly through her blouse, she stared at everyone's lips, at every movement, like she was sucking it all in.

By the end of the sumptuous twelve-course meal, my wife had only eaten some salad, *kimchi*, and pumpkin soup. She hadn't touched the sweet rice ball soup that had a unique flavor, because the soup had been made with beef stock. Everyone continued to talk as if my wife wasn't there. A few who felt sorry for me sometimes tossed a comment or question my way, but I knew they were keeping me at a distance, for deep inside, they saw me as being the same.

When fruit was served as the dessert, my wife ate a slice of apple and orange.

"You must be hungry. You barely ate," the president's wife said in a friendly tone.

133

My wife, though, didn't answer. Instead, she stared at the other woman's refined face without smiling or blushing. Her steady gaze was extremely unnerving. Did my wife realize how important this meeting was? Did she even know who that middle-aged woman was? For a second, the impenetrable inside of her head felt as dark as a bottomless pit.

Death, Eroticism, and Virtual Nationalism
in the Films of Hong Sangsoo*

by Kyung Hyun Kim

On
Cinema

I went down to the river bank and joined the crowd. The dead woman was facing the river, so I couldn't see her face but I could see her permed hair and plump white limbs. She was wearing a thin red sweater and a white skirt. It must have been rather cold early in the morning. Or maybe she had a liking for that outfit. Her head was resting on rubber shoes with flowery patterns and lying on the ground in the rain and a few feet away from her limp lifeless hand was a white handkerchief, which, as it did not blow about in the wind, seemed to be wrapped around something. To get a glimpse of her face, the children stood in the stream facing my way. Their blue school uniforms were reflected upside down on the water and were like blue flags surrounding the corpse. Strangely, I felt rising within me a great surge of physical desire for the dead woman. I hurriedly left the scene.[1]

The passage above is from "A Journey to Mujin," [Mujin kihaeng] a story by Kim Sŭng'ok that established him as one of the most celebrated writers of the post-Korean War era in addition

---

* A small portion of this essay appeared under the title "The Awkward Traveller in *Turning Gate*" in the anthology *New Korean Cinema,* ed. Chi-Yun Shin and Julian Stringer (New York: NYU Press, 2005), 170-179.

1. Kim Sŭng'ok, "A Journey to Mujin," Moon Hui-kyung, trans., in *Modern Korean Literature: An Anthology 1908-65,* ed. Chung Chong-wha (London and New York: Kegan Paul International, 1995), 365.

AZALEA

*The Films
of Hong
Sangsoo:
Kyung
Hyun Kim*

to being one of the first generation of writers to be educated in the national language (Korean) after Korea's liberation from Japan.[2] The story is written from the perspective of a young man, Yun, whose frustration at returning home is highlighted in this passage when he encounters a young woman's corpse. In Seoul, Yun has established a successful career as a young executive at a pharmaceutical company through a marriage with the daughter of the company's president. The encounter with the dead body takes place during an annual trip to his seaside home in order to pay a visit to his mother's gravesite. His old friends no longer amuse him, however, and a brief love affair with a local music teacher sours when she resists separation from her husband. Yun's sudden encounter with the body of an apparent prostitute who has committed suicide signals an almost existential shift in the story: it reveals not only the vast wasteland Korea's countryside has become, but also the death that exists in life.

"Death as the absolute point of view over life and opening on its truth," writes Michel Foucault, "is also that against which life, in daily practice, comes up against."[3] What Foucault is suggesting here is that the perspective offered by death is essential to cracking open the truth of life, and also that death's meaning is so absolute and inescapable that it is not easily perceived in everyday life. Does the narrator become embarrassed about the philistinism of his own erotic response because the young woman's dead body signifies an absolute pure quality? Also, does his necrophilia have something to do with the debilitating relationship that exists between his life as a successful, urban, corporate executive and the dilapidated countryside in which he was born and raised? Fulfilling his desire is impossible, and Yun runs away, but the close affinity between death and sex in this scene unconsciously disengages sexual desire

---

2. During the latter part of the Japanese colonial era (1910-1945), usage of Japanese among intellectuals became the norm as Japanese administrators pursued a *naissen ittai* policy that sought to squash two national bodies (Korea and Japan) into one.

3. Michel Foucault, *The Birth of the Clinic* (New York: Vintage, 1973), 155.

from procreation, since necrophilia is ultimately a nonproductive discharge of semen.

Written over forty years ago when the draining of Korea's young labor force and the denuding of Korea's hills were at their respective peaks, this description of a young woman's body emerges as a shocking allegory of Korea's ravaged landscape. The corpse is a sign of the plundered countryside and tamed revolutionary spirit of the early 1960s that had aroused repressed political agency, as well as a depiction of an infertile land and barren women. The woman's body, which is already lifeless, immaterial, and insubstantial, is not unlike Korea's national body, which had displayed a momentary democratic cultural renaissance that would be killed off by a single blow, a military coup less than a year later. Eroticism and death are central to this passage, but also a disturbingly sensual reckoning of a nation's historical remembrance.

I begin this essay on filmmaker Hong Sangsoo with this literary excerpt from 1963 because there is a sense in which the post-war Korean literature of the 1960s, which featured writers such as Kim Sŭng'ok, Yi Ch'ŏng'jun, and O Chŏnghŭi, forms a continuum of sorts with Hong's films. Kim Sŭng'ok's pointless outburst of eroticism, his obsession with death, and the unattractive landscapes in which his tale is set together signal a withdrawal into interiority that partially reflects the political crisis of the short-lived April 19th Revolution's confused aftermath. This modern awareness of interiority is accompanied by both an intense form of narcissism *and* a realization of the futility of conscious exteriority. This triumvirate comprising modernist subjectivity—narcissistic interiority, the de-linking of the individual and the social, and an obsession with death and mourning—is also especially relevant to Hong Sangsoo's films, which have been a favorite of critics since his debut in 1996.

A dialectical relationship built around cosmopolitanism and eroticism permeates the texts of both Kim Sŭng'ok and Hong Sangsoo. The demand for space for narcissistic libertine sexuality

AZALEA

*The Films
of Hong
Sangsoo:
Kyung
Hyun Kim*

competes with a desire for universality and cultural pluralism. This relationship, I argue, is ultimately tied to the depoliticized environment in which both artists were active immediately after the intense politicization of their respective youths. Korea's two post-ideological fervors (post-60s and post-80s) generated a strong movement towards the massive interiorization reflected in their work.

Every intense political movement in twentieth-century Korea has been followed by a cultural renaissance. The gap between the individual and the social was erased during these periods of heightened politicization, and an aesthetic movement that sought to defend the space of the individual ego followed. In the period after the anti-Japanese nationalist movement of the 1920s, symbolized by the Kwangju Student Uprising (1929), had lost steam, the poetry of Yi Sang startled literary circles and became the bedrock of Korea's modernism. Once the democratic regime established through a student-led revolution in 1960 had come to an end, modernist writers like Kim Sŭng'ok and Kim Suyŏng became the stars of the literary world that anchored post-war Korea's intellectual discourse. During the most recent post-political phase, Hong Sangsoo has emerged not only as a favorite of film critics, but also as the prodigal son of literary critics. These critics have seen in Hong's work a profound crisis of meaning in language that is intimately tied to the withering of political agency, a symptom of any "post-political" model.

Terms like "gender," "class," "ethnicity," or "national identity" appear to have little connection with Hong Sangsoo's thematic concerns about everyday life in such a "post-political" paradigm. Indeed, Hong Sangsoo's films, notorious for overstressing the difficulties of communication, can be said to awaken the potential destabilization of already fragile relationships: friendships, family ties, or national communities. He strips away the thin veneer of reason and decency that forms the fabric of every social network and shows, through his indignant, socially inept characters, how

138

miscommunication is often not the exception but the norm in everyday interactions between people. In this cultural formation, any type of ideology, including national subjectivity, which ought to function as the glue between the individual and the social, becomes highly suspect and even irrelevant.

In Hong Sangsoo's film *Night and Day* (2007), shot almost entirely in Paris, Kim Sŏngnam, a South Korean painter living in exile in France because he violated the marijuana possession laws in his home country, tries to atone for an offensive comment he once made about Kim Il-Sung to a North Korean foreign student in Paris. Realizing that they have nothing more to say to one another, the two Koreans—one from the South and the other from the North—decide to settle accounts by arm wrestling. As Louis Althusser has suggested, language is a key ideological access point to an individual's dominant framework.[4] Here is a key Hong Sangsoo moment: since the two cannot speak to each other, the only way they can "communicate" is by going outside the domain of language. Refusing to enter the social (symbolic) sphere, they become silly kids wrestling each other on a playground.

Such a childish portrayal of the most fractious nation-state in the world today still split into Communist North and Capitalist South both dislodges the traditional austere representation of Cold War Korea and engages a new line of historical confabulation. If portraying everyday banality is a way of sublimating the social totality of this particular epoch, then even the slight annoyance of failing to understand each other (or of walking around aimlessly, both typical occurrences in Hong Sangsoo films) expresses what Akira Mizuta Lippit describes as being "at the end of the political lines that traverse and constitute Korean history, *at the other end of politics*."[5] Therein lies what I call the *virtual* engagement with

---

4. See Louis Althusser's seminal article, "Ideology and Ideological State Apparatuses," in *Lenin and Philosophy and Other Essays*, Ben Brewster, trans. (New York and London: Monthly Review Press, 1971), 121-176.

5. Akira Mizuta Lippit, "Hong Sangsoo's Lines of Inquiry, Communication, Defense, and Escape," *Film Quarterly*, Vol. 57, No. 4 (Summer, 2004), 22.

Azalea

The Films
of Hong
Sangsoo:
Kyung
Hyun Kim

Korean history implicit in Hong Sangsoo's texts. This engagement delves deep into the interiority and past of a nation which is itself undergoing a painful process of decolonization still far from complete.

Long before the U.S. military occupation (1945 to the present) and Japan's colonization (1910-1945), Korea had a long, unremarkable history under the Chosun dynasty (1392-1910). This extended period of rule was marked by an abiding fear of foreigners, especially after the devastating invasions by the Japanese and Manchus in the late sixteenth and early seventeenth centuries. In order to sustain sociopolitical stability and cultural autonomy, the Korean kings of the Chosun dynasty submitted to the Chinese policies of "unity" and "peace" and to Chinese suzerainty. Though Hong Sangsoo's films express neither epic dramas nor folk traditions that can help to manufacture a sense of nation, they propose everyday temporalities of both cosmopolitanism and narcissism—however contradictory the two may seem—that are sought out by Korean intellectuals. That is to say, the anti-heroes of Hong Sangsoo's films are those who confer value upon the city and the egotistical intellectuals who live in them, and, by extension, the nation that is socially repellent to them.

Most people squirm upon hearing an association being made between Hong Sangsoo's films and nationalist (*minjok*) discourse. The presumption is that being engaged in a nationalist cinema means seeking to re-inscribe the conventional bonds between a nation's symbols (e.g., the flag, the 38th parallel, memorabilia from the war) and their historical signification. Kang Je-gyu managed to do this with his box-office smash *Tae Guk Gi: The Brotherhood of War* (2004), as did Kang Woo-suk in *Silmido* (2003). In other words, landscapes, objects, and people must serve as allegory or metaphors. However, both these options are unacceptable as creative praxis for Hong Sangsoo. Through his films, he asserts that language and systems of signification are inherently arbitrary, sometimes by even forcing bonds between a signifier (a word or a cinematic image) and its corresponding signified (the object or concept represented) to erode.

For example, whether or not Sujŏng is really a *ch'ŏnyŏ* (virgin) in *Virgin Stripped Bare by Her Bachelors* is still a matter of intense conjecture in discussions held after screenings at Hong Sangsoo retrospectives at various film festivals around the world. This debate eventually leads to questioning the very meaning behind the idea of "virgin." Common sense might suggest that this is unnecessarily complex for a film running 100 minutes and meant to be shown in commercial multiplexes. Questions such as "What is the meaning behind *ch'ŏnyŏ*?" resist the mind's inclination to neatly slot all complicated philosophical issues into categories of race, gender, class, and national identity. It is difficult to deny that race, gender, class, and national identity constitute important aspects of the social discourse and impact how we interpret culture. All thinking requires interpretation. But, as Susan Sontag reminds us, "that does not mean there aren't some metaphors we might well abstain from or try to retire."[6] Hong Sangsoo's films attempt to retire many objects from the tyranny of metaphors. In the process, they achieve what I call a *virtual* refiguration of objects and space, including the nation.

To classify Hong Sangsoo's films as exemplary texts of the "virtual" may sound a bit mystifying since "virtual" nowadays is more commonly understood as "false," "artificial," or "un-virtu(e)al." In addition, as Deleuze argues in explaining his use of the term "virtual," it describes the past as something not necessarily only represented as a thing of the past, but as something that "coexists with itself as present."[7] But if Deleuze's "virtual" predates "virtual reality" and remains faithful to its etymological origins, then perhaps Hong's images or signs could be said to end up nullifying the tension between past and present, or between truth and

6. Susan Sontag, *Illness As Metaphor; and, AIDS and Its Metaphors* (New York: Doubleday, 1990), 93.

7. Gilles Deleuze, *Proust & Signs*, Richard Howard, trans. (Minneapolis: University of Minnesota Press, 2000), 58.

AZALEA

The Films
of Hong
Sangsoo:
Kyung
Hyun Kim

falsehood—that is, they are capable of reassigning certain values of truth as ungraspable and un-representable.

If the term *affectivity* has caught the attention of many academics who describe the creative processes taking place within the field of the humanities, it is because the emotions with which one responds to the real have been floundering in the wake of the growing popularity of "reality TV" and the Internet. In this Internet age, where *cinéma verité* has become the most dominant commercial visual medium, how could we ever trust that an image issuing from late capitalist culture could belong to the terrain of truth? The attempt to achieve this degree of trustworthiness is, I argue, different from the objective of realism, which desperately seeks to break down the boundaries between an object or a thing and its representative filter, thereby replacing, even if only metaphorically, the truth behind *that* very object or thing that has been filmed. The kind of self-reflexivity that only admits the essence of subjectivity is a doubly layered one where the past coexists with the present. Such self-reflexivity lies at the foundation of Hong Sangsoo's modernist take on cinema, which can itself be seen as a last-ditch effort to reclaim "truth" for the visual medium.

This arrival at a truth that is "ungraspable and un-representable" is the point from which we can begin to understand Hong Sangsoo's tenacious desire to flirt with his own eroticism, death, and national identity. This tendency, evident in all of Hong's films since *The Day a Pig Fell into the Well* (*Tweji ga umul e ppajin nal*, 1996), has become even more pronounced in those he has written and directed in the 21st century: *Turning Gate* (*Saenghwal ŭi palgyŏn*, 2002), *Woman Is the Future of Man* (*Yŏja nŭn namja ŭi miraeda*, 2004), *Tale of Cinema* (*Kŭkjangjŏn*, 2005), *Woman on the Beach* (*Haebyŏn ŭi yŏin*, 2006), and *Night and Day* (*Pam kwa nat*, 2007).[8] This essay considers how these films reconstitute

8. Between *The Day a Pig Fell into the Well* (1996) *and Turning Gate* (2002) Hong made *The Power of Kangwon Province* (*Kangwondo ŭi him*, 1998) and *Virgin Stripped Bare by Her Bachelors* (*O! Sujŏng*, 2000), both of which were well received. I have written extensively about these films in *The Remasculinization of Korean*

the fallacies of erotic desires, fear of death, and nationalist values. Reversing the pattern of Yasujiro Ozu, whose films "pick[ed] out the intolerable from the insignificant itself,"[9] Hong Sangsoo is at ease picking out the *insignificant* from the *intolerable*.[10] All of the impulses listed above—sex, death, and national (*minjok*) identity—are either matters of grave importance or taboo subjects for most Koreans.

However, for Hong Sangsoo, they are just depictions of the everyday, and thus fraught with mundane insignificance, especially since they are typically deployed as additional stressors to personal jealousies and narcissism. The premise of *Night and Day* is a case in point. The painter protagonist, wanted by the Korean authorities for having puffed *a single* marijuana joint, bemoans the fact that his "crime" resulted from a momentary lapse caused by a capricious desire to try a new experience just once. Jail is like death to him. His fear of the penitentiary is so great that he seeks refuge in a city, Paris, where he knows no one. However, as revealed later in the film, his crime is actually only a misdemeanor, i.e., something that could have been taken care of by paying a small fine. Here again, what Hong has managed to do is unscramble the *intolerable* from the *insignificant* for the purpose of scrambling the two together again. Curiosity about an unknown substance (*insignificant*) escalates into a serious violation of the nation's drug prohibition laws (*intolerable*). Later, the fear of prosecution (*intolerable*) is translated into paranoia and hypochondria (*insignificant*).

Two other films, *Woman Is the Future of Man* and *Woman on the Beach*, also revolve around characters who have just returned from studies abroad. Because these characters are in Korea for

Cinema (Durham: Duke University Press, 2004).

9. Gilles Deleuze, *Cinema 2: The Time-Image* (Minneapolis: University of Minnesota Press, 1995), 19.

10. This by no means suggests that Hong Sangsoo has no respect for the work of Ozu. On the contrary, in my private conversations with Hong, he has demonstrated the deepest respect for the work of the revered Japanese director. Hong has gone on to record to say that every aspect of Ozu is perfect. Chuck Stephens, "Future Shock: Hong Sang-soo's Lady in Red," *Film Comment,* Vol. 40, No. 6 (Nov.-Dec. 2004), 44.

Azalea

*The Films
of Hong
Sangsoo:
Kyung
Hyun Kim*

the first time after a long absence, they tend to complain about the difficulty of adjusting to life as well as the irrational values they now detect among Koreans and the deep-seated prejudices the community has against outsiders. Hong is often unforgiving in his analysis of Koreans—both those who have never left home and those who have returned from their studies abroad—who continue to suffer from fear of freedom, fear of cosmopolitanism, and fear of complexity stemming from their own lack of experience (the result being that they end up borrowing the customs, values, and economic structures of both Japan and the United States.). Neither the remarkable economic renaissance enjoyed by Koreans after long years of destitution nor the democratic transformation Koreans experienced are to be celebrated; they are, to put it crudely, fake. Self-denial and intellectual bickering among Hong Sangsoo's characters indicate an exquisite sense of loss and mourning for the valorized Korean spirit, which can perhaps never be restored, and for the possibility that various inauspicious characteristics acquired during the colonial and postcolonial periods may never be erased.

Turning Gate

In *Turning Gate* (*Saenghwal ŭi palgyŏn*, 2002), Kyŏngsu, an actor in the midst of a career change from stage to film, finds himself between jobs. As the film opens, he receives a phone call from his director friend, who notifies him that he's been fired. Kyŏngsu is told that he is being blamed for the box-office failure of the last film in which he had been cast. Upon visiting the production office, he receives one million *won* (about US$1000) as residual pay for the film. But since the movie has flopped so badly, the director insists that it would be unethical for Kyŏngsu to take the money. He is entitled to it according to a clause in his contract, but Kyŏngsu's personal friendship with his director is jeopardized the moment he accepts it. The director warns Kyŏngsu, "It is difficult to be human, but let's try not to become monsters." This satirical statement stands out as one of the story's central themes as

Kyŏngsu struggles between being "human" and being a "monster" throughout the film.

Ironically, because he has been fired, Kyŏngsu has earned some free time from his work. He travels to Ch'unch'ŏn, a three-hour train ride from Seoul, to see an old friend, a writer, before visiting his family in Pusan. Kyŏngsu's nomadic identity allows the story to find some space in a modern world divided between routine drudgery at work, family responsibilities, and sleep. In other words, the narrative space of *Turning Gate* escapes conventional causality because Kyŏngsu is temporarily relieved from having to work. The film proceeds to follow the aimless trajectory of its idealistic protagonist as he pursues the meaning of life on the road. (The direct translation of the film's Korean title is "Discovery of Life.") By being released from work and the maddening city of Seoul, Kyŏngsu has time to indulge in a capriciousness and idealism that is amusing to viewers, who are themselves constantly being weaseled and baffled by the congested human traffic of urban centers.

The main characters of all Hong Sangsoo films to date are humiliated at some point, and Kyŏngsu is no exception. His idealism and obstinacy may be noble, but, in practical reality, he is a person who—as a fortune-teller tells him—"cannot easily blend with the others." He resists love when it is offered to him, yet he clamors for it when it is denied. Kyŏngsu meets Myŏngsuk, a dancer, in Ch'unch'ŏn, the first city he visits. Despite the fact that Sŭng'u, the novelist friend he is visiting, already fancies Myŏngsuk, Kyŏngsu sleeps with her without guilt or love. Myŏngsuk has already seen Kyŏngsu several times in the movies, and has fallen helplessly in love with him. Her attempt to win his love is to no avail, however. Kyŏngsu leaves town by train, leaving Myŏngsuk behind, her eyes swollen from crying. However, the unrequited love Myŏngsuk feels for Kyŏngsu will soon be felt by Kyŏngsu too. Continuing on his way to Pusan, he happens to meet Sunyoung, an attractive woman who is traveling home to Kyŏngju. Helplessly

Azalea

*The Films
of Hong
Sangsoo:
Kyung
Hyun Kim*

drawn to her, Kyŏngsu gets off at her stop and surreptitiously trails her to figure out where she lives.

This unscheduled stop releases Kyŏngsu from the linear plot line, and also from his final destination, Pusan. Since he has no plans, and only a vague idea of seduction, which may or may not happen, he has effectively freed himself from the chain of dramatic causality. Kyŏngsu is not just a lonely traveler; he is also an outsider from the metropolis in a small town where he is not particularly welcome. He finds himself in Kyŏngju, an ancient capital of Korea and a city where the only person he knows is Sunyoung, who, it will soon be revealed, is a married woman. Although he has found out where she lives, and will soon visit, surprising her and the rest of her family, he has yet to make up his mind about what to do next. He checks into a cheap boardinghouse. Alone, he takes a walk to a part of the city where tourists rarely visit and nonchalantly enters a restaurant. In this flimsy yet crowded barbeque place, he orders some *kopchʾang* (beef intestines) to grill at the table and a bottle of soju, thanks to which he will slowly become intoxicated.

"In a day made up of twenty-four hours, couldn't you possibly spare ten minutes to make one simple phone call?" asks a male diner with a thick accent who is sitting at a table next to Kyŏngsu. The woman—with the same accent—replies, "I was too busy. . . . I'm sure that you understand." The tension between the couple reflects the all-too-common situation of a country boy who has been anxiously left behind while his girlfriend pursues her dreams in the metropolis. It does not take long for the already irritated young local man to catch sight of another man sneaking a peek at his girlfriend.

"What were you looking at?" the young man asks Kyŏngsu, rudely jolting him from the reverie he had fallen into while eating and staring at the woman's slender, exposed legs. The male diner's thick, provincial accent is even more pronounced now, marking him as someone rooted in this traditional, conservative town. Kyŏngsu immediately denies the charge, replying meekly, "What . . . me? Nothing. I wasn't looking at anything." Despite Kyŏngsu's denial—he

146

Kyŏngsu caught sneaking a peek

protests that he had been checking out a poster pinned right above the woman's head—the audience already senses Kyŏngsu's guilt. His feeble lie—the denial that he was looking—exasperates the other male diner. Irritation soon turns to rage, producing obscenities and insults directed at Kyŏngsu, a stranger who has violated a code of ethics. "*Ssagaji ka bagajine!*" (Mind your fucking manners!), the angry diner, who himself seems to have lost any semblance of decency, blurts out in his regional slang. Fortunately, the quarrel does not explode into physical violence after the woman pleads for her boyfriend to calm down.

Though deeply textured with action and drama, this scene—shot in a single take—creates a sense of emptiness by detaching itself from the rest of the narrative. Instead of suturing the drama together, it almost punts the audience right out of it. Ironically, because the scene gives viewers reprieve from the narrative's structural tyranny, it forces them to explore the details of the space, the community in which Kyŏngsu finds himself, and the intricacies of drama beyond the primary one.

The use of provincial accents, though frequent in Korean post-war literature and comedy genre films such as the series *My Wife Is*

Azalea

The Films
of Hong
Sangsoo:
Kyung
Hyun Kim

a Gangster, is actually rare in Hong Sangsoo films. In all eight films made thus far during his thirteen-year career (1996-2008), he has never featured a major character whose accent comes from outside Seoul. As in his other films (the irate motorcyclist/restaurant worker from the Shindori Beach Resort in *Woman on the Beach*, Dongsu's friend in *Tale of Cinema* who tells the outrageous story of Yŏngsil's physical scar, and the irritated North Korean foreign student in *Night and Day*), the shifting of accents from the standard Seoul variety to more regional ones poses an often humorous threat to the main characters. The intervention of regional accents moves the focal point from the main protagonist to the minor characters, though not at the expense of the main narrative arc.

The scene's long take not only leaps over the constraints of the narrative and proposes to divert the audience's gaze to different aspects of the mise-en-scène; it also serves as a temporal guide through the process of Kyŏngsu's awkwardness: first, the stage of initial desire (from looking at the woman's legs), then guilt (for having peeped), and finally, obsessive denial (for insisting that he was just looking at a poster on the wall). The entire scene—taking place in real time, in a simple, long shot with very little camera movement—is critical for diversifying the audience's gaze. What is also remarkable about this emotive quick shifting of gears between desire, guilt, and denial is the condensation that characterizes this discursive assembly of eroticism, hypochondria, and the fear of death.

Public and private are constantly crashing into and eroding one another. This also happens between the metropolis and the province, and between English and Korean, each of which serves, respectively, as a synecdoche for elitist snobbery and local traditions. At a critical juncture in the film, Kyŏngsu blurts out, "Can you speak English?" in English as he runs away from Sŏnyŏng's house after having been caught by her husband, who has just returned home. The use of English here is awkwardly humorous in a fashion both recondite and obscure to the audience. "Can you speak English?" is one of the first English sentences Koreans learn

148

in school, yet such a question is hardly appropriate to the situation of two Koreans meeting for the first time in a provincial town. It is also a question, or so Koreans are taught, usually posed when one wants to open a conversation with a stranger, not something blurted out when trying to avoid meeting someone.

Up until the point when Sŏnyŏng's husband approaches him, there's nothing about Kyŏngsu that suggests he has done anything unusual or unethical. However, Kyŏngsu finds himself caught not only in an interstitial space between public and private (the alleyway he is in leads only to Sŏnyŏng's house, so there could be no other purpose for his presence), but it is also an awkward bit of timing, since he has just had sex with the man's wife the night before. Therefore, his attempt to beat a hasty retreat from the scene of his voyeuristic crime is undertaken to avoid a potential eruption of hostility or violence from a jealous husband. This "Can you speak English" scene is a repetition of what took place earlier in the *kopch'ang* restaurant, where Kyŏngsu's awkwardness can be summed up as an initial stage of desire (from looking through the gate to see if Sŏnyŏng was there), guilt (for having peeped), and finally, obsessive denial (for insisting that he does not even speak Korean). Again, we find that the rotating wheel of desire, guilt, and denial sustains a triptych structure of eroticism, hypochondria, and fear of death. In both scenes, the exaggerated fear of pain or death also registers as a deep-seated fear of cosmopolitanism, sexual freedom, and the complexity inherent in being a nomad in an unfamiliar space between private and public.

All of these repetitions take place in a kind of double articulation of past and present integral to the temporal rhythms of Hong Sangsoo's films. However, if earlier films such as *Virgin Stripped Bare by Her Bachelors* (2000) managed to tangle up time by staging the same event twice, *Turning Gate* brings to a standstill Hong Sangsoo's previous experimentations with time forking into two different paths. *Turning Gate*'s time remains linear, but it constantly weaves the past as well as the future into the present.

AZALEA

The Films
of Hong
Sangsoo:
Kyung
Hyun Kim

Repetition also plays a critical role here. For instance, during a bit of pillow talk between the two towards the end of the film, Kyŏngsu confesses to Sŏnyŏng that he remembers seeing her husband on a date with another woman. This questioning of her husband's moral integrity—despite her protest—is the result of an accidental encounter between Kyŏngsu and Sŏnyŏng's husband before the "Can you speak English" incident. While in Ch'unch'ŏn, Kyŏngsu's duckboat had bumped into another one, and the stranger on the other boat—accompanied by a woman—had asked for a light. But, much as viewers of the film will probably have forgotten whether the stranger in the boat and the man in front of Sŏnyŏng's gate were indeed the same person (Hong Sangsoo deliberately cast a nondescript, non-professional actor to play the role of the husband), Kyŏngsu also has an unreliable memory. "Perhaps I was mistaken," he says, before cynically adding, "All Koreans look alike." Are Koreans alike only in physical appearance? What about other qualities, such as behavior? Could this statement be re-construed to imply that the gap between one Korean (the husband) and another (Kyŏngsu) is also indiscernible? Such questions are left unanswered.

Though *Turning Gate* invokes a legend or myth that directly refers to exterior conditions circumscribing the fate of the film's protagonist, the myth does not serve to facilitate a transcendent understanding of life; rather, it implies an objective social condition that suffocates any form of idealism or desire. Kyŏngsu's relentless pursuit of Sŏnyŏng leaves the two in limbo. In order to help her choose between Kyŏngsu or her husband, the two visit a female fortune-teller. The fortune-teller proclaims her verdict like a blind prophet at the climax of a Greek tragedy, forcefully stating that Sŏnyŏng should finally choose her husband over Kyŏngsu. This female *mudang* (a shaman who communicates with the local spirits) is incisive in a situation in which there is no clear line between right and wrong. Kyŏngsu is "truly" in love to the extent that he declares there is "nothing else that I would want in a woman."

But it is unethical for him to love a woman who has a family with another man. As such, the *mudang*'s analysis is simply too cruel for him. She predicts that Kyŏngsu's future will be cursed with vacuity, wandering, and physical danger, while Sŏnyŏng's husband will enjoy a fate filled with prospects for career advancement, wealth, and popular respect.

It is intriguing that the *mudang*'s "verdict" about the *present* is reached through her clairvoyance about the *future* after analyzing the *past*—i.e., the birthdays of Kyŏngsu, Sŏnyŏng, and Sŏnyŏng's husband (who of course remains absent during the fortune-telling session). Present, past, and future are once again jumbled. Ironically, the supernatural and the pre-modern must be invoked in order to resolve a conflict between the ideal (love) and the practical (marriage) at a time when no other productive mechanism can be found to arrive at a decision. The powers of the supernatural, of clairvoyance, and of the future nail down the coffin in which rests the ideal love aspired to by Kyŏngsu.

Though Kyŏngsu's ego is bruised and his quest for the meaning of life can never succeed, his failure gives us a glimpse of what Georg Lukacs, according to Fredric Jameson, once pointed out as "the most basic image of human freedom"—"the *momentary* reconciliation of matter and spirit toward which his [a novelist's] hero strives in vain"[11] [my emphasis]. Kyŏngsu's obsession and stubbornness have at least *temporarily* made him a hero who will strive for the unity of transcendental ideals and a pragmatic life, despite the probability that he will fail miserably in this pursuit. In the process, he will have fallen short of "becoming human," a project that was cursed from the beginning and acknowledged as unrealizable in the end. By portraying a man who has been thoroughly humiliated, however, the film succeeds in reverberating with the redemptive message that life still needs to be lived—even when its meaning remains undiscovered.

---

11. Fredric Jameson, *Marxism and Form: Twentieth-Century Dialectical Theories of Literature* (Princeton, N.J.: Princeton University Press, 1971), 173.

AZALEA

The Films
of Hong
Sangsoo:
Kyung
Hyun Kim

After all, disappointment produces a pivotal moment in any given quest. "It is difficult to be human, but let's try not to become monsters," pleads Kyŏngsu several times throughout the film, echoing his director friend. This repeated plea, which is just as well directed at himself as at others, is at once comic and a critique. *Turning Gate* thus realizes a theme that is extremely rare in stories today, and almost extinct in contemporary films: that of a hero who achieves meaning only in opposition to his context and who is hurt when he seeks integration, whether into a society or into true romance. By portraying this awkwardness, Hong Sangsoo draws out a story of human experience in which truth, however futile, is still worth striving for.

Woman Is the Future of Man

In *Woman is the Future of Man* (2004), two friends, Hunjun (played by Kim Taewoo) and Munho (Yoo Jitae), reunite after Hunjun has returned home after having finished an M.F.A. degree in film production at an American institution. As he has done several times before, Hong has borrowed the title of his film from a Western literary/art source. Like *The Day a Pig Fell into the Well*, a title derived from a John Cheever short story, and *Virgin Stripped Bare by Her Bachelors*, named after a work of art by Marcel Duchamp, *Woman Is the Future of Man* comes from a line of Louis Aragon's poetry that Hong Sangsoo found on a French postcard.[12] Despite the film's title, which suggests that the future is reflected in woman, it is mainly the past that the two male protagonists, Hunjun and Munho, attempt to access through a woman (Sŏnhwa). As in his other films, time refuses to stay within a linear framework, and the temporal rhythms in *Woman Is the Future of Man* constantly weave in and out of the past. Because Sŏnhwa is essentially a sign, of their past and their present simultaneously, she is also virtually their future.

---

12. Chuck Stephens reports that Hong Sangsoo had the following explanation for the title of his film: "As the future is yet to come, it means nothing, and if the future is multiplied by man, the result is still zero. And if woman is the future of man, which is zero, woman is also nothing." Stephens, 45.

Towards the beginning of the film, Hunjun visits Munho at his house. Heavy snow has covered the lawn of Munho's impressive house in P'yŏngch'ang-dong, a district in Seoul well known for its vintage mansions of old-money *chaebol*s. The film immediately contextualizes these two protagonists as sons of Korea's affluent class—people who could afford an education and career in the fine arts and film. Hunjun and Munho visit a Chinese restaurant for food and drinks. Hunjun's goal is to make films in Korea, but he faces an uncertain future. At one point during their conversation, Munho, who has just been made a professor of studio art, becomes upset about a past event: Hunjun had apparently given Munho's wife a hug when the couple had paid him a visit in the U.S. Munho growls at Hunjun, "Why did you try to embrace my wife?" Hunjun tries to defend himself by retorting that it really wasn't much of a *kkyŏantta* (an embrace or a hug). Munho refuses to buy the poor excuse and bursts out, "Shut up! Do you actually think that you are a *miguk nom* (Yankee or American bastard) or what?"

Though Munho's reaction is excessive, he legitimates his anger by asserting that Hunjun is a national traitor who has violated a thousand-year-old Confucian code of conduct that forbids any type of physical contact between two members of the opposite sex. Is Munho an upholder of traditional Confucian values for blurting out a derogatory term (*miguk nom*) that contains such strong "nationalist" or xenophobic views? What is invoked here is not so much that Munho is a principled man who strongly defends the traditional values of Koreans, but that he is an egoist who will freely adopt a nationalist cliché in order to camouflage his own insecurities. In other words, *miguk nom* is only an inscription, a sign capable of emitting anything but its real meaning. But does this awkward exchange completely strip *miguk nom* from—to borrow a Deleuze-ian term—the "thing-ness of the sign"? Is Munho simply suspicious of Hunjun's intention, and will he do anything to ward off this threat against his wife, or is his intention to warn his friend that he has obnoxiously adopted American-style mannerisms that

AZALEA

*The Films
of Hong
Sangsoo:
Kyung
Hyun Kim*

do not fit Korean ones? This multiplying ambiguity again reaffirms the repeated circuit of eroticism and death that often overwhelms unsubstantiated rhetoric in Hong Sangsoo's films. Here, one needs to be reminded that the threat of death is always accompanied by hypochondria, so that the actual potential for death becomes unrealizable. This circuit that moves from eroticism to death and back again has the potential to continue eternally until love or death actually does arrive.

Munho storms out. Hunjun, dumbfounded, is left alone. It is at this precise moment that a plainly dressed waitress with a noodle dish enters the frame. Hunjun takes a peek at her and suddenly asks, "Are you interested in acting?" He introduces himself as a film director and explains that he usually casts his actors from "real ordinary people" he meets. The young server, without a single word of excuse, tells him that she is not interested and walks away. This awkward encounter between Hunjun, the film's protagonist, and the restaurant worker reveals a foreign subject—a first for a Hong Sangsoo film. When the server leaves Hunjun's table, the camera follows her with a pan that captures her talking with another woman standing at the cash register. The film provides no subtitles for the Korean audience, despite the fact that the two women are not speaking Korean; they are speaking Mandarin. It is only because of this exchange that the audience comes to realize that the woman is ethnically Chinese.

Sudden outbursts of anger, the awkward solicitation of women, and sneaky defensiveness against unanswerable questions are all too familiar moments in a Hong Sangsoo film. Hong Sangsoo's characters face repeated obstacles that generate "persistent disorientations" and a "sense of being lost in the world."[13] Yet this particular scene manifests something of a postcolonial symptom that plagues and doubly alienates the Korean intellectual who arguably belongs neither in the West nor in the East. Hunjun's

---

13. Akira Lippit classifies Hong Sangsoo's character as being in a psychic state of "aporia" or at the "end of the line." Lippit, 26.

Hunjun asks a Chinese waitress to be in his film

character is prone to attacks throughout the film because his identity is unstable after having been stretched beyond a single national subjecthood. He has just been yelled at for having temporarily forgotten that he is a Korean. Having returned home from the U.S., Hunjun finds himself not only situated between the past (U.S.), the present (Chinese restaurant), and the future (Korea), but also stretched through and across different registers of textuality, nation, and language, none of which remains stable, and each of which is wrapped up in a series of endless and constantly expanding contradictions.

Earlier in the conversation, in a vain attempt at self-promotion, he tells Munho that his graduate film received compliments from his faculty advisor. "You know what he called it?" Hunjun asks before answering his own question: "A germ." "What is a *chŏm* (in Korean, a dot)?" Munho asks Hunjun. Both Hunjun, a Korean who has returned from the U.S., and Munho, a Korean who has never studied abroad, have mispronounced the word "gem" as "jurm" rather than "jem." To Munho, "gem (or *chŏm*)" or "germ"—the former signifying purity and the latter its opposite—are indistinguishable and unrecognizable English

155

AZALEA

The Films
of Hong
Sangsoo:
Kyung
Hyun Kim

words. After he is told that "germ" means *posŏk* (a precious stone), Munho snickers and retorts by asking whether the English word for *posŏk* isn't "treasure." "No," Hunjun tells him, "treasure" in Korean would be *pomul*, not *posŏk*. The English word "gem" slips between a "gem" and a "germ," but also between the two Korean signifiers *pomul* and a *posŏk*, losing in the process the initial signified that was intended to proudly flaunt Hunjun's talent.

This contentious discursivity created through language is further pursued by the intermittent insertion of Mandarin, spoken by the waitress and the proprietor, both of whom are *hwagyo*s (Chinese migrants in Korea). The Chinese restaurant featured in the film belongs neither to a nation nor a reality. The restaurant's wide windows, which display the street as if it were a moving portrait, position the restaurant as a dreamy space devoid, at least for the time being, of the weariness of a native intellectual who has returned from an American metropolis, only to find that job prospects for him at home are dim.

This particular citation lays bare one of the symptoms of Korean society's vexed relation to its "ethnic other." The ethnoscape of transnational Korea, where Korea is caught between the U.S. and the rest of Asia, is located somewhere between visible legibility and inscrutability. The desire shown by Korean libertines to take an interest in the Chinese girl, who is precious because of her gem-like, uncanny ordinariness (or purity), allows room for Hong Sangsoo to take issue with Chinese subjecthood in Korea, which has in the past been both conspicuous and inconspicuous. The impulse to represent the other implies the cultural disenfranchisement of the anxious male Korean subject, and, in this instance, forms a narcissistic loop around the protagonist's own ontological nausea.

That nausea is similarly invoked in *The Mother and the Whore* (1973), directed by Jean Eustache,[14] in which Veronica, a

14. Jean Eustache is a French filmmaker who has made several films including *The Mother and the Whore* (1973) and *Mes Petites Amoureuses* (1974); Hong Sangsoo had not been aware of Eustache's work until I introduced him to it in 2003 right after he completed *Turning Gate*.

Polish immigrant worker in France, is seduced by Alexandre, an idle Parisian intellectual. This nausea is itself a displaced symptom that engages the body of the Chinese girl without being either conscientious or self-reflective. Hunjun's strong desire for the Chinese girl and the way her subjectivity is reduced to his need for an actor for his film is an obvious move to construct an ethnic other in order to help overcome the internal turbulence he feels after his friend claims that he speaks and behaves as if he were a "Yankee bastard." Therefore, Hunjun's scopophilic glance, which will later be repeated by Munho, incubates in these intellectuals a self-deluding *other-ization* of a kind that could be described as the "metropolitan transfiguration of the colonial dilemma" [15] —a state that could be said to resemble Albert Camus's racialized construction of the French imagination through stereotyped representations of North Africans in his novels.

However, if Camus had captured what Edward Said characterized as the "waste and sadness" of French imperialism through his depiction of Arabs, the melancholia and anxiety of Korean men could be said to have sprung forth from a paradigm that belongs to both the First and the Third Worlds. Thus, the otherness of the Chinese worker is both defamiliarized and made familiar. After all, using the term "colonized" to depict the Chinese diaspora in Korea is no small irony—not only because China has never been colonized by Korea, but also because it is often impossible to distinguish between Koreans and Chinese just by looking at their faces, and many ethnic Chinese in Korea are fluent in Korean. The Chinese waitress speaks Korean without any accent, and her Chinese ethnic identity would not have been revealed had it not been for her subsequent chat with her boss in Mandarin. Yet a heightened awareness of Chinese ethnic otherness continues to sprout up around the all-too-familiar notion of Korea as an impotent, desecrated Fatherland and women from China as a locus of the maternal imagination.

15. Edward Said, *Culture and Imperialism* (New York: Vintage, 1994), 184.

Azalea

The Films
of Hong
Sangsoo:
Kyung
Hyun Kim

After the Chinese restaurant worker rejects this offer from a disillusioned Korean intellectual, she sneaks out of the restaurant. Hunjun gazes at the woman as she waits in the street for her ride to arrive. The narrative, initially stymied by the Chinese woman's refusal, gets further off track with the small talk that follows. Hunjun's gaze, which has been reoriented around the sight of the woman outside, effects a complete break from the present. The film loops into a flashback sequence that features Hunjun's youth, and the two Korean libertines end up reliving their memories. Does the refusal of the Chinese woman precipitate this radical break from the present to a time when innocence and youth could be grafted onto past college days, when Hunjun still believed in the "purity" of women? When he thought of women as "gems" and not "germs"? The intellectual's attempt to find an authenticated place in the world by filming an "ordinary" and therefore uncontaminated Chinese woman is thwarted, and all he can do is comb through the memories of his unsullied past.

But even here he finds the young Korean woman, Sŏnhwa (Sung Hyunah), to be both precious and contaminated. In other words, everything from the past, the present, and the future can be a gem, a germ, or a *chŏm*. Later, Sŏnhwa's sexual relationship with both men, one married (Munho) and the other single (Hunjun), is exposed, angering Hunjun. The three separate, and Munho joins up with his students who are playing soccer on a school playground. This is the only moment in the film where the protagonist takes part in a group scene, and, as happens in all of Hong Sangsoo's films, he will soon face expulsion from, or public humiliation by, the group.

Echoing *The Day a Pig Fell into the Well*, when the B-grade writer-protagonist is humiliated at a gathering after having had too much to drink, in *Woman Is the Future of Man*, Munho is placed at an art student soiree where drinks flow freely. He is the only faculty member present. "Now whose turn is it? My question is always the same." Turning to one of the female students, Munho asks, "Tell us the last time you had sex, when it was, with whom, and what it felt like." This question reaffirms Munho's double standard in chastising Hunjun earlier for giving his wife a "Yankee"-style hug. Despite a collective protest by the other students, the student he asked decides to answer in a surprisingly frank manner, telling the entire group that she had had sex just two days earlier in a filthy motel room with a person she hardly knew, and that the feeling wasn't anything to write home about. Her confession arouses strong disapproval and dissent. By "forcing" an unmarried woman to talk about her sexual activities, an invisible taboo has been broken. The only way to mollify this public outrage would be to identify the culprit and make him pay.

Munho thus becomes the *homo sacer*, a person who, according to Giorgio Agamben, "is banned, may be killed by anybody, but may not be sacrificed in a religious ritual."[16] A male student across from Hunjun snickers, "Hey, Teach, don't you think you are a bit *chŏjil* (低質 literally low-grade or vulgar)?" Nervously trying to placate this student's rage, Munho responds with "What are you? If not a *chŏjil*, what are you? A *kojil*?" Here the joke is that *kojil* is a homograph that stems from the Chinese characters 痼疾 that are typically combined to mean "chronic disease" rather than the intended 高質 (literally high-class), which sounds the same as "disease" in Korean. Here again, we are introduced at a critical moment to the confusion that arises between two different meanings of the same spoken signifier—much like the earlier *ge(r)m*, both of which are pronounced in Korean as *chŏm* since "r" sounds are notoriously silent in Korean *hangul*. Could a person be both high-class and a chronic disease?

Even this punning of *kojil* as disease (germ) or high-class (gem) is not sufficient to surprise the angry student into laughter. He brushes off his teacher's question by reiterating his position: "I just said what I said because I thought that you were being a *chŏjil*,

---

16. Giorgio Agamben, *Homo Sacer: Sovereign Power and Bare Life*, trans. Daniel Heller-Roazen (Stanford, CA: Stanford University Press, 1998).

AZALEA

*The Films
of Hong
Sangsoo:
Kyung
Hyun Kim*

that's all. Not that I think that I'm a *kojil*." Through his stubborn willingness to further insult the teacher and implicitly challenge him on the legal basis of sexual harassment, the student swiftly runs a course from desire, to impotence (symbolic or real) and death, finally arriving at paranoia or hypochondria. Though Munho unleashes a rage of his own by making semi-coherent, profanity-laced accusations in response, he cannot regain his standing. He sinks further and further into an abyss of suffering as a teacher accused of sexually harassing his own student. One by one, the other students jump on the bandwagon, verbally stabbing their already slain teacher. "But how do you go on living when you believe in nothing?" exclaims a student. Another howls, "But do you think you are the only one struggling with that?"

Munho has been thoroughly disgraced by this public humiliation, but he must follow the circuit running from pleasure to pain and displeasure in order to be re-animated. The final scene involves Munho being approached in the street by the sexually active female student, who suggests that they check into a motel together. In a crummy motel room, the student volunteers to "suck him off" and proceeds to do so. But even before Munho, who had failed to satisfy Sunhwa earlier by ejaculating prematurely, can get it off, the *kojil* (a non-pervert and a pest) student interrupts by calling her on her cell phone from right outside their room. Munho, trying to project a cool veneer, becomes frightened that he will be officially charged with "sexual harassment" and suggests that they coordinate their alibis. Once again he becomes a germ and a gem, moving nervously between a man of principle who openly discusses his true desires and a paranoiac/hypochondriac worried about a student bringing a suit (either harassment or adultery, which still remains prosecutable in Korea) against him.

Tale of Cinema

Hong Sangsoo's films are notorious for the ways in which they shun family, schools, and other social institutions. Most of his films take place in unpopular coffee shops and restaurants, private motel rooms, and on unattractive streets where his characters endlessly loiter. This revulsion against the social is particularly pronounced in *Tale of Cinema*, which marked Hong Sangsoo's debut as a producer of his own films (something which became necessary after he could not secure financing beyond a French distribution deal with MK2). The de-centering of subjectivity, through which the protagonist becomes humiliated, serves as an underlying theme of *Tale of Cinema,* as it does in Hong Sangsoo's other films.

In *Tale of Cinema,* Hong's two male protagonists, Sang'wŏn (played by Lee Gi-woo) and Tongsu (Kim Sang-kyung, who returns to play yet another role in a Hong Sangsoo film after having played Kyŏngsu in *Turning Gate*), are constantly being placed in awkward positions they attempt to evade, which only pushes them deeper into an abyss of humiliation. Both Sang'wŏn and Tongsu assume the role of *flâneur*, meandering throughout the city looking for excitement, only to end up endangering themselves. In *Turning Gate*, the film's hero, Kyŏngsu, tries desperately to steal a glance at a woman's legs, then tries even more desperately to deny he did so. In *Tale of Cinema*, smoking is the issue that brings about a rupture between private and public.

The film begins when Tongsu, unbeknownst to its audience, visits a theater in Seoul that is sponsoring a retrospective of the films of his colleague, Director Lee, his best buddy at film school. The film-within-a-film's plot begins with lanky teenager Sang'wŏn, who has just graduated from high school, wandering through the old downtown of Seoul after having had a small quarrel with his older brother. He spots a girl Yŏngsil (Ŏm Chiwŏn), a former classmate, who had dropped out after being sexually harassed by her teacher. After killing time waiting for her by watching a play called *Ŏmoni* [Mother], Sang'wŏn finally meets her. Yŏngsil confesses that she is smitten with Sang'wŏn (she asks repeatedly, "Would you like me to be your mistress?"), and they decide to spend the night together in a motel room near Namsan Tower. They

Azalea

The Films
of Hong
Sangsoo:
Kyung
Hyun Kim

Libido, unfortunately, is thwarted for young Sang'wŏn

fail to complete the sex act, however, because she suffers acute pain whenever Sang'wŏn attempts to penetrate her.

Libido, the life force or the procreative drive, is thwarted for young Sang'wŏn. The failure of sex, in Freudian terms, signals the impossibility of all creative and life-producing drives.[17] The juxtaposition of Sang'wŏn's bizarre dream of a white woman in a nightgown offering him an apple with his futile attempts to initiate sexual intercourse with Yŏngsil emphasizes his increasing anxiety over the physical obstacle to pleasure. This stifling of libido, this incapacity to enjoy sex, sparks a death wish that the capricious Sang'wŏn cannot resist. Once again, Hong Sangsoo is able to extract the intolerable from the insignificant by translating a seemingly trite sexual experience into a horrifying double suicide attempt. Throughout the night, the two hop from one pharmacist to another buying as many sleeping pills as they can. But all's well that ends well. Yŏngsil wakes up in the middle of the night, crawls into the bathroom, and vomits, emptying her stomach. She places an emergency call to Sang'wŏn's family using his cell phone, and he is rescued by his uncle.

17. See Sigmund Freud, *Beyond the Pleasure Principle* (New York: Norton, 1975).

Tale of Cinema thus continues the theme of associating sex with death. In the film-within-a-film, the young couple's failed attempt to have sex causes them to overdose on sleeping pills, which leads to yet another failure: their attempted suicide. This continuing entanglement of sex and death shows that obsessions with eroticism and the termination of life are crucial lynchpins for abandoning exteriority and accountability and purifying the individual mind—a place without materiality, immune to the intrusions of capital. In *Turning Gate*, Hong's protagonist Kyŏngsu lusts after the "perfect woman" he has finally managed to find; but as soon as he openly acknowledges that lust, he cannot act upon it, and becomes impotent. In Hong's work, explicit drives towards eroticism and death are always tempered with impotence (inability to have sexual intercourse) and hypochondria (inability to face pain and death). This is why Hong Sangsoo's films lack the urgency found in the more solemn and somber works of Ingmar Bergman, though the films of both directors tend toward an abandonment of the social.

This withdrawal from the social is also captured in a remarkable way by a scene in the middle of *Tale of Cinema* when Tongsu, who has just seen the film about the double suicide, runs into a friend from his film school days and joins him and his family at a Chinese restaurant. The old classmates cover topics ranging from their dying friend who's in a coma (Director Lee) to memories of *kalbi jjim* they had eaten together many years ago. Though the lunch is satisfying, Tongsu's departure from the group is anything but graceful. After the meal, Tongsu's friend offers him a ride.

The ride only lasts few minutes, however, because Tongsu asks to be let out almost immediately. He has violated one of those new public rules that has caught on globally in the last few years: avoid smoking in other people's cars and especially around children. When Tongsu pulls out a cigarette and begins to smoke, he is violating the code of decency that regulates behavior in a public space. I use the word "violating" to emphasize not only Tongsu's will to fulfill his desire to smoke despite other people's health concerns,

AZALEA

*The Films
of Hong
Sangsoo:
Kyung
Hyun Kim*

Tongsu would rather be smoking on the street than not smoking in the car

but also the primacy of family and especially children, which typically supersedes the desires of the individual. Tongsu, who's asked to put out his cigarette for the sake of the children, begins to feel uncomfortable. The camera focuses on his discomfort through a medium close-up of his face, which is held for a good ten seconds. Unable either to protest his freedom to smoke or to comply with the "no-smoking" rule in his friend's car, he has no choice but to get out and walk on a brisk winter day.

Tongsu's abrupt departure and voluntary exile from the comfort of the car, rejecting his friend's generosity, prompts us to think about the structure of inclusion and exclusion in a society. Networks of friends, community, and family—and even the nation—rely upon regulated codes of ethics that discipline aberrant behaviors and actions. Tongsu's habit of smoking and, as revealed in a conversation he has later that evening with friends, his binge drinking, are signs of irrational indulgence that sum up Tongsu's negative, self-destructive nature. For the moment, however, without car, friends, or family, he revels in walking.

Being a pedestrian in Seoul is radically different from being "a man of leisure [who] can indulge in the perambulations of the *flâneur* only if as such he is already out of place."[18] "In Paris," Hannah Arendt also notes, "a stranger feels at home because he can inhabit the city the way he lives in his own four walls. And just as one inhabits an apartment, and makes it comfortable, by living in it instead of just using it for sleeping, eating, and working, so one inhabits a city by strolling through it without aim or purpose, with one's stay secured by the countless cafés which line the streets. . . ."[19] If Paris, as suggested by these two Germans, successfully erases the boundary between inside and outside by providing a smooth passage for pedestrians, Seoul cannot be said to invite a similar kind of comfort. Parked and moving cars perpetually invade the sidewalks because of the crammed roads and a shortage of public parking. Construction gear, pits, and men at work also frequently disrupt the flow of foot traffic in Seoul, which is constantly under construction. Along with the teeming masses of pedestrians endlessly snaking along the sidewalks, these conditions make the experience of strolling and loitering in outdoor cafés virtually impossible. As a result, the interiorization of the exterior—and the inclusion of exiles or foreigners as well—is difficult to achieve in Seoul.

Tongsu has chosen to take his walk on a brisk Sunday. There are hardly any other pedestrians, and there is no reason for him to hurry, for he has no friends, no family, no job obligations, and no willpower. On the street, he catches sight of the actress who played Yŏngsil (also the actress's name) in the film he has just seen, entering the very optometry as in the film. Though they have just met, Tongsu not only asks for her phone number, but also asks her to star in the film that he is working on—which may or may not get made. She is amused by both requests, but they are destined to meet again later at a dinner to raise money for the terminally ill Director Lee.

---

18. Walter Benjamin, "On Some Motifs in Baudelaire," in *Illuminations: Essays and Reflections*, ed. Hannah Arendt, trans. Harry Zohn, (New York: Schocken Books, 1968), 172.

19. Hannah Arendt, "Introduction to *Walter Benjamin*: 1892-1940," in *Illuminations*, 21.

AZALEA

*The Films
of Hong
Sangsoo:
Kyung
Hyun Kim*

"Should we die together? If we knew we could only live another half-a-year, we could love each other intensely," Tongsu says, after having sex with Yŏngsil. This statement is intriguing for it presumes that the reason for the failure of true love is that we do not know when we are going to die. In other words, the unpredictability of life makes us wander from one desire to another. Hong Sangsoo's films generally feature characters suffering from nagging injuries or health problems. In *Woman on the Beach*, for instance, there is a scene in the middle of the film where Kim Chungrae (played by Kim Sŭng'u) suddenly falls down while jogging on the beach. He has inexplicably pulled one of the "unused muscles" in his right leg, and he drags his foot in pain for the remainder of the film. In *The Power of Kangwon Province*, Chaewan complains to the main protagonist Sang'gwŏn that he has dermatological problems. "Use less soap," is the advice Sang'gwŏn offers to his dear friend. Sujŏng in *Virgin Stripped Bare by Her Bachelors* constantly avoids meeting her boyfriend Jae-won at a motel room, using her poor health as an excuse, and Tong'u in *The Day a Pig Fell into the Well* visits a clinic to get a shot for his venereal disease. Each of these ailments provides comic relief from otherwise serious, everyday matters (unemployment, adulterous situations, sexual advances in romantic relationships, etc.) in which the characters are embroiled. The proliferation of hypochondriacs, who are constantly entering and exiting clinics, hospitals, and pharmacies to treat their nagging medical problems, forces us to think that the fear of death or pain, not unlike the desire for sex and love, is slightly inflated in a Hong Sangsoo film.

In *Tale of Cinema*, death or the death drive is no longer treated in the grossly exaggerated way it was in previous Hong Sangsoo films. Tongsu suggests to Yŏngsil that they plan a double suicide because that would be the only way their love could remain genuine. But is love between the two bound to be more successful if death looms around the corner? Would the pleasure principle then be completely freed from the constraints of reality (the need to save for retirement, obligatory familial responsibilities to reproduce, etc.)? Or would the prolongation of hedonistic sex, like drug use, also be considered an avoidance of reality, and thus the same as death, at least in the domain of the social? What remains clear is that love is intimately tied to death—not as its binary opposite, but as its mutually dependent other, with the two sharing common ground in their opposition to the reality principles that govern the conventions and rules of any social community. Yŏngsil shrugs off this question because she fails to grasp the sincerity of Tongsu's offer of sex and death at the same time. She has granted Tongsu his wish to have sex with her, but she does not seek a future with him beyond this one-night stand.

When Tongsu visits him in the hospital, Director Lee, who has difficulty breathing even with the aid of a respirator, begs, "I want to live. I don't want to die." Director Lee, who is in some way Tongsu's alter ego, struggles to say these simple words. This statement is a classic example of a kind of hypochondria, but Director Lee's shrill desperation, sweaty face, and terrified eyes all suggest that death and the pain associated with terminal illness (though we are never told what his illness is) are neither a trifle nor a joke. Death is frightening; it is absolute, real, and irreversible. Tongsu leaves the hospital, and on the street, he remarks through an earnest voice-over: "I need to think more. Thinking can make me even quit smoking. Only thinking can rescue me from dying." He then reaches for a cigarette.

Hong Sangsoo in the Age of *Hallyu* [The Korean Wave]

Despite their lack of box-office success, Hong Sangsoo's films continue to inspire page after page of critical reviews in the local press because their imagery interrogates, critiques, and seeks to unsettle the rigidified and fixed ways in which humans continue to live, talk, work, and shun their families. And yet, Hong Sangsoo's work, especially during the *hallyu* era, has continued its downward spiral in terms of box office receipts. None of his films, including

AZALEA

The Films
of Hong
Sangsoo:
Kyung
Hyun Kim

his most successful one, *Turning Gate*, which was widely released and sold about 250,000 tickets domestically in Korea,[20] has ever become profitable for their investors. Despite authorized theatrical and DVD releases of *Woman Is the Future of Man* and *Woman on the Beach* in the U.S., Hong's box office figures have not exactly been something to boast of. Not only do his films suffer from the relative scarcity of art house moviegoers in recent years, but also from the widespread prejudice against Asian modernist films in general. Though online American DVD rental outlets have been flooded by over 100 Korean titles, most of these are genre films that specialize in horror, action, and melodrama.

In an effort to construct a unique vision of aesthetic practice, Hong Sangsoo gestures toward what could become the guiding ideal of Korea's contemporary art house cinema: seeking in the arts a space where culture cannot function as capital. Hong's films claim no obvious kinship with those genres that appeal mostly to teenagers. While genre films have to have a clear beginning, middle, and end, Hong's texts instead focus on the aimless peregrinations of intellectual characters and the endless monotonous loops such journeys tend to create. In a movie-going environment in Korea that is increasingly subject to pressure from mass media and the consumer marketplace, maintaining distinction and prestige based solely on film festival awards and favorable reviews is difficult. Hong Sangsoo's blunt treatment of sexuality has often added to his growing reputation for being sex-obsessed on top of the inveterate snobbery implied by his rejection of commercial genre forms as well as political realist narrative codes. But Hong Sangsoo's work is never a good aphrodisiac. Not only do his films lack the salaciousness usually underpinning deep-seated Confucian repression, such as

---

20. *Turning Gate* is widely viewed as the most commercially successful film made by Hong Sangsoo. It was released in 2002 before the Korean film industry had introduced a computerized tally of national box office receipts, but it reportedly sold around 127,000 tickets in Seoul alone. Considering that sales in Seoul usually comprise about half of the nation's total ticket sales, one can estimate that it has sold around 250,000 nationwide.

that displayed in the work of his predecessor Jang Sun-woo, but they are also too closely aligned with death (both symbolic and physical), especially those films that were made in his post-*Virgin Stripped Bare by Her Bachelors* years.

Mainstream viewers tend to place their faith in decency and reason rather than wanting to be challenged by the revelation of stronger impulses toward domination, selfishness, and deceit. After all, U.S. Republicans continue to insist, not without success, that going to war with Iraq was a "noble" thing to do and a genuine attempt to make the world into a better place.[21] Mainstream audiences crave more patriotic images that can reassure them that the insecurities of nomadism and alienation are fabrications of the mind, not real social situations. No surprise, then, that the films of Hong Sangsoo are utterly devoid of commercial marketplace value in both Korea and abroad. His images insist that they cannot represent anything beyond what is being projected within the cinematic frame: life's frailty poised between life and death, between truth and deceit, and between the egotistical mind and love for others. Hong Sangsoo's world, as attested to by his films, is slowly being transformed, and will persist only as long as the plane of life on which he dwells remains fundamentally unchanged: sooner or later, man's desire, man's will to live, and the nation's fate, will all be thwarted.

21. As demonstrated frequently by Bill O'Reilly of *The O'Reilly Factor* in arguing against Michael Moore and even David Letterman who oppose the war in Iraq, the word "noble" seems to occupy a special place in the conservative pundits' rhetoric about the war.

The Cheerful Night Road

by Gong Sun Ok

Translated by Jane Suh

I was sick of the rain. It had been beating down for so long. The monsoons had started a week ago and it had been raining ever since. The house reeked of dampness.

Can't get over you
Can't get over my love for you
I wanna fly,
Fly far away
I wanna hear you breathe
Can't sleep 'cause of you
I wanna fly,
Fly into the night
Can't sleep 'cause of you

I think of my first love whenever it rains, and when I think of my first love my heart aches. I hope the rains end early this year.

"And now a request from the head nurse at S Hospital, 'Plantain' by Su and Jin."

We need to live grand like fireworks
We need to stand tall, each coming day

171

Like grass in the open fields
We need to love them to their faces
Not hate them to their backs . . . .

"And next it's Yi Ŭn-mi with 'Not Yet Thirty'."

My days drift away like wisps of smoke
I used to be full of memories—
I thought youth would be mine forever,
But my youth is leaving me too

I'm sure the radio will be blaring songs by Cho Yong-p'il, Yun To-hyŏn, Su and Jin, and Yi Ŭn-mi until the end of time. People live and die but the radio is forever. My mother has just entered her sixties but during the past rainy week, her grasp on reality has gone downhill fast. The dampness permeating the house hurts her inside and out.

"Hey you—your father went off and left me, you know."

I first noticed the signs of dementia four days after Father's funeral. That's when Mum started feeling sad that her husband had gone off and left her. It wasn't until she kept repeating the same line for an entire month that I realized something wasn't right. Barely twenty-one years old and stuck at home with a senile mother—and I had few options. I had gone to nursing school with the sole desire to get a job away from home. But as soon as I finished school, Father passed away. One by one my big brothers and my sister went off to live their own lives and here I was back at home . . . just me and Mum.

"There are two hospitals in town, you know," my brother had said to me. "And a dental office and an herbal medicine clinic too!" my sister chimed in. My brothers were buried in debt and my sister was a divorced single mother. My brothers jointly took out a loan and one of them became a florist. He went bankrupt after a typhoon destroyed his greenhouse, and the other brother went down as well trying to pay back the loan.

172

Sheltered by an umbrella, I went out to our yard to pick some mallow leaves. Mum's voice followed me out: "Hey you—it hurts, you know? Here and here and here. . . ."

Ten leaves were plenty. It would be difficult to find ten good ones, and those ten would still be tough to chew.

"Hey—do you think your father really went off and left me?"

Should I forget about the leaves? Whenever I see the flowering mallow plants, a surge of fear washes over me. Compared with the joy I felt when I gathered the soft, delicate leaves of the mallows I'd planted and added them to the *toenjang* soup, hopelessness overwhelmed me with the realization that my once flowering mallows were now tough and dry. *Gee, that's right—I've only used them twice in soup since I planted them.* I wasn't feeling helpless because of the soup. I had been oblivious to the fact that my mallows were flowering—what had I been doing in that time? When I finally remembered to tend to them, they had already blossomed, wilted, decomposed beyond recognition and died. I didn't realize this until I plopped myself down next to where my mallows used to be; I started to quiver with an overwhelming urge to cry. Anyways, I managed to find a few leaves that were tender enough. The rains exposed the stark, gravelly dirt of the unfertilized mallow bed, which no amount of rain could soften, like the mouth of an old person—all teeth, no gums. Compared with the mallow bed, the bed of hot peppers, with its mixture of amaranth and foxtail, gave off a good earthy smell.

"Hey you—I heard your father's coming."

I picked exactly three hot peppers. Mum always wanted me to pick extra even though she never ate more than one. I'd probably have to eat the other two—nothing like a couple of fiery hot peppers for dinner to keep your stomach burning throughout the night.

"Hey you—when's your father supposed to come?"

Our dinner consisted of mallow leaf soup, three hot peppers, and some *toenjang* to dip them in. As I was about to eat, something bright red flickered into view amidst the tomato plants. I went back down to the muddy yard and there they were—two bright, ripe tomatoes. Those two cherry tomatoes lit up our dreary dinner table. With the tomatoes between us, Mum and I started eating. Very. Slowly.

On Saturdays the Yŏnse Family Clinic closed at 3 p.m. The doctor had already left and it was time for Su-a and me to lock up. I was planning on going for a walk afterwards with Su-a along the riverbank road that wraps around the town, buying some soft drinks along the way before heading home. And maybe I'd get to listen to the latest ballads on Su-a's new MP3 player.

The riverside road was beautiful in the springtime with the cherry blossom trees in full bloom. *I bet we'll be a dazzling sight for the young men, there being precious few of us in this town.* Our coordinated sky blue dress and yellow flared skirt would gently wrap around our legs as the wind blew. And that's all that would happen before we went our separate ways and hurried home. If we lingered, the young bachelors, some of them our age, probably wouldn't leave us alone. In addition, there were so many foreign men around these days.

The first time I had actually seen foreign workers was at Man-bae's plastics factory—he usually asked me to stop by his office for coffee since the factory was in the industrial complex on my way home from work. His factory was part of what was officially designated as an industrial complex ever since that factory, along with a furniture factory and a medical equipment factory, took possession of the hills and replaced the rice paddies and the dry fields. Man-bae's small factory had its origins in a pig shed outside the complex where he had raised a couple hundred pigs before getting in trouble with the police for illegal sewage disposal. It was around the time that the industrial complex went up that the foreign workers arrived, and they not only worked there, they lived there as well. The factory was a cacophony of thumping from the plastic injection machine, the punching of plastic from molds,

174

and a radio turned up full blast. I could feel the factory shake as the machines and the radio tried desperately to drown each other out. The radio was belting out old-time trot tunes, and one of the workers who'd been singing along—a wiry, dark-skinned foreigner with squinty eyes—was looking me over.

"Hey, you idiot!" Man-bae barked. "Stop drooling and get back to work—work!"

The foreign worker chuckled and retorted, "You idiot! Stop drilling and back to work work!"

Heck with this coffee. . . . I'm out of here.

Su-a disdained all men who worked in factories, manager and laborer alike, claiming they were too stupid, too rough, too ignorant, and completely worthless. I agreed with her—I guess her experiences with them had been the same as mine. In any event, the guy we really had to be careful about was Man-bae himself. Most important in my mind, I knew that neither Man-bae nor the factory workmen were capable of offering me a better life. Just looking at them made my insides churn. Besides the tearoom girls, we were the only young women around. And so Su-a and I walked along the riverbank road amidst the whirl of cherry blossoms because we still could. Why not? We were still young. Our youthfulness simply couldn't resist a walk when spring was in full bloom. I imagined Su-a and myself bursting out laughing for no other reason than the ticklish sensation of the wind wrapping our skirts around our legs.

Su-a and I were about to lock up the clinic when a white SUV stopped in front and a man got out and approached us, his face contorted in pain. He was a handsome man, and I could tell right off that he wasn't a factory worker.

"I have a terrible pain in my chest," he said, half gasping and half moaning.

"We're closed, you know," said Su-a indifferently.

I had a hunch that the man was disregarding Su-a and that his pitiful look was intended for me. I unlocked the door and tried to reach the doctor on his cell phone but he didn't pick up. The doctor, recently divorced, was busy dating to make up for lost time and he did a particularly sloppy job on Saturdays. He couldn't have cared less about the women from around here. Instead, the moment he was done for the day, he left for his place in the city—an hour and a half drive. I sometimes wondered if he was afraid that if he lived here a local gal might infiltrate his place at night. And so another thing we liked to do on our way home with our soft drinks in hand was to make fun of this unfeeling doctor who never offered us a kind word. For all we knew, he might be making fun of us when he was in the big city.

Since it seemed to have fallen to me to take care of the man, I laid him down and undid the buttons on his shirt. Then I tried calling the doctor again, and again no one picked up. Su-a had taken off and it was just the man and me. I wasn't sure what I should be doing, being only a nurse's aide. I started by giving him some water. The man drank but the pain in his chest was still there. I tried gently pounding his back and he didn't protest. Next I massaged his limbs and dabbed at the sweat on his forehead. I tried to nurse the patient as best I could.

The patient's condition improved after a while. I observed him for some time—He gave me a nice long look too. His eyes were brimming with tears. The patient—no, he's a man now—grinned. Beads of perspiration had reappeared on his forehead even though I'd wiped it a moment ago. And then my nursing instincts took over and I took a washcloth to his forehead but he said, "Oh you don't have to do that." At that very instant I felt embarrassment in the presence of this handsome and mysterious man. At the same time I felt content, having done all that I could from a professional standpoint.

"Thank you so much."

I stood there bewildered. *What next?*

The man flashed an innocent grin and with difficulty he spoke. "I really ought to quit smoking. Anyways, I—I—should repay you for your kindness, shouldn't I?"

I flinched. "Repay me?"

He says he wants to repay my kindness. Look at me . . . he's thanking me and I don't know what to do. But after all, I was barely twenty-one back then.

"No, I mean it. You pretty much saved my life. I want to thank you for that." He wasn't stuttering anymore. In fact his voice had a nice ring to it.

Before I knew it, I had nodded in acknowledgment. My heart was pounding in my ears. I felt as if somehow I'd be a bad person if I didn't give him the opportunity to repay me. Finally I managed to form the words "All right."

The man thanked me again in his nice deep voice. He asked me for my number—I guess he had earned it—and left me with his before departing. *I guess he doesn't have time to repay me today.*

That night I got a call from Su-a. She wanted to know what had happened.

"Well, the first thing I did was unbutton his shirt."

"You *what!* You undid his shirt?"

"And then I gave him some water and patted his back."

"Uh . . . okay. And?"

"Then I massaged his arms and legs and mopped the sweat off his forehead."

There was a shriek on the other end: "OH MY GOD!"

I gave her a few moments to recover and then said, "May I continue?"

"Yes."

"After I wiped the sweat off his forehead he thanked me. In fact he wanted to repay me for my kindness."

"Repay you?"

"Uh-huh—he wanted to repay me for my kindness and so he asked for my number."

I heard a beeping sound on the other end and guessed she had another call. *She must have gotten call waiting.* I still didn't have a clue about how to get call waiting but I did know what those beeps meant.

"What's that sound?" I asked innocently.

"Oh, I think there's another call. You know, Yŏn-i, I'm just going to say one thing—the more you like a guy, the more cool-headed you have to be, okay?"

"I know, I know."

And then there was a click. As soon as I hung up, the phone rang again.

"What do you want?"

"I would like to repay you for your kindness."

Okay. Cool-headed. Just like Su-a said.

"It's, uh, kind of late."

"My apologies, this is the first chance I've had to call—I've been really busy."

I found myself holding onto the phone with one hand and getting dressed with the other. And the next thing I knew, the cold night air was making its way through my thin blouse and I had goosebumps all over as I got into the white SUV. The man turned on the heat and then the radio. I recognized the program—"On a Starlit Night"—and hummed along quietly with the music.

"That's 'Merci, Chérie' by Franck Pourcel."

I was embarrassed and for a moment I even admired him. He was definitely worthy of my admiration, having the ability to share his knowledge with me. It made me sad to think that I was embarrassed and he was admirable. I'd only known the song as the opening music for "On a Starlit Night" but he not only knew the exact title of the song but also who sang it. I was sad because I realized then that he belonged to a different world than mine. There's not much you can do about a sadness like that. The man drove through the starlit night and about ten minutes later he was parking inside an open gate and ushering me inside his place.

It was the house that Su-a was always saying she wanted to go inside. I remember she once brought me past this very house and pointed it out to me on the way home from work. Starting out from the clinic, I would arrive at our house first, and the man's house was between ours and Su-a's—which meant I never went by his house on my way home from work. But Su-a passed by it every day and apparently one day she had noticed something different about it. It was at night when she showed me the house and we could hear a faint melody from inside.

"I really want to go in there some day," Su-a whispered.

"Who lives there—do you know?"

"No, but I'll bet it's a gorgeous man and he's all by himself."

"How do you know?"

"From his laundry—it's guy's clothes and only enough for one."

The house looked pretty plain on the outside. It did have a few pansies in front, but otherwise it was just an average house you'd find out in the countryside. People around here didn't plant anything in front of their houses, never mind pansies.

There was something conspiratorial about the way he ushered me in, as though he were about to show me a secret garden. He opened the door and there before me were more books than I'd ever seen in any one room. Books on the shelves and books stacked on the floor. And not just books—movie posters, postcards, photos and newspaper clippings covered the walls. And all of it so clean and well organized. There was music here too. I didn't hum along this time, just mouthed the words to the songs. The strong aroma of coffee was in the air. *Taster's Choice? No . . . maybe it's Esquire.*

"You know this song, don't you? 'Smokegetsinyoureyes' by Billie Holiday."

It was so inconsiderate how he rattled off the titles of these foreign songs so fast. I felt a twinge of anger but I wasn't sure why. I wasn't accustomed to the unfamiliar song titles rolling off his tongue. And then it occurred to me—*Coffee and music, is this how people repay each other? I wonder if Mum's pacing the yard, wondering where her daughter's run off to. Maybe she's at the entrance to our alley, crying and stamping her cane in frustration. If anyone*

*asks what's wrong she'll wail that her daughter has deserted her, just
like her husband. She'll probably sniffle that her daughter doesn't want
to feed her, do her laundry or even live with her.* But I wasn't about to
leave just then. I guess I kind of liked the unfamiliar sensation—so
unfamiliar it was enticing—washing over me and into my soul. One
thing I was absolutely sure of—the man was not from around here
and that fact excited me.

In the beginning the man called me out at night. He picked me
up and dropped me off. There was always music in the car and at his
home. I'd hear a few songs that I knew and others I'd never heard
before, like the one that was on when we shared our first kiss. I'd
wanted him to tell me the name of that song. I liked it that he could
tell me things I didn't know. But my ears were just not receptive to
the song titles. All the songs were foreign and hopelessly difficult for
me to learn.

"What's the name of the song playing right now?"

"'Maria Vergonha', a fado song by Bevinda," he quickly replied,
his heavy breathing warm on my lips. As always, I found myself
wishing he wouldn't rattle off his answers like that.

When he stopped kissing me and began undoing my blouse,
a new song came on; one that I'd heard somewhere. I let out a gasp
of delight—*That's right! It's from an SK Telecom ad!* The man must
have taken my gasp as a response to his caresses because he was soon
engrossed in rooting around my breasts like a hungry young animal.

To get from where I lived to the man's house, we had to go
across the river, down a road flanked by paddies and past the rice
mill, which had been closed down three years earlier. The mill
showed signs of neglect—it was run-down and the tin roof was
rusted over. He never passed by the mill without stopping to linger.
I knew what he wanted to do in there but he never managed to
get me inside. All I could do when he jerked the car to a stop was
give his little head a big hug. With his head in my arms I noticed
an unfamiliar shampoo scent. I couldn't muster up the courage to
ask him what the scent was called and instead asked what brand

of shampoo he used. He responded with the same piercing gaze as when I'd mopped the sweat from his forehead that time.

"Dou-ble-Rich-Shampoo," he answered abruptly.

On those spring nights of my twenty-first year I felt like I was traveling with him to a place far, far away—a place I could reach only with him, an unfamiliar and distant place I couldn't go to on my own. For that very reason it was also a sad journey. When I returned from these sad and achingly beautiful journeys, I was confronted with another sad scene, but this time it was all too familiar—Mum pacing the dusty earth of our yard, waiting for me.

At some point, I don't remember exactly when, the man stopped picking me up.

"Take a cab," the man would say when he called.

And who's going to pay for it? I silently asked.

"I want to see you now," he whispered, the words warm on my ears.

My resolve began to waver. *Then come get me.*

"I'm fixing up something tasty."

Oh, I get it—you're cooking something for me.

And so I took a cab. I let myself into his house and his tender voice welcomed me. The meal he'd been making was a hotpot of canned pike mackerel.

"Say, is your family into farming?" he asked as he spooned some soup.

"Yes." The truth was, we no longer had farmland, but even if we had, we no longer had people to work it.

"Who's the farmer?"

"My mum." *My mum who'd just turned 60 and had dementia.*

"Wow," he muttered, "lucky you. If you're going to live in the country you've got to live off the land, you know."

There was no music that night.

I decided to change the topic, seeing as I couldn't keep on lying forever. "No music?"

"Music? My laptop's broken—it's pretty much history."

"You can't play music without a laptop?"

"The real problem is, I can't do any writing either."

That was when I found out he was a literary type. But I didn't know what he wrote.

"Well, that's that. Anyways, what do you and your mom grow?"

"Lots of things—hot peppers, scallions, spinach, lettuce, crown daisies, eggplant, chicory, tomatoes, cherry tomatoes, and mallows."

"Man, that sounds good. It always tastes better when you grow it yourself, don't you think?"

"Yes—but why did you ask if we farmed?"

"Oh, I was just thinking that the hotpot we ate would have been wonderful if we'd sliced up some organic hot peppers and scallions and added them in."

"Why don't I bring you some?"

"Really?"

"Yes."

The man was practically jumping up and down with delight as he gave me a peck on the forehead. He fixed me with a tender gaze and said, "You're so nice and lovable—I'm going to take good care of you."

That night, the "person who wrote," but only with a laptop, was too drunk to give me a ride home. And so I had to walk. That gave me some time to think about Mum. *What can I do so that Mum isn't out pacing the yard waiting for me on a night like this?* After mulling it over I concluded that it'd be good to get Mum started on her vegetable garden again. They say it's helpful for people with dementia to work with their hands. Mum had never learned how to play flower cards and she was too old for piano lessons. Besides, I think I'd heard on the radio that the best thing you could do for people with dementia who were depressed was to surround them with greenery. And finally, Mum had a wealth of experience in farming.

Our house didn't have a vegetable garden anymore, never mind farmland. Our fertile vegetable garden had disappeared a while ago—thanks to our neighbor buying the land and covering it with cement blocks that became a dormitory-style building that he figured would be good for housing foreign workers. Then again, the fact that we didn't have a cemented yard like everyone else— granted it was because we didn't have the money for it—turned out to be useful in the long run. To be honest, by growing our own vegetables, we wouldn't have to buy them at the market.

I kept imprinting it in my mind that it wasn't to provide organic vegetables for the man that I was preparing the vegetable garden. But as I broke up the soil for days on end and finally saw the first hot peppers ripen, I thought of the man more than anyone else—wondering when he would invite me over again. But he never called. There was such a crowd of peppers growing that I was afraid their weight would bend the stalks over. It was scary the number of new sprouts that appeared every morning. And there was the lettuce too. Mum would shed doting tears as she thinned out the dense patch. It seemed Mum was still in the habit of caring for her produce as she would her own children.

"Hey—how come your father won't thin out the lettuce?"

Mum knew for certain that if the lettuce wasn't thinned out, the whole patch could be ruined by a day's rain.

"Hey—make some lettuce kimchi for your father's dinner."

After a dreary dinner with Mum I washed and wrapped the leaves of lettuce she had thinned out, neatly arranged some hot peppers in a plastic container, dug up and bagged some chicory, and took it all to the man's house. Mum must have forgotten that she'd told me to make some lettuce kimchi for Father's dinner. Anyways, I went to make some for the man instead—the man must have forgotten how happy he was when he asked me to bring him some organic vegetables. The man blocked the doorway—this had never happened before—and he didn't invite me in, which told me right off he had company—probably a woman. It occurred to me that the woman might be Su-a—the sandals I glimpsed between the man's legs looked an awful lot like hers. In fact, just the previous week Su-a had emptied out her savings account before it had come to term. I also knew that she had gone into town to Electronics Land last weekend—maybe for a laptop? I could hear music—maybe from the laptop Su-a had bought? I handed over the vegetables. The man made a huge fuss over them. But it was only for show. Perhaps the man had decided to be polite when he stopped calling me.

"Thanks for the vegetables—why so many peppers?"

"Yes, there are a lot of them, aren't there. Last spring I planted fifty of them. I guess I put in too much lettuce too. Anyway the peppers grew like bamboo after the rain. See that chicory? It might look tough but it's very flavorful—grown from good old plain dirt. Just look at their color."

"Fine, thanks very much."

"But, um, you know, your yard, I can tell it's got better soil than ours. It'll look so good with a nice vegetable garden instead of grass and weeds. Would you mind if I came over and dug up the soil for you?"

"That's all right, don't worry about it."

"You know, I'm pretty good at farming, growing up in a farming family and all."

"All right, I understand. But today is not good."

"Goodbye, then."

I trudged home in the dark only to find Mum plopped down in the dark yard, thinning out the lettuce by starlight.

"Hey—did you make some lettuce kimchi for your father's dinner?"

"Yes, Mum."

I decided to quit the Yŏnse Family Clinic and work at Kim's Herbal Clinic when it reopened, after the building expansion was completed. The Yŏnse Family Clinic paid more and had a better work atmosphere but I didn't have the confidence to work comfortably with Su-a, knowing that she might be going to the man's house at night. While I waited for the newly expanded Kim's Herbal Clinic to reopen, the monsoons came. I was sick of the rain. But it would keep beating down for a long time.

After dinner I went down to the vegetable garden and picked the hot peppers, lettuce, chicory, and eggplant. I wrapped it all in newspaper and put it in a plastic bag.

"Hey—make some lettuce kimchi for your father's dinner."

"Okay, Mum. I'll do that right now." I answered cheerfully, just like a twenty-one-year-old woman would.

For the first time in a long while you could see glimpses of stars between the clouds lighting up the clear black sky. The stars shone unsteadily through a slit between the thick clouds. It took an hour to walk to the man's house—and I took my time that night. There were times when the walk home was scary, especially if I got off work late or went into town to hang out before going home. But at that moment I wasn't afraid. *Did you forget what you told me that night—that night you called me out because you missed me?* I'd ask as I gave him the organic peppers, lettuce, chicory, and eggplant that I'd worked so hard to grow. *You asked if I'd really bring you organic vegetables—you asked me that on one of those nights when your words warmed my ear. Did you forget what you said to me—what you said to me with your head buried in my chest? Well, I remember everything—I remember all the things you said and did that night when you picked me up and when you drove me home. If you deny it all, you're sinning against me.*

He was home—I could hear music from inside. And yet again he didn't invite me in. I thrust the vegetables at him. The few unsteadily shining stars had disappeared behind the thick clouds.

"They're organic vegetables."

"Stop bringing things here—whatever they are."

"I worked all through the spring to make a vegetable garden in our yard so I could bring you vegetables. My hands were bleeding from digging up the soil."

"I never asked you to do that, Yŏn-i."

"I wasn't even able to install call waiting—just so I could afford a cab to your place."

Did that happen? I didn't know how to express the sadness, the anger, all the unfamiliar feelings welling up inside me—I just blurted out things like call waiting because I didn't know what else to do. I was afraid of telling him what I really thought: *You're a jerk*!

"Install what?"

I stood there speechless.

"You don't 'install' call waiting, you set it up on your phone line. Don't you know anything?" the man sneered.

And that was the last straw.

"Whatever it is, I don't have an MP3 player and I can't buy you a laptop like others can. All I can give you is organic vegetables. Don't make a fool of me—I'm only twenty-one. People will pass judgment on you if you treat a young woman like this. Besides, you're a well-educated man and a literary type—even though you can't write without a laptop—and you can afford a house like this, right?" My heart was pounding but I tried to speak as slowly and as steadily as I could.

"Hell, I don't deserve this after everything I did for you! I cooked for you and put music on every time you came over, remember? You can't be doing this to me—you're just messing with me now. You think you're the only one who can mess around? I can too—but did you ever see me lay a hand on you? If you want plain proof, what about the mill? I could have had my way with you there if I'd wanted to. Was I ever rough with you, huh? You know, I never told you this because I didn't think I had to share my thoughts with a kid like you but—you think I'd be living in a place like this if I was famous? If I had it better, like some people, I wouldn't have to get insulted by the likes of you. Just because of my house and the way I live, you think I look like a beggar? Fuck, I don't need this stuff—take it away! You've got some nerve, you homely hayseed girl.

You piece of shit. . . . " And with that the man threw down the bag of vegetables.

I went about picking up the peppers, lettuce, and chicory that had spilled out—my hands trembling and my heart shaking even more. I couldn't bring myself to cry. It started to pour.

As I walked home in the rain I noticed someone walking behind me. It was a man—actually two men—and they were talking. The night was dark and gloomy. On the way to the man's house I had been fearless, fired up by resentment, but the walk back home was scary. I was afraid of that man and his merciless verbal attack, I was afraid of the gloomy night, and I was afraid of the people walking behind me. I experienced the piercing realization that the world was a scary place. I ran blindly, tears streaming down my face—and I tripped. One of my shoes slipped off and I stepped on something sharp. I managed to hide inside the old mill, and that's when I realized I'd lost the bag of vegetables.

"Hold on, what's this?" The two men had stopped outside the mill, under the eaves. It sounded like they were opening something. I stayed still and held my breath.

"Kkan-jju, is that money?"

"They hot peppers, Ssabudin. Lettuce too. We have soju with *samgyŏpsal* wrapped in lettuce on payday." Kkan-jju seemed delighted by the mere thought of it and started to sing.

I guess I loved you
I guess I can't forget you
I keep thinking about you—
It's driving me crazy
I guess I'm regretting it
I guess I'm waiting for you . . .

Hidden in the darkness, I found myself mouthing the words to the song.

I guess I'm stupid—can't say anything to you
How're you doing?
I guess you're happy
Your beautiful smile makes me feel so small . . .

"Poor manager."

"I hated manager. Kkan-jju, you screwed everything up."

"Can't ask manager for money. Manager has no money, he
sick, his mom sick, manager sad."

"You still must ask."

"Can't ask manager for money—he sick."

"When you leaving, Kkan-jju?"

"Day after tomorrow. I sleep tonight, tomorrow night, then go.
Tomorrow I go to town, buy Yun To-hyŏn CD, rubber gloves, soju,
clothes, and shoes. I'm a big, big fan of Yun To-hyŏn."

"What you gonna do when you go back your country, Kkan-
jju?"

"I dunno. Gonna go see my mom, dad, sisters and cousins—
gonna go up a mountain and see stars. See the stars in my country,
Nepal. I ask the stars what I should do. What 'bout you, Ssabudin?"

"Younger sister married a Korean man. They live in country.
Husband beats her. She very sad. Older brother marry Korean
woman. She run away. I have nephew. Older brother and nephew
very sad. My parents dead. I have nobody back in Bangladesh. They
all in Korea. Can't go back. Older brother is hurt—fingers all cut off.
I take care of nephew."

"Ssabudin, when I sad in Korea I sing. Sing a Korean ballad.
Manager swear at me like crazy. My heart beat like crazy. My hands
shake like crazy. I cry like crazy. Then I sing. Nobody to love—so
I sad. Then I sing more. Then fall asleep. Then see stars in my
dream—big and pretty Nepal stars." Kkan-jju started singing again.

As I waited for you in front of the mailbox one autumn day
Yellow gingko leaves fluttered in the breeze—

188

I watched them move farther and farther away,
like the people passing me by

Hidden in the darkness, I found myself singing along again.

How long will the beautiful things of this world last?
Like strong flowers that endure—
even after a summer rainstorm
Like trees that stand tall—
    even after a winter snowstorm
Will everything under the heavens be able to stand on its own?

Ssabudin began to sing as well.
Goodness me, goodness me—
Please don't do this to me
You can't do this to me—
    Anymore

The mill was filled with the smell of rice flour, and now with singing voices and the beating rain.

"Ssabudin, we have lettuce and hot peppers too. We have hot pepper paste at home. We buy soju. We have no *samgyŏpsal*. We buy *samgyŏpsal* too. We drink soju."

"Good, good."

The two men walked off into the dark rainy night. They sounded so cheerful. Beyond the road that Ssabudin and Kkan-jju had disappeared on, I could see the road I had come on. Beyond that road I could see the man's house—I could feel my heart start to pound violently again. And I sang a song.

I guess I loved you
I guess I can't forget you
I keep thinking about you—

It's driving me crazy
I guess I'm regretting it
I guess I'm waiting for you . . .

When I left the mill and went out into the rain I could feel bitter anger swelling up inside me. But I kept on singing, despite the tears streaming down my face. In the distance I could see the stars above Nepal's snow-covered mountains. I set off towards those stars with unnatural confidence. Slowly. Cheerfully.

Secret Lover[1]

by Yun Young-su
Translated by Elizabeth Y. Kim

"I'm serious. Yang-mi's got a man now. Cross my heart!"
Yich'ŏn-daek[2] struck her knife on the table like a cleaver slicing a fish. I tore a sheet of paper towel from the roll in one corner and started to wipe the counter. In the background, a plate of *chapch'ae* noodles was spinning in the microwave.

"Come on, Odong's dad, why don't we just stuff our own mouths? We'll find out all about her gorgeous future husband later," Yich'ŏn-daek shouted at me in a loud voice.

Across the corridor, in the Chicken Corner, Yang-mi looked at us and smiled shyly. She's going to skip her breakfast today *again*. It's already the fourth day.

"Well, it's about time Yang-mi got married. What's your problem, old lady?" I snapped at her.

Unwittingly, I was taking Yang-mi's side before I even started thinking. But there's truth in what Yich'ŏn-daek was saying—Yang-mi does need to lose weight. I am a man 178 centimeters tall but I weigh only 75 kilograms. There is *no way* that Yang-mi, who's only 158 centimeters tall, should weigh as much as 70 kilos!

---

1. The original title is "My girlfriend's sweet love affair" (Nae yŏchach'ingu ŭi kwiyŏun yŏnae)

2. "Daek," a respectable form of the Korean word meaning "home" (*chip*), is traditionally used as a suffix to names of regions (i.e., Yich'ŏn) in order to address a married woman and indicate her local background. Hence the suffix "daek" could be thought of as a feminine nominal suffix, like the French *elle* or Hindi *a* or *ni*.

"Men! They say a girl's looks don't matter, that it's her good heart that counts. Crap! Tell them to try picking their own brides, huh? Take a hundred men and a hundred will pick out the prettiest faces first. I hope that a naïve gal like Yang-mi isn't chasing a false hope." Placing some *chapch'ae* noodles on my rice dish, Yich'ŏn-daek went on with her nagging.

"Look lady, why don't you go ask her the details?"

"Like she'll tell me what's on her mind? A big snake inside her stomach, I tell you. If only she could vomit out that snake, I'll bet she'd lose at least 20 kilos!"

"You have such a big mouth, you know. An hour goes by, and everyone at the Mart is babbling about what you said."

I stuffed the *chapch'ae* noodles with rice into my mouth. Yich'ŏn-daek gave me a dirty look with her piercing eyes. It's all the same to me! I thought.

"Yeah, yeah. Don't even talk to me again, eh? Don't you dare eat! Why do you even eat what I give you?"

Yich'ŏn-daek snatched my rice dish. I grabbed it back almost immediately.

"You know, you shouldn't even bother a dog when it's eating! Don't you complain next time people call you a jealous nag, old lady!"

"Who says that? Besides you, Odong's dad, who ever says I'm a jealous nag? Is this the thanks I get for feeding you?"

Yich'ŏn-daek works at the Side Dish Corner of the Food Section located in the basement of the Mart. Son Yang-mi works at the Chicken Corner, and I am the Team Manager of the Shipping and Parcels Department in the Storage Section. We're used to eating breakfast together. We even eat dinner together at least twice a week. We started eating together from the fall of this year when I became a formal contract employee, so I guess it's already been almost four full years. It all started like this. One morning I went to deliver some styrofoam plates to the Side Dish Corner. Yich'ŏn-daek and Yang-mi had come in early and were trying to eat their

continued
page 209

192

Photographs

_____

Atta Kim

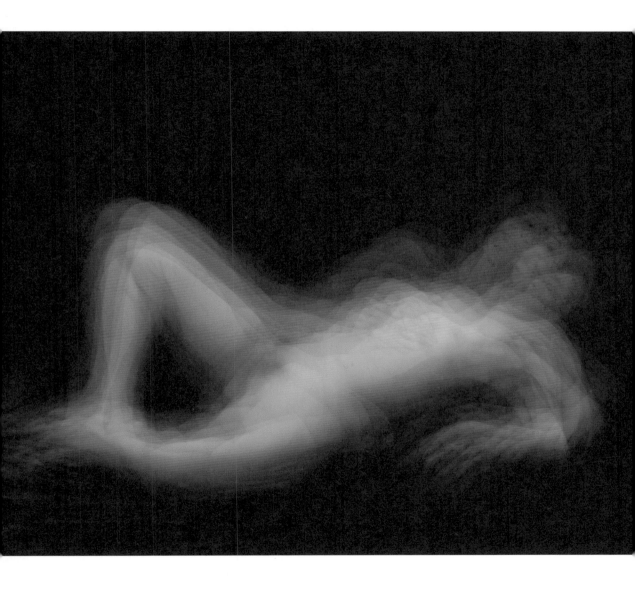

AZALEA

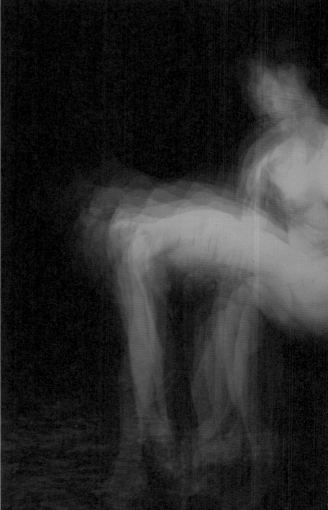

201

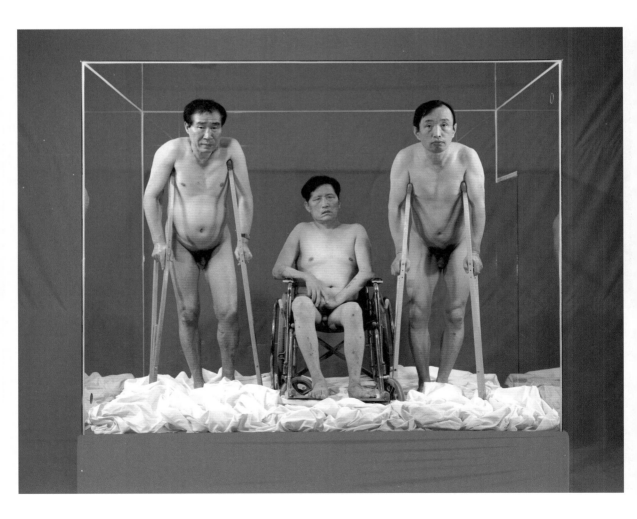

breakfast before the Mart opened. Clever Yich'ŏn-daek had put aside in the fridge one or two side dishes that didn't sell out the day before, and they were eating them for breakfast. Now that a huge Air Purifier Plane has been installed in the ceiling, all the food Corners like the Fish Jelly Corner and the Chicken Corner are on either side of the corridor. But up until last year, Yich'ŏn-daek's Side Dish Corner and Yang-mi's Chicken Corner were right next to each other.

Secret Lover, continued from page 192

"If you want, Mister Ch'oe, you bring your own rice, too. I'll take care of the side dishes for you."

That was Yich'ŏn-daek. It wasn't like me to refuse. Next morning, I went to the Side Dish Corner with my breakfast box containing only rice. The two women greeted me happily. Sometimes they even offered me side dishes such as seasoned and steamed pollack, and *chapch'ae* noodles—popular side dishes that definitely would have sold out.

"What the heck, these are only worth two or three thousand *won*. It's not like they'll raise my salary if I sold them anyway."

Indeed, Yich'ŏn-daek has an easygoing personality. Her husband is a bulldozer driver and moves from place to place abroad while she takes care of his ninety-year-old mother. Yich'ŏn-daek is practically living a widow's life. But at least at this Mart, where she's got eight years of experience, she's a female warrior that nobody messes with.

"No matter what it takes, I'll get Yang-mi married. But before anything, she has to get the hell out of that damned house. Dead or alive. Oh, the twenty million *won* her brother stole was her life's blood . . . when she found that out, she just sat there silently and stared into nothingness. What must she have felt . . . the poor innocent creature, what sins did she commit in her past life? My heart just sank . . . watching her like that."

As if Yich'ŏn-daek forgot that only a minute ago she was pissed off at Yang-mi because she wouldn't eat breakfast with us, she's now worrying about her, acting as if the world's going to end.

Yang-mi and I are both thirty-seven, born in the Year of the Monkey; while Yich'ŏn-daek is forty-seven, born in the Year of the Dog. Yich'ŏn-daek, who knows how to read people's fortunes by their zodiac signs, says, "Monkeys and dogs are supposed to be enemies." Strangely, however, Yich'ŏn-daek and I click together perfectly. After a considerable amount of time mulling over this issue, Yich'ŏn-daek concluded that she was not a dog born in the first month by the lunar calendar, but a rooster born in the last month. She says that being the fifth of eight children in her family she went to school one year late, because her parents even forgot to register her birth on the census registration papers. Her mother explained that was because Yich'ŏn-daek was a dog born in the first month and too young to attend school with those born in the Year of the Rooster. She reasoned that just because "the ice in the upper part of the water bowl cracked open" and spring arrived, that doesn't make it New Year's Day. But Yich'ŏn-daek believes that she's really a rooster born in the first month. The fact that her husband is a summer sheep, always wandering in foreign countries; the fact that her son is a spring rabbit, as stubborn as no other creature in this world—all this is proof to her that she isn't a dog, but a rooster.

"Let's eat some other side dish tomorrow. How could you give us *chapch'ae* for three days in a row in this burning heat?"

Pushing aside my empty dish, I yapped at her, instead of giving her a friendly greeting.

"Oh, go away! Get the hell out of here. Now I understand why people say don't expect any thanks from black-haired animals." I saw Yich'ŏn-daek's fist flying to my face, but I was quicker in dodging it.

The Mart hadn't opened yet. A couple of employees were moving about rapidly, setting down some boxes at the Fruit Corner. I walked towards the Chicken Corner. Yang-mi was in the middle of washing the glass doors of the machine used for cooking chickens.

"Aren't you going to bring me coffee?"

"Oh, that's right. I forgot . . ."

210

Yang-mi placed the kettle on top of the gas stove. Ordinarily, it was Yang-mi who brought the coffee after breakfast. But because she hadn't been eating breakfast lately, my morning coffee didn't appear. Over Yang-mi's cleavage, I saw a necklace with three long metallic bars gathered to one side and swinging together on a thick chain, a shiny pendant reminiscent of the national flag swaying in the wind.

"Nice necklace. Did your sweetheart give it to you?"

Although we consider ourselves good friends with nothing to hide from each other, I still felt somewhat embarrassed asking her about a man. Yang-mi giggled shyly.

"A friend from primary school gave it to me. You see, she owns this accessory store with her husband, at the East Gate Marketplace."

"It looks like a man's."

"She said I would look better with a man's necklace, since I have big bones. All my other friends who came along got women's jewelry, but . . . I guess I must have been fat all these years just so I could get my hands on this necklace. I mean, it's strange, even the fact that my primary school friends decided to hold a reunion out of the blue."

I had no idea what she was talking about. Anyway, what mattered was that Yang-mi seemed to like her necklace, that's all. I could tell by the way she gently closed her eyes when she was talking about it, blushing.

"Well, you do need to lose weight. For your health, at least."

Taking a sip of my coffee, I continued to make small talk. Yang-mi's rotund body didn't look any different. Well, that's true, though—it had only been a few days since she started to skip breakfast. No wonder there was no change in her appearance.

"So, where did you meet this guy?"

"On the street."

"In the middle of the day?"

"Why? Because I'm ugly?" Yang-mi looked up at me, and let out a mysterious laugh.

"Because I met my own pain in the ass walking on the street with my eyes wide open."

"Oh, not complaining about your wife again! I know you don't mean it."

Other employees started to enter the store.

"I'm off."

I started to walk towards the Storage Section with my coffee in hand. Actually, coffee is always available in my office at the Storage. The electric coffee pot is still working fine and there's lots of instant left in the cabinet. It's just that I prefer to relax by drinking my morning coffee with two women.

Even if my morning coffee disappeared, if Yang-mi could meet a good man and get married, Yich'ŏn-daek and I would have no problem with that. Yang-mi has suffered too much in her life. Ever since graduating from an all-girls high school, she has been entirely responsible for supporting her family, providing her younger siblings' tuition fees for nearly twenty years. Isn't it about time she lived her own life?

"Oh mother, it's because you keep telling Odong to eat and eat that the kid has turned out this way!"

"Who cares? Everyone I know envies us, they talk about how healthy our Odong is."

"If you go to his school, you'll see that he's being bullied by all the other kids."

"If you're really such a great educator, why don't you raise him yourself! You're the one who leaves home at sunrise, as if your behind is on fire. And when do you come back? When ghosts are wandering around!"

"Do you think I go out to party or something? Of course, if the kid's father brought home enough money for us to spend, I wouldn't have to work for all these other housewives, would I?"

"How much money are you making with the massage treatments, after you've bought your meals and paid for

212

transportation? Is it half as much as what I'd earn at other people's homes in two days?"

"Are you telling me to go work as a cleaning lady now?"

"I'm telling you to stop pretending you're the only one earning money in this world, that's what."

"What about *you*, mother? What position are you in to nag me? You don't give us any support! You don't even know how much money is being poured into paying for your hospital fees, whenever you say, 'It's a muscle ache this time, it's a stomachache this time,' and so on."

No fighting again, please. I thought they had stopped fighting when the TV drama started. Don't tell me now that the show's over they're at it again.

"Odong! Where are on earth *are* you?"

Walking into the living room, I yelled in a loud, serious voice on purpose. Odong, who had been sleeping on his grandma's lap, slowly got up, still looking sleepy. I grabbed his hand and walked out of the house. If I'm not home, Ma and my wife don't even bother having an argument. If they fought at home all the time the way they fight when I'm there, our family would have completely fallen apart by now!

"You brat, can't you see that your mother and grandma are fighting because you keep on eating and don't play any sports?"

Puzzled, Odong looked wide-eyed and uncomprehending. He had only just turned three.

"Oh, Hyŏn-su, you know it's all because your mother and your wife both care for you so much! They're only trying to be sweet with you, you know, because they're sorry to see you earning money all by yourself. They're trying to tell you that they are somehow trying to help you out, you know. Oh, you're just worrying over something you should be happy about!" If it had been Yang-mi . . . that's what she would have told me.

Habits are hard to break. I used to start my day babbling in front of Yang-mi and Yich'ŏn-daek, even using crude language sometimes. Since about two weeks ago, I've been feeling frustrated as never before, unable to speak my mind. Yet all I can do to relieve my stress is toss a few words at Yich'ŏn-daek and tease her.

I feel as if dregs of conversation were trapped in my body, dregs I should have gotten rid of long ago. There's no space left for any more words to build up. I feel anxious and bothered, as if my mouth keeps trying to expel these dregs . . . all in a single breath.

Is this how much Yang-mi meant to me? I've always thought that Yich'ŏn-daek and I were the only ones blabbing on as Yang-mi was always just listening silently, as if she didn't exist. But now that she's actually out of the picture . . . I begin to see how even talking with Yich'ŏn-daek isn't the same.

We used to joke around—the three of us—during those days when we ate together. For instance, when we arrived at work we'd say, "Good job, now go home and rest." When we were leaving work in the evening, we'd say, "It's time to get ready to go to work." Come to think of it now, those weren't just everyday jokes. I see now—I wasn't envious of rich men or those high class men, at least never when we were drinking coffee together after a hearty meal. I would think, "Even though we don't eat as much or spend as much as those wealthy people, I can't think of anyone with a better life than us." But now that was no longer the case. It was always just arriving at work, over and over again—there was no way back home. It seemed as if Yang-mi had taken with her all the stability and peace I used to feel when leaving work. Seeing her bright and happy expression made me feel strangely nervous, as if she now lived in another world. Yang-mi has certainly changed during the past fifteen days. And I'm not just talking about her necklace. She even puts on fake lashes, though I have to say they look a bit odd on her, along with her pink lipstick. What's more, I can finally admit that Yang-mi's silhouette has started to change, with her neckline and arms looking noticeably slimmer. I guess her diet has started to have an effect.

"Daddy, buy me ice cream!" Odong started to whine when we were passing by the grocery store in town. If Ma were here, she'd say,

"Alright, alright, my little puppy" and generously hand over a bill. The old lady suffered so much when she was young, so how could I blame her? She's an old woman now, always insisting that starvation is the worst suffering in the world.

I handed my son an ice-cream cone and sat him on a swing in the town's playground. I sat on the swing next to his. The evening wind was chilly. Yes, the day after tomorrow would be the end of August, which everyone had talked about as the hottest month in decades. I could hear the sound of the cicadas in the grass, signaling the onset of autumn.

Odong treated the ice-cream cone like a treasure. He stared and stared at it, slowly licking it with delight, checking in the dim lamp light to see how much remained. His slight roly-poly frame, his pudgy arms. *Yes, I can understand his mother's worry.*

"Finish it up and swing, you brat!" I shouted out in irritation, and suddenly, somebody seemed to be getting out of the jungle gym behind me. I turned around and saw it was a couple in their twenties. They extricated themselves and left the playground, grumbling about something.

I was in love once, too. There was a time when I was anxious because I couldn't touch the body of Kim Hui-ok, my wife. A time when other people's stares were just too distracting to bear. Maybe at this very moment Yang-mi is enjoying a date with her boyfriend. Although it's pretty hard for me to imagine, given how obese she is, they're probably at some dreamy moonlit café, or maybe arm in arm at some secluded street corner.

I met my wife Kim Hui-ok at a bus stop on my way home from work. I was thirty-three, and she was twenty-seven. An attractive lady blessed with a tiny waist, she worked at a cosmetics store. Even after having married her in haste (because she had gotten pregnant), I was so happy! What a pumpkin pie had rolled into my hands! I knew I had been lucky to get a wife who had a job, considering my own status. Back then, I had thought, "If the two of us earn something, our financial situation will improve in a short time and we'll be able to buy a small apartment." But my wife had to quit her job less than a month after we got married because the cosmetics store was closing. It was the same with other cosmetics stores. All over town they were closing one after another, casualties of the competitive world market in which big-name cosmetic companies and Internet shopping sites had started to flourish. Even so, my wife didn't worry. She proudly said, "I can still earn some money at least at the same old rate, if I sell cosmetics door-to-door!" She insisted, "Women might decide not to buy an outfit or skip a meal, but they can't stand not spending money on their cosmetics!" But going from door to door carrying a bag of cosmetics for sale was rapidly becoming an obsolete business, vanishing even faster than the town's cosmetics stores. The only other option my wife had was doing facials for some of her old loyal customers—yet even that was an opportunity that came only once or twice a week.

Come to think of it, I think I would have been better off married to Yang-mi—that is, financially speaking. True, it's an exhausting job she has—to be frying or spicing up chickens, standing in one spot all day long. But I must say, given the good turnover, the Chicken Corner and the Side Dish Corner are an indispensable part of the Mart, to speak for the Food Section at least. While I can be replaced by any other person at any time, because I am merely a Team Manager of the Shipping and Parcels Department (and what a monkey's position that is!), Yang-mi and Yich'ŏn-daek will keep on going strong. What's more, Yang-mi is a diligent girl. As far as I know, Yang-mi has never once been late to work or absent. Given all her effort, unlike workers at other Corners, Yang-mi is irreplaceable at the Chicken Corner.

Oh, and I could tell you about her cleanliness, too! Yang-mi sweeps and scrapes the floor every day, all the way to the Fish Jelly Corner and the Dried Seaweed Corner. She's the type of girl who cares enough to do things like taking the broom and dustpan into the sunlight to be aired, and washing the cotton dishtowels in boiling water to keep them clean and fresh.

And yet, if I was given another chance, would I really choose Yang-mi without hesitation? I have to think carefully before jumping to conclusions: Yang-mi is . . . ugly. Her eyes disappear behind her swollen and bulging eyelids. There's nothing attractive about her nose, flat on her face like a child's fist. Her far too curly hair and terribly pockmarked skin that looks like an orange peel make her face look even bigger. Maybe it's true what Yich'ŏn-daek says: all men are beasts who know nothing better than gaping at pretty masks.

Her physical appearance, however, is not Yang-mi's only problem—one should not forget her family. Although as head of a family I'm in the same situation as Yang-mi—earning all the income, unable to spend one or two hundred thousand *won* on myself—her family situation remains far more problematic than mine. In contrast to my family where Ma and my wife are busy trying to save every penny, everyone in Yang-mi's family is busy trying to grab all her money while she's breaking her back at work to support them.

It was just two years ago that Yang-mi's family moved into the fifteen *p'yŏng*[1] slum of a townhouse they live in, a place she bought with her own sweat and blood. Yet when Yich'ŏn-daek remarked, "Your family must be damn proud of you, now that you've managed to buy a house," Yang-mi only smiled and said, "There's always a new mountain to climb." *She was right.* After she provided her family with a home, her father soon abandoned his work at a salon on the pretext that "People would gossip if the father of a household held a menial job while his daughter earned real money." Although thank goodness Yang-mi's mother still works at the town's supermarket where she peels garlic, she was used to hearing stories about other parents whose daughters regularly give them money for vacations. Consequently, her mother was known around town for organizing all kinds of outings with the townfolk whenever Yang-

---

1. One *p'yŏng* is approximately 3.058 m².

mi's payday approached, such as going to a hot springs resort or some other destination. And it's not like her siblings were any more sensible than her parents. For instance, there was no question that her two little sisters and brother Yang-gil graduated from university due entirely to Yang-mi's efforts. Even if her little sisters can be excused from family responsibilities, considering that the two of them are married now—there's still her brother Yang-gil, the real pain in the neck in the family. That no-gooder got married even before graduating from university and has children to support; but he rashly quit his job at the fishing rod manufacturing company, a job he had barely secured, on the pretext that it was exhausting! He's been living off Yang-mi for five years now. Yang-gil is also a brazen guy who—despite having blown large sums of money after a few doomed attempts at setting up small businesses like a food store or a supermarket—acts condescendingly towards Yang-mi, saying, "She doesn't know a thing about what's going on in the world because she's just a high school graduate."

It was around this time last year that Yich'ŏn-daek and I convinced Yang-mi to open an Installment Savings account and finally succeeded. "*Yang-mi, save up some money! What do you have to show for having worked your fingers to the bone for twenty years? You ought to get married one day, too. You're responsible for your own future!*"

A total of 20 million *won* in 35 months by installment—that was the deal Yang-mi was supposed to take for her own sake, for the first time in her life. Unfortunately, Yang-gil somehow got wind of the fact she had an Installment Savings account, managed to make his mother his accomplice, and borrowed 20 million *won* from the bank with Yang-mi's Installment Savings account as the surety. As a result, Yang-mi fell into her current state where for the next two years she has to pay off the debt that Yang-gil owes to the bank.

"What can I do? I can't send them to jail, after all it's my own mother and brother."

That was Yang-mi's only response. Perhaps one could say that her biggest weakness is her soft-hearted nature. Doesn't she know the old saying, "Stretch out your legs only after seeing if there's enough space to lie down"? Yang-gil and her parents knew all about Yang-mi's frailties.

Odong had been leaning on the rope of his swing with his head tilted far back. His eyes blissfully closed, he's now lying flat on the ground. I try to lift him up and I can feel how heavy he really is. My wife is so right! I ought to make him eat less, no matter how, even if it means having to scold him and make him cry. Yes. Perhaps, rather than a good-hearted girl like Yang-mi who lives without any alternative to fall back on, a strong-willed woman like my own wife is better—although I must admit that my wife also has her flaws, one of which is that she never gives in during any argument with her mother-in-law, even stubbornly talks back at her.

Time flew by and *ch'usŏk*[2] arrived before I knew it. During these high seasons, the Storage Sections at all the Marts are busy as ever. The Shipping and Parcels Department is responsible for all sorts of things such as updating the stock, dealing with refunds, and wrapping hundreds of gift sets.

"I hear that Miss Son of the Chicken Corner has lost 8 kilos now. Have you seen that she's even straightened her hair nice and sleek?"

As soon as he got to work, wrapping up the daily products, Cho started babbling on again. The hottest topic these days among the employees at this Mart is Son Yang-mi, in fact.

"8 kilos? Hm, I'll give it another thought if she succeeds in taking off 10 more kilos." Chief Manager Kim went back to his work.

Oh, give me a break. Don't you know that you're about to turn fifty tomorrow? Just be good to your two kids, man. People

2. *Ch'usŏk* is a harvest festival similar to the Western tradition of Thanksgiving.

219

say that his wife suddenly went missing one day, but it was probably just a rumor. I'm sure she ran away because he beat her up so often.

"Why, Son Yang-mi isn't all *that* bad. True, her face is ugly enough to stop a clock—but I won't be able to see her face if I turn off the lights, will I?"

I quickly talked back over the Chief Manager's disgustingly unpleasant laugh.

"Oh, Son Yang-mi has a lover, actually. He's a strong young fellow, too."

"Team Manager Ch'oe, you've seen him?"

"Of course I have. He's a big man and very tall."

"Ha! Then I bet they look good together—two fat bodies hanging out together," Cho quipped in response to the Chief Manager's stupid talk, as if he couldn't stay silent for a second. He was also getting on my nerves again.

"You know that necklace of Miss Yang-mi's?" he asked. "That necklace is in fashion now. Young men these days all buy one for their girlfriends, you know. It's very popular because that's what Pak Wŏn-jun wears, in this hit TV drama. He puts it around his girlfriend's neck, saying, 'You are what I am, don't ever forget that'— then walks away, just like that, heh! But I have to say that this lover of Miss Son Yang-mi must be a funny fellow, acting the way young men do, when he must be nearly forty years old. I guess even oldies imitate young people in the ways of love!"

"You idiot, Yang-mi didn't get that necklace from her lover!" To my own surprise, I found myself shouting at him.

"Gosh! Calm down . . . ! It's not like *you* gave it to her—or did you?"

"You think I'm crazy?"

"Exactly. You're acting like you're ready to get stabbed by your wife," said the Chief Manager, siding with Cho.

I quickly tried to change the topic. "Cho, isn't this detergent supposed to be a refill product? Is this the original price?"

220

I could tell Chief Manager Kim was still thinking about Yang-mi. Thinking about *sleeping* with her.

"I have to admit she did get prettier, finally looking like a female now that she wears a skirt, too. Still a virgin, you think?"

Cho again responded to the Chief Manger's stupid, vulgar comments. "You know, she kept touching her necklace all day long . . . mumbling something to herself. It was funny. Actually, I think she was rather cute."

"Shut up and get back to work, you idiot! Don't you dare talk that way!"

These days callow young men like Cho don't even pretend to be listening to their superiors, unless they get kicked in the ass or something. My sudden burst of anger silenced Chief Manager Kim too—I must have looked like a warrior.

Yet I wonder too—what's driving Yang-mi to such showy ways these days? She even got her hair . . . that treatment—what do you call it in salons? *Straightened*. Her originally curly hair that used to be frizzy all the time now falls down nice and sleek on her shoulders, with even a few fashionable streaks bleached in for effect. Not to mention the high heels and different skirts. And that white necklace of hers—she's touched it so many times it's even changed color. It might have suited her in the days when she was fat and looked like a man, but now that she's gotten slim, it really doesn't suit her anymore.

"Team Manager Ch'oe! Do you know Son Yang-mi, in the Food Section?"

It was Manager Maeng of the Security Department, who hurried in to the Storage.

"My gosh! So I guess Yang-mi really *is* the hottest topic in town," I whined to myself. Manager Maeng quickly gave me a slap on the back.

"Oh, forget it then. I came all the way here to just tell you something, because you seemed to be a good friend of hers, you know. Well, never mind!"

"You came here to tell me . . . what?"

I was looking at him suspiciously and Manager Maeng took some time to try my patience, before he finally spoke again.

"Just a while ago that jerk who's supposed to be Son Yang-mi's brother barged in to Security. He was claiming that he came here to pick up Son Yang-mi's salary. Man, he even brought Son Yang-mi's signet, her registration card, all prepared! What really got me was what he said: 'Old sister's gone crazy because of a man, and now the whole family's starving to death!' I cut him down to size right away. I said, 'Let Yang-mi come here herself and ask for it.' I told him that because Yich'ŏn-daek told me before the bastard had stolen poor Yang-mi's Installment Savings money. He finally went away after complaining for a long time. What a creep! 'Old sister's gone crazy because of a man'? Is *that* what anybody should say about his own older sister?"

"I see now why Son Yang-mi hasn't been able to get married yet. It's all because of that goddamned family of hers."

Chief Manager Kim jumped into the conversation, as if he'd been waiting for the chance. Thanks to Yich'ŏn-daek and her talent for gossip, now everyone at the Mart knows Yang-mi's family situation inside out.

"Ah, I'm not listening to this sort of male gossip anymore!" I decided I'd had enough. I stopped wrapping the rest of the boxes, got up, and made my way out of Storage.

"What's the matter with that Team Manager guy? Whenever someone brings up the topic of Son Yang-mi, it's like he's working overtime. Hm, could it be that he's got a wife waiting for him at home, and he's also trying to hook up with a lover outside?"

Their derisive laughter reverberated behind my back.

I couldn't understand myself why I had become so involved. Why do I get so tense whenever there's any mention of Yang-mi's love affair? Recently I discovered that there's nothing left in this world to make me laugh. Hysteria and paranoia tend to go together, and there's not a single day when I smile, at home or at work.

I had always heard that losing weight isn't an easy task; most people don't succeed in the long run. Yang-mi will give up, I assumed. How wrong I was! I never imagined that Yang-mi would turn into a different person and so soon! For some reason, I felt deprived and empty inside. It's not as if I'd been thinking of Yang-mi as *my* girl—but . . . it was true that, I was feeling . . . a sense of betrayal.

Back at the Market Section, a large number of customers milled about. Everyone seemed busy preparing for Ch'usŏk. I walked towards Yang-mi once the guests at the Chicken Corner had all been served. I picked up a seasoning radish lying on top of the counter.

"Why don't you let me check out your guy for you? A man can only be judged by another man, you know. How old is this guy, anyway?"

"He's . . . younger than me."

Yang-mi smiled, hesitatingly: she was feeling a little uncomfortable.

"Younger than you? Haha, congrats! But are you sure he's not some kind of a fraud or anything, huh? He's got a steady job, yes?"

"Yes . . . of course."

With a toothpick covered in a napkin, Yang-mi started to scrape something off the handle of her cooking pan. *This is what I mean. It's impossible to help her with anything because she never tells you what's on her mind!*

"Don't be too nice to your man, okay? He'll get sick of it."

"I'm not. *He*'s the one who treats me too nicely . . . there's nothing I've done for *him*. And yet, if I think about it, not everything that exists can be seen with our eyes, right? You know, the really precious things in life are invisible. Like love, for instance. Love is something that exists but can't be seen."

I turned away. "*Love is something that can't be seen.*" There was nothing special in what she said and yet I felt she had just sung to me in the most beautiful voice. Yes, I suppose that to love someone probably means something like what she said. Love means being able to first genuinely accept and embrace your beloved, before all the kissing and the sex business. It means to be together as one, as in *one heart*. It's the ultimate confirmation of your loved one's being, although love isn't something we can see with our eyes.

Eyes . . . oh, Yang-mi's eyes! I suddenly came to a halt. A customer passing by gave me a strange look. I resumed walking.

When was it? . . . There was a time when one day, in mid-sentence, when Yang-mi had given me a most puzzling look. That look in her eyes was an expression of some kind of longing . . . could it have been . . . *love*? Oh! Why didn't I notice it then! Even if I hadn't eventually paired up with Yang-mi, I could at least have been more careful to avoid hurting her feelings with my silly words and behavior. Unfortunately, I had started dating Kim Hui-ok just around the same time I had begun to have breakfast with Yich'ŏn-daek and Yang-mi. Being the idiot I've always been, all I did then was to blather every single horny detail about Kim Hui-ok and myself, obsessed only with the thought of conquering her body!

Would I ever be able to face Yang-mi again with a clear conscience? Suddenly, I felt overwhelmed by shame. And then I was terribly sorry. Now Yang-mi is truly in love, with someone else . . . I realized I should be happy for her.

It drizzled all day long. Tasks at the Storage Section become more time and energy consuming when it rains, but in a way, I felt refreshed by the rain showers. I felt the air being cleansed of all impurities. It was already time to leave work. While I was putting on my jacket, Cho, who had gone out to make a delivery, walked into the office, shaking off the water from his umbrella.

"Team Manager! Guess what? I saw Miss Son Yang-mi yesterday at the public park over there."

It had been quite a long time since I had heard of Yang-mi from Cho. Only a month or two had passed, to be exact, but Yang-

224

mi was already gone from people's minds. That's what all gossip is supposed to be, anyway. Only those people who couldn't get rid of their memory of the once fat Yang-mi chattered on like a flock of sparrows. But now that it was a fact that Yang-mi had become slender, it wasn't really anything to be amazed at anymore.

"What do you mean? You don't think Son Yang-mi can go to the park?"

"I couldn't tell it was her just by seeing her backside. Her body looked so slim and she was dressed gorgeously! The girl I was there with had gone to the restroom for a while, and when she came back she told me about a woman sitting on a bench at the front of the park. She told me that a lady was on a bench all alone with a cake displayed in front of her. With lit candles, too. I instinctively thought, *oh it can't be* . . . but I couldn't help checking it out myself . . ."

"You mean to tell me that the lady was Yang-mi?"

"Well, yes . . . I even passed on my greetings to Miss Son Yang-mi. Oh, what an awkward moment that was! She hurriedly put out the candles and put the cake back into the box and then swiftly went away. I wonder if it's her birthday . . . but still, why would she . . . all by herself . . . ?"

"Shut up, you cad! Playing the trumpet when you don't even know the score! Are you trying to prevent her from finding a husband?"

Even as I glared at him, I was recalling what Yich'ŏn-daek once said.

"Yang-mi is acting quite strange these days. That she talks to herself is nothing new. But at times, she even laughs and twists her body around, as if there is someone . . . tickling her. She laughs looking at the chicken machine and speaks half in jest like she's really talking to someone. What the heck, when Yang-mi went to the restroom, I even checked under the machine to see what could possibly be there. Do you think maybe . . . she's hallucinating because she hasn't been eating properly?"

I thought about going to the Mart, but decided against it. What should I say to her? . . . I felt lost. This was *not* the fragile Yang-mi I used to know. She was no longer the ugly Yang-mi, either. Even though all she did was lose some weight, in time, she had been transformed into an attractive lady with her own distinctive character, even without painting her face like young girls do today. Confidence—yes, there was a subtle confidence about her now, emanating from her very presence. I sighed deeply and started to get ready to go home. After all . . . there was a time when Yang-mi and I didn't even know each other. So once more, we were going our own separate ways. Maybe we'd run into each other and say hi, considering that we live just a street away from each other, but it certainly wasn't my business to interfere in her life and . . . *that was it.*

I was walking towards the bus stop holding onto my umbrella when I saw Yang-mi in the distance. She was standing at the crosswalk, waiting for the traffic light to change. Brown handbag, brown high heels . . . she was wearing a fashionable trench coat wrapped tightly at her waist. Anyone could tell from the way she was dressed up that she was going out on a date. Yang-mi crossed the street and to my surprise, entered a florist's. Could it be that someone she knew was ill or even in the hospital? I was staring blankly at the opposite side of the street when the traffic lights turned back to green. I scrambled like a madman to get to the other side of the street. I had no special reason, of course. It's just that I hoped I could perhaps . . . get a glimpse of Yang-mi's lover, even from a distance. Suddenly—my heart thumped! I was just about to step onto the pedestrian walkway when Yang-mi came out of the flower shop! I quickly hid under my umbrella.

A red rose . . . it was only a single red rose that Yang-mi had bought from the shop. She walked slowly, sniffing the rose. She entered a building. There was a café on F2. The White Hill Café. I finally climbed the stairs. Who cares if we bump into each other, all I need to do is just be myself, and say hi.

I never knew there was a café as nice as this and so close to the Mart. In a vast hall that seemed to be at least fifty *p'yŏng*, a number of chairs with high backs covered in patterned fabrics were carefully placed at select spots. The aroma of coffee, classical music playing softly in the background . . . on a day like today, when the drizzle outside looked like it would never end, this was the perfect setting for a date. But where's Yang-mi? She was not . . . oh. Yes, she was there. On a sofa near the corner, beside the open window, she sat leaning back, her eyes closed. She was by herself, the single red rose placed neatly on the table in front of her: it was like a scene from a book because the fabric of the sofa she was sitting on happened to be patterned with red roses, too.

I took my seat at a spot near the entrance and ordered a cup of coffee. This was the perfect spot from which to see the people walking into this café. 7,000 *won* for a cup of coffee. I didn't regret it at all. It was an opportunity for me to see Yang-mi's lover.

There was an economic slump and it showed. More than twenty minutes passed before two female university students walked in. And then ten more minutes passed and a not-so-young couple walked in.

Maybe it was the music, poignant yet with dark undertones. I got up, finally. Saying good-bye to her on my own, from a distance—this was the best present I could give to Yang-mi, I thought. Whomever she's dating, how much could I really know anyway, just by getting a glimpse of her lover from a distance? At least I couldn't behave like my coworkers who had no heart and blabbed on about her love affair—Cho, for instance. At least *I* shouldn't act that way. The ethical thing to do now was to keep an eye on her, to help Yang-mi make her own decisions. If she ever needed my help, if she first asked for my help—then . . . then I would offer good advice, with all my heart.

I walked out into the street and wandered around aimlessly like a man who had just been stood up. But there was no turning back. I had to get her completely out of my mind. The only role left for me was that of friend; I had to admit that Son Yang-mi had promised her future to a man and say goodbye. The rain became heavier and filled my shoes; it soaked my pants and weighed me down. But I had decided it was all for the best. I felt fragile and vulnerable suddenly, and I needed to feel grounded again. Or else like a wooden top spinning on too narrow a base, I wouldn't be able to bounce back up.

I was in the middle of taking some detergent boxes out of the truck when my cell phone rang. It was Yang-mi. She sounded frightened and urgent.

"Hyŏn-su, have you seen my necklace?"

"Nope . . . what did you do this time? Wasn't that your little treasure?"

"Stop joking around, Hyŏn-su! If you have it, please give it back to me."

"No prank. Why on earth would I have taken your necklace?"

She hung up.

Yang-mi was always touching her necklace, smiling brightly and happily. How could she have misplaced something she used to treasure so dearly? "Oh hurry up!" the irritable truck driver nagged at me, cigarette in his mouth. But my cell phone rang again when I resumed taking down the boxes.

"Oh Hyŏn-su . . . what should I do, what should I do? I can't live without that necklace . . ."

Yang-mi was sobbing on the other end of the line.

"Well, you know what? You can buy the same one again! You could even ask your friend to give one to you again."

"Oh, Hyŏn-su! It wouldn't be the same . . . it would be different!"

"Well . . . of course it would be different. Can't be the *same,* you know."

She hung up again. Try as I might, I couldn't keep working. It wasn't like Yang-mi to be calling twice about a trivial matter. Besides—she was crying!

"Cho, I'll leave the rest to you—take care!"

I took off my gloves, flung them aside, and started running towards the Mart.

There was a commotion. Some people were gathered around the Chicken Corner. Was Yang-mi hurt? Women who worked at different food Corners were milling around but Yang-mi was nowhere to be seen. To my surprise, the chicken frying machine was lying abandoned sideways on the floor. It looked like some water had been spilled on the floor too. Cooking oil, I realized. The big frying pan from the Fish Jelly Corner was missing.

"Why the hell is she acting that way? Yang-mi, that bitch, what does she have a grudge against me for! Tell her there are certain things in this world that she must do. What a crazy girl . . ." Mrs. Pak of the Fish Jelly Corner was stomping her feet with rage.

Yich'ŏn-daek screamed at her, "Shut your mouth! What makes you think you can swear like that at people? Mind the guests, at least."

"Well . . . if I get fired, will you compensate me? It's not like Yang-mi is your daughter or anything, is she? Why is it that whenever I talk about Yang-mi, there's fire in your eyes?" Only momentarily cowed by Yich'ŏn-daek's spirited defense of Yang-mi, Mrs. Pak yelled back again.

Of course, Yich'ŏn-daek wasn't about to back down either. "Do you really think that making a scene here is going to help? Is this going to help you put the oil back into the pan? What I'm saying is, anyone can make a mistake. And yes! Yang-mi *is* like my daughter. There's no girl like Yang-mi anywhere—she's a gem! Remember the time when you were out for three days last month, huh? Who did your work for you? Yang-mi! She covered up your absence so well that no one even suspected you weren't there. What I'm saying is, we should all help each other out, you know. Why make a big deal out of cooking oil that's already spilled, when you can simply wipe the floor and be done with it?"

But it wasn't as simple as that. Six, seven people were down on the floor trying to scoop the spilled oil into a large washbowl or trying to mop it up with paper, but the oil stains kept spreading. The real problem was the employees' shoes, all soaked with the oil. Within a matter of minutes, the oil was spread wherever they walked—from within the Food Section to the Dairy Product Corner to the Frozen Food Corner—everywhere! Some of the floor tiles began to come loose as the oil seeped into the grout. Mrs. Pak started to yell hysterically again, trying to press down the tiles with her hands.

"Yich'ŏn-daek, why are you picking a fight with *me*? I'm not even the one who stole that stupid necklace of hers! Yang-mi is crazy! Ah! I should've known something like this was coming! I knew there was something really wrong with the way she kept mumbling to herself and giggling by herself, getting on everyone's nerves. And you yell at *me*! What have I ever done to you?"

People forced Yich'ŏn-daek and Mrs. Pak apart because the two were obviously starting to fight again. I grabbed Yich'ŏn-daek and pulled her away from there, dragging her into the kitchen.

"You know . . . Mrs. Pak has a right to be mad. I mean, I don't understand why she's become like that, either—Yang-mi, I mean."

After gulping down a whole bowl of cold water, Yich'ŏn-daek finally calmed down enough to tell me the full story.

"I had gone to the bank, you see. I mean I went to the bank that's in front of the bus stop, up there. There were so many people gathered on the main road. They were talking quietly among themselves, saying that a movie was being filmed. They said that Pak Wŏn-jun was there. Actually, I was surrounded by so many people that I didn't get to see him myself. When I came back to the Mart, Yang-mi happened to be there so I simply said to her in passing, 'Guess what? I went to the bus stop and Pak Wŏn-jun was there. There were people gathered around him.' As soon as I said that, Yang-mi collapsed on the floor. Her tears fell in thick drops. And what was it she said? She said someone came to visit her because she lost her necklace. I couldn't understand a thing she was

230

saying . . . she was saying things like, 'Oh thank you so much, oh I'm
so sorry. . . .' And then, suddenly, she sprang up and started out. But
she tripped over the electric cord of the chicken machine. As the
machine fell down, it hit the frying pan in the Fish Jelly Corner. She
was lucky that the frying pan wasn't heated yet. Who knows what
could have happened! What if someone had been burned or scalded
by the oil! Anyway, how could Yang-mi run that fast? You should
have seen her running—I couldn't run like that myself, even if a
bomb exploded right in front of me."

Someone looked into the kitchen and called for Yich'ŏn-daek.
It was the Manager of the Executive Department.

"What is the matter here?" He looked forbidding. The floor
was still shining in places, stained with the oil.

"Son Yang-mi of the Chicken Corner touched the electric cord
and. . . ." Mrs. Pak seemed about to wail but Yich'ŏn-daek jumped in.

"Oh, it's no big fuss. The oil was old and we were about to
throw it out anyway. This customer had this child with her, and the
child . . . maybe five or six, well, his foot got caught in the electric
cord, so . . . even the frying pan went flying with the machine.
Everyone here is a witness. Team Manager Ch'oe, isn't that so?"

Yich'ŏn-daek turned around and looked at me meaningfully,
handing the story over to me. I jumped in.

"Yes. And Son Yang-mi just went to find a technician to fix the
machine, you see. I have to say it's fortunate that no customer was
hurt, sir."

"How could you have placed the cord so that a customer's foot
could get caught in it! Are you all idiots here?" he thundered.

If it hadn't been for the fact that there were customers passing
by, the Manager would have gone on like that forever.

"Get things settled as soon as possible. And tell Son Yang-mi
to come see me when she returns."

Yich'ŏn-daek, who had been standing obsequiously before the
Department Manager, flicked my shoulder and whispered, "What
are you standing here for? Go, fetch Yang-mi!"

The street in front of the bus stop near the bank was dull and empty. Judging from the leaves strewn around in small pieces on the ground, there really must have been quite a crowd of people gathered here earlier. As I had figured, Yang-mi was . . . right *there*. She was sitting limply on the edge of the bus stop bench. I took Yang-mi to a tent-bar by a stream, about a stop away. I knew people at the Mart must be waiting desperately for her to come back. But I couldn't take her there, not in this condition. She wasn't her usual self, and though she had stopped crying, she looked thoroughly spent, drained even of the will to speak.

She gulped down an entire bottle of soju and then finally looked at me. She was giggling a little, smiling wanly. "It was the day I had found out Yang-gil had stolen 20 million *won* from my savings account. I really didn't want to go back home. But . . . I had nowhere else to go. I thought I had just got on the bus . . . but before I knew it, I was at the final stop on the line. So I had to walk back towards home. I think I must have walked for three hours."

"You know what, Hyŏn-su? I'm not good-hearted at all. Every time I got my paycheck, I felt like I was being wronged by someone. Every day I felt distressed and hated myself. I asked myself, 'Why live like this'? All my hard-earned money, sometimes new and crisp, straight from the mint, was my own money. But I wasn't even allowed to touch it. I had to spend all that money on my siblings' tuition fees and buying rice, or else on coals for heating. At the end of every month after subtracting my transportation fees I wouldn't even have ten thousand *won* left in my pocket, you see." She rambled vaguely and I patiently heard her out.

There were only a few guests inside the tent-bar. Yang-mi and I seemed solitary in our tête-à-tête, with soju glasses in our hands. Only a young couple sat across from us in the opposite corner, rolling up noodles with their chopsticks.

"I had absolutely no energy left. It was almost twelve. I felt that the way home, walking up the hillside, was like walking up a mountain . . . home seemed high up and so far away. And then it happened just as I was about to pass by a store on a street corner. Suddenly a gentleman stretched out his arms in front of me, and handed me a can of beer! He was tall and handsome, and dressed in an impeccable suit. He said to me, '*How about a drink to cool you off, eh? Forget everything after you drink!*' It was Pak Wŏn-jun! You see, there had been a poster of Pak Wŏn-jun on the door of the store, a poster of him with a big smile, holding a can of beer. From there, from that very poster, he walked out like magic! Oh, Hyŏn-su, can you believe what I'm telling you?!"

Yang-mi looked up at me with curious eyes.

"I guess you can't! No one, not a single soul in this world can believe me. That's fine! It's a matter between him and me. It's a matter that concerns no one else!"

I had been listening to Yang-mi's words, nodding encouragingly all the while. For the first time, Yang-mi was opening up to me, laying before me all that was on her mind. That had always been *my* role. She had always listened.

"I sat on the flat wooden bench in front of the store, and called out to the owner. '*Excuse me! I'd like to order a bottle of beer.*' Oh, Hyŏn-su! Do you know how much that beer cost? One thousand and four hundred *won*! Can you believe it was the first time I had ever spent money on myself?"

Tears started to roll down Yang-mi's cheeks. There was nothing I could do for her, aside from filling up her empty glass of soju. She continued.

"With a can of refreshing beer, we cheered up. We were sitting down on the flat bench together, facing each other. Tears streamed down my face. It was so strange . . . I hadn't once cried even when I had found out that Yang-gil had duped me out of my money. But now my tears just came pouring out. All the sorrow piled up inside my entire being was now flowing out through my eyes, just like that."

"And you know what he did? He pulled me towards his body

and embraced me. He said, '*Miss Yang-mi, be strong. I'll always be your protector.*'"

"When I stood up from the bench to go home, I was no longer sad. Even as I opened the front gate when I arrived at home, late and somewhat drunk—I carried with me the calm he had given me. An expected commotion was waiting for me. Mother was on the floor, hysterical, crying her same old complaints: 'Oh, I'd rather die! I'd rather just die now, so I don't have to see you acting like this!' She's an expert at that. You see, she's accustomed to threatening me like that whenever there's a reason to feel sorry for me—it's just her way of turning the tables. As usual, father was sitting beside mom, adding a nasty remark to console her: 'What can we do? Hold yourself together. After all, it's only our Yang-gil who will be responsible for all our ancestral duties, isn't it?' Instead of getting mad, however, I actually felt sorry. Why? Because Pak Wŏn-jun had followed me all the way to my room, holding tightly onto my waist! I couldn't believe he was in my room . . . that depressingly dim, narrow, stinky room!"

"'How come that bitch doesn't even say anything?' 'Leave her alone, she's just a stupid girl. Don't mind about what's already happened.' My mother and father kept up their grumbling, but Wŏn-jun and I ignored them and just smiled at each other. We even laughed!"

"He asked me, '*You still have that necklace I gave you, don't you? Let me see it.*' And then I figured everything out! You see, everything had been destined to happen that way! He had borrowed my friend's hands to pass on the necklace to me, but it was really *he* who had given it to me! I was so grateful and touched, yet I was not surprised. If you think about it, that's the way things are in reality—say, magic or miracles . . . all these things begin so small! In fact, they originate from almost nothing in the beginning—like love that grows in our hearts. Like the grass being rippled by the wind, they're tiny and futile at first . . . but they gradually settle into a definite form and grow roots when they find the right soil. That's how a small plant becomes a strong tree, like a huge willow tree unshakable even by the stormiest wind!"

Yang-mi gave me a bright smile, the way she used to at the Mart. It was a smile I hadn't seen in a long time.

"'*Touch your necklace and stroke it. And I'll find you, wherever you are.*' This is what he said to me and whenever I touched my necklace, he really appeared in front of me! He said he liked me because I was good-hearted. He said that being good-hearted is not being stupid, but just being good-hearted. He said there are bad people in the world who take advantage of good-hearted people. And then he said . . . he loves me! The moment I heard him tell me this, I couldn't help feeling ashamed of myself. I suddenly became aware of my fat waist, my big shoulders. Oh, Hyŏn-su! Don't you agree that I should have felt this way?"

Yang-mi covered her mouth with her hands, as if she thought it was funny to be telling her own story.

"You know what? I spent a lot of money. I had to become pretty, you see. Being Wŏn-jun's secret lover, I wanted at least to try to look my best. So I went to a salon. Not one of those small salons in our town, but a grand one in Kangnam. I walked inside and proudly said, '*I must have the best hairdresser here do my hair.*' Do you know how much money I paid at that salon that day? Oh, it was half my salary, Hyŏn-su! I couldn't believe it. Two hairstylings . . . did I work all these years just to earn money that was worth just two hairstylings? Did I really suffer through all those traffic rush hours day and night, just to earn that small a salary? I suddenly felt sorry for my parents. I regretted having been so stingy, not knowing how little my salary was worth in real society."

There was a childlike candor to Yang-mi now but she was unaware of it.

"I went to a Shopping Mall and bought some clothes for myself. I even bought some expensive cosmetics. I dumped the plain, worn-down closet that was in my room, and I bought a lovely new wooden one. Wŏn-jun looked deeply into my eyes and said, '*Don't hesitate—*

what you're doing is perfectly fine! You are the most precious person in the world. Everybody lives for his or her own happiness!'"

"I had spent all the money that my family needed for living expenses and I couldn't help feeling restless at first. I knew my family wasn't going to just watch me do whatever I want. And you know my father, so aggressive, I thought he would have at me with that leather belt like he used to when I was young. But, how strange . . . my family began to be mindful of my presence! When I mentioned that my room was small, my father said quietly, 'Well, if your room is small, you can trade it for the master bedroom.' What was funnier was how mother reacted—she started giving me meat as a side dish! You know, mom used to be stingy even with kimchi and bean sprouts, complaining that we don't have a penny to spend in our house, even though I only get to eat at home on holidays. She used to slap my hand whenever my chopsticks went near a meaty side dish, and yell, 'Stop eating so much!'"

"But things were different with Yang-gil. He literally went crazy accusing me. 'Old sis is being swindled by a fraud,' he said. 'Someone loves you? How could you fall for such a lie!' I ignored him. You know, Yang-gil is . . . well, he's always been a pain. What surprised me was that . . . my sweetheart, *he* took it differently. He stared fiercely into Yang-gil's eyes, and his face turned red with rage. That was when it suddenly hit me—*I shouldn't be standing here like this, doing nothing!* I yelled back at Yang-gil with all I had in the depths of my being. '*Yang-gil! Get out of this house, right now! Take your parents and support them on your own! Don't you dare appear in front of me ever again!'*"

"Of course, I wouldn't have had the guts to pull that off if I'd been there by myself. All the while, my sweetheart was holding my hands tightly, you see. And he pulled me towards him and hugged me tightly. '*You are what I am, don't ever forget that! Whatever you say or whatever you do, just remember that I'm always with you.*'"

"That evening, I went to an enchanting café with him. I also bought a cake I wanted to eat and shared it with him. He whispered in my ear hundreds and thousands of times that he loves me . . . that I am prettier than anyone else in this world!"

"On the morning of Ch'usŏk, Yang-gil said to me while we were sitting in front of the memorial table, 'I'll be a good brother from now on, and I promise I won't hide the money for living expenses. I know how hard you've worked for us all . . . of course I know it.' Soon I found out that Yang-gil had found a job as a parking lot attendant for a Korean restaurant. He used to refuse to do that kind of work, you know, arrogantly insisting, 'How could a university graduate stoop so low?' How things have changed! Even mother and father don't say anything rude in front of me now. They only whisper to each other: 'Be good to Yang-mi. Or else she might give us hell again. Honestly though, it's true that Yang-mi has done pretty much everything that a son would do for us."

"Life can be such a comedy! When I swallowed all the humiliation and did my best for my family, they treated me like dirt; I felt as if they were actually riding on my back, waiting to see me collapse. And now that I stand up for myself, vent my anger, demand what's mine—what was mine from the very beginning— they're frightened, mindful of my anger, wary of my very being!"

I could see that Yang-mi's glum expression was gone; she was glowing again as she gave me a bright smile.

"You know, when I touched my necklace and stroked it . . . my sweetheart would appear in front of me, just as he said! Just like in *Aladdin's Lamp*. Like the Genie who appears and disappears, *poof!* like smoke from the lamp. Except . . . my sweetie doesn't appear or disappear in smoke. He walks slowly towards me, after appearing suddenly from out of nowhere, it seems! He appears at the Mart's Side Dish Corner, at the bus stop, sometimes even in front of the women's bathroom! No one else sees him. I'm happy about that. Because I bet any girl who sees him will fall for him!" she giggled.

Yang-mi covered her breasts with her two hands, and closed her eyes, as if in a trance.

"My sweetheart likes to play around a bit too much, that's his only flaw. He's always showering me with kisses while his arms are wrapped around my waist, not even minding people's stares. He sneaks under the counter stand of the Chicken Corner, putting his hands inside my skirt, always playing the fool! Even when we're at a café, he pushes me to the darkest corner and he . . . *Ai, ai . . . stop it, Hyŏn-su is watching! Stop! What's gotten into you!*"

Yang-mi opened her eyes. She had been giggling with her eyes closed, twisting her body spasmodically, as if she had felt someone's hands tickling her. Suddenly she picked up the bottle of soju, looking at me in a strange, forlorn way.

She tried to pour some soju into her glass but wound up spilling it all over the table.

"But, now . . . it's all over. I lost the necklace, you see. And now he can't come! He can't, can he? I mean, he'd come all the way to the bus stop where I think I dropped the necklace . . . yet I wasn't even there to meet him. Even if I went to find him now . . . he wouldn't be able to tell who I am, because I already lost that necklace!"

She looked so lost. Poor Yang-mi.

I grabbed the glass of soju that was in front of Yang-mi and drank it myself. And slowly yet clearly, I said, "You don't need that necklace anymore. Didn't you tell me your boyfriend said to you, '*You are what I am*'? He promised you that he'll always be your protector! So then where could he have gone without you? You know, he's stuck to you now. Ah! Isn't your boyfriend going a bit too far? My, I don't even know where to look!"

I poured more soju into the glass. Then I handed it back to Yang-mi.

"Here, tell your lover to be honored to receive this glass from me. Ah, the two of you, you guys are so cruel, you know! What, are you going to have me sit here for you and turn me into a vegetable?"

Yang-mi stared right into my eyes. There was a long pause. I lifted up my head and looked back at her, meeting her gaze.

"You can see? Hyŏn-su . . . you too can see my sweetheart?"

238

"Why, did you think I was blind? Actually I'm thinking I should teach him some manners with my fist. This rogue, he's younger than me, isn't he!"

Once again, I saw Yang-mi's eyes well up with tears. But this time, I could tell from her face that she was overwhelmed by happiness.

"You can see him . . . oh, Hyŏn-su! You can see him with your eyes, too! See! This is what I mean! He does exist! Yet, they all say that they can't see . . . *they* can't. My mother and father can't see him at all. Even when my sweetheart had followed me all the way into my bedroom, they didn't catch a hint of his presence. They can't see him even though he follows me around everywhere, sometimes naked too! Following me to the bathroom, to the kitchen . . . you name it! It's so funny! But you can—you see him! Oh, Hyŏn-su!"

Carrying Yang-mi on my back, I walked along the main road. There were many empty taxis passing by but I didn't try to catch one. I wanted to carry her forever and ever like this, until the day I became drained of all my energy, until the day I couldn't possibly stand anymore. On the road, ochre leaves were falling down one after another from the platanus trees: November had arrived.

Love isn't the only invisible thing that exists. Friendship, a heart that wishes only happiness, a love that has always been there: all these are invisible too. However, not only good things are invisible. There's hatred, envy, and selfishness that seeks to benefit at the expense of others. And then there's also sadness, desperation, loneliness . . . the hardships of life which we all encounter and struggle with, and often fail to overcome on our own. So I must say that while I'm sorry that the good things can't be seen, I'm also glad that the bad things are invisible too. If the good things are said to be small yet precious, just like pearls growing within the depths of the ocean, the bad things are just too glaring, too common, too . . . ugly. If with one sweeping view we could see all the bad things that exist, life would be unbearably distasteful, even nauseating.

"Yang-mi, look! The leaves are falling, can you see? Isn't this scenery beautiful? Look, the autumn leaves! Such vibrant colors, aren't they?"

I thought I had come up with a romantic cue, but Yang-mi on my back responded strangely. "My darling Wŏn-jun, aren't you tired carrying me?"

It's alright. Yes, yes, it's alright. It is *I*, Ch'oe Hyŏn-su, standing with Yang-mi, after all. Isn't it fortunate that instead of her invisible lover I am here, and at least she has me, who can carry her on his back?

Come to think of it, there are so many more things to feel fortunate about. The fact that Yang-mi lost some weight, for instance. If Yang-mi had weighed up to 70 kilos like she did in the past, even though they all call me a macho man, would I have been able to carry her on my back for so long? I must admit, the secret of Yang-mi's successful diet was her invisible lover Pak Wŏn-jun. Yet I decided to tell him a thing or two anyway.

"Hey! Isn't that just fine! I'm the one who's carrying Yang-mi, and you cheat, all you do is grab her pretty hand like the madman you are. What, are you going to pretend later that *you* carried her on your back? You're nothing but a bag of bones, you dandy, you fop! Ha, you're the biggest jerk in the world . . ."

You can say pretty much anything you want to an invisible guy, provoke him as much as you like, so I guess it's not so bad. Even if he wanted to punch me in the face, *how* could he do *that*? But I must say . . . if *I* wanted to deck him with a blow to the chin, that wouldn't be an easy job either.

Five Poems and an Essay by Kim Hyesoon

Translated by Chae-Pyong Song and Don Mee Choi

THE HORIZON

Who broke it?
The horizon beyond,
the fissure between heaven and earth,
an evening where crimson water spreads out from the gap.

Who broke it?
The slit between upper and lower eyelids,
The scars of my body broken because of emptiness within and
    without,
an evening where tears erupt from the gap.

Can only a wound flow into a wound?
The glow of sunset rushes toward me as I open my eyes.
When a wound touches a wound,
red water flows without end.
Even the exit, disguised as you, shuts in darkness.

Who broke it?
The white day from the dark night.

During the day she becomes a hawk,
at night he becomes a wolf.
Through the gap, the evening of our encounter
brushes by like a knife blade.

Flu

We looked at each other in the other world
as if I existed inside the black-and-white picture he was looking
    down from.

Inside his picture I always felt cold.
Coughing trees were standing along the river, hacking away.

Whenever I awoke, I was always climbing a snowy mountain.

After narrowly making it around a corner, there were still vast white
    snowfields
and endless cliffs that dropped sharply from the edge.

That evening I looked out at his eyes, wide open like a frozen sky.

A rumor spread that a ghost with the flu was coming to the village.
At every chimney, clouds shook their bodies.

He is not in my body, because I drove him out.

With an avalanche in my heart I shivered for more than an hour.

As coughing trees shook down snowballs,
jagged ice shot out from the open valley.

Barefaced, I was sitting on a frozen bench,
withstanding the wind, with quivering lips.

I wanted to escape from this frame he was looking down from.

—Translated by Chae-Pyong Song

STARFISH*

I leave my starfish in the Pacific Ocean
my cuckoo in Tibet
my sloth in the forest of the Amazon
and I cook and lecture and age like this

I tie my fingers to a pine tree in the tundra
and bury my eyes beneath the vast snow of the North Pole
and leave my heart to melt in the abyss of the Pacific Ocean
and I cook, eat, sleep, drink, and even laugh like this

Therefore sadness blows in from Sumeru
Cold tears arrive from the bottom of an ice sheet that never melts
all year long
Therefore fever arrives from the Sahara
from a faraway place overgrown with cacti that can't close
their mouths, for needles stick out from their tongues
the inside of my open mouth is hot as lava

So don't keep coming to me, my starfish, crazy starfish
It is said that you were made from a fleck of rice
and can become as big as a house, a mountaintop
Don't return here even if a ditch forms from the tears
that I shed every night from missing you
the ditch is not a place for you to live
If you keep coming back I'll pin a star to my hair
and all the night of the world will explode inside me

A fine new day arrives like a clear sky after the typhoon
When I stand in the street, wearing a pair of dead gutter-rat shoes,
my butterflies blow in from all over even though my body is so
    small

Why are my arms, my head, my legs, my limbs so distant?

I must have been chased by all the wind in the world and got
   wrecked
inside this body
My arms and legs become distant in all directions
my head feels hazy

Since I always lack oxygen, my footsteps move across the tundra
Being on time is my sickness, but I need to go out to be on time

Someone stares into me for a while then flees
My feet are outside of my vision

My feet gradually fade away and
take off like the wolves to the faraway mountains

—Translated by Don Mee Choi

*Starfish [*Pulgasal*] is the name of a monster from a fable, a monster that can
only be killed by fire. According to the fable, during the Chosŏn period (1392-1910)
when Buddhism was suppressed by King Yi Sŏng-gye, monks were imprisoned.
One monk created an animal from a fleck of rice, and the animal escaped from the
prison and roamed the entire country eating iron bits and became a monster. In
Korean *Pulgasal* and starfish are homonyms.

Seoul, Kora[1]

The mountain barks
then follows me

The mountain gives birth
The mountain licks a mountain
The mountain's litter sucks on its nipples
The mountain cold-heartedly discards all its litter
The young mountains copulate in broad daylight, the stench
The mountain roams like a pack of dogs inside a maze

The mountain looks at me with its wet eyes
It trembles as I stroke its neck
The mountain gets dragged away with a rope around its neck
The mountain gets locked up behind bars. It's beaten. It's kicked.
It dies.

The mountain eats shit, eats a corpse
The mountain, the mountain full of rashes attacks me with its
    flaming eyes
The mountain, the mountain with snow on top cries
The mountain without a single tree laments with its head flung back
    towards the sky
The mountain bites and fights a mountain
The mountain, the big mountain chases its own tail

Empire's military exterminates the mountain that swarms
The mountain that survived, the mountain, the mountain climbs
    over a mountain
and runs away

---

1. Kora refers to a loop of prostrations around the sacred mountain, Mt. Kailash,
Tibet.

It's still running away

The mountain, the mountain that wants to shed a mountain, brings
  its hands together
and stretches them towards the faraway mountain, touches its
  forehead, pulls them down to its chest, looks at the faraway
  mountain once again as it draws its elbows to its waist, then
  bends its right knee, both hands down on the ground, then
  bends the left knee, presses down its hands on the ground and
  sends them far, far away, then prostrates, its entire body touching
  the ground. Then it cries. The mountain circles a mountain,
  repeats the whole thing every three steps.

SAND WOMAN

The woman was pulled out of the sand
She was perfectly clean—not a single strand of her hair had gone
    bad

They say the woman didn't eat or sleep after he'd left
She kept her eyes closed
didn't breathe
yet wasn't dead

People came and took the woman away
They say people took off her clothes, dipped her in salt water, spread
    her thighs
cut her hair and opened her heart

He died in war and
even the country parted somewhere far far away
The woman swallowed her life
didn't let out her breath to the world
Her eyes didn't open even when a knife blade busily went in and out
    of her

People sewed up the woman and laid her in a glass coffin
The one she waited for didn't arrive, instead fingers swarmed in
    from all directions

The woman hiding in the sand was pulled out
and every day I stared vacantly at her hands spread out on paper
I wanted to ride a camel and run away from this place

In every dream the woman followed me

and opened her eyes

the desert inside her eyelids was deeper and wider than the night

   sky

—Translated by Don Mee Choi

In the Oxymoronic World[1]

By Kim Hyesoon
Translated by Don Mee Choi

The ether of a poem, the emptiness, the poesy exists inside the movement of language. The trace of the movement can only be drawn as a formless form, like the way our brain activities reveal themselves as waves, the way electric currents flow between you and me. I'll call such wave motion the "moving dot."

The moving dot can be extinguished in an instant, yet it contains all information, even eternity. Try placing a dot on the undulating waves. The moment I extend my arm, the dot is already gone.

The moving dot is infinitely small because it moves, yet at the same time it is infinitely large. Inside the infinite smallness the self becomes infinitely tiny and dies. Inside the infinite largeness the self becomes infinitely huge and dies. The extremes of the infinitely small and infinitely large are the non-self. The non-self is required by the speaker and the listener of a poem. Poetry is a modality that follows the path of the discourse and through that path is able to conceive an empty space. To say that the dot does not have form or even a size because it is infinitely small is no different from saying that the dot is infinitely large and therefore is the universe. The moving dot is the slowest, yet the fastest. It is as big as Chuang Tzu's

---

1. Previously presented at American Literary Translators Association (ALTA) Conference, October 21, 2006.

Azalea

In the

Oxymoronic

World:

Kim

Hyesoon

bird and as small as Chuang Tzu's fish. The moving dot is a whale's body and the egg of an anchovy.

The moving dot is the "now, here, and I" that appear in poetry. All the images in poetry become instantly compressed inside the "now, here, and I"—the moving dot. The chaotic, the marginalized, the "now, here, and I" flutter about in the fringes— the "now, here, and I" pulls the moving dot with its breath. The tiny moving dot breathes in the swirls of the Milky Way and pulls the fringes of the city of Seoul. The images of poetry are the trace of the moving dot; they point to the place in which the eternity that can be extinguished in an instant is caught by the text. The images extend the days they'll exist inside the moment of absence. Conversely, they extend the days of the absence inside the moment of existence. The trace of the moving dot is an infinite world—a world beyond time, a world rediscovered, a world of poetry. It is a sketch of something sublime beyond existence, beyond the grave. In spite of that, poetry exists inside a single woven text. Poetry exists inside the text that I experience, inside the expanded, multiple space that I the object must overcome. Poetry exists inside prose's maze of suffering, the neglect, the fringe, the repetition. A woman goes, passing along the windy road of language, a woman without a mother tongue, a woman who labors in no-action—she goes.

The inside of the maze is a path of to and fro, a spiral path and a dead end, a path that is far yet near, a sky path, a water path. Like the inside of a conch shell, like being swept by a whirlwind, a typhoon. What stories does the maze tell? Does it speak to future generations about life's journey, the roaming, the difficulty of finding an exit, or perhaps the recollection of a struggle at the crossroad? The maze is the diagram of the trace that is both present and absent. In the lines of the maze, life and the world intersect. The lines form a crack that crosses the two worlds. The maze is either a map of the nomads who roamed the desert looking for a path, or a drawing of the trace of my footsteps on magnificent Seoul.

The maze is a passage through which life's secret is delivered. The passage looks like the moments of my rites of passage. Therefore, my maze is a record of my endless escape, my running away. In order to escape from the maze, I must realize that time does not flow in a linear fashion; time is spread out. The inside of the maze is filled with dead ends and paths that lead me back to the exit. I don't know how far I must walk, but there is a dance, the rule of an undulating movement.

The footsteps of someone who dances inside the maze seem confusing at first, but the steps connote the essential rules of the infinite undulation. They contain immanent rhythm that leads to plentitude and a new structure. The maze's breathing overcomes the masculine, the overly regulated rhythm that denies any repudiation, the prose narrative that follows linear time, the gravity—the modality of dancing steps that unravel. Its only criterion is indefiniteness and fortuity. As the maze grows more complex, it contains the flexible logic of non-alignment. This logic of non-alignment demands from me a new experience with language. I must go beyond my conventional prose in order to attain the experience of the new. But when I enter the newness, once again, I become constricted by the rhythm and repetition of verse. I bend language on both sides to build a diction that undulates in a new way. Only then can poesy enter, transcendent, inside my poem.

When such shape is pulled into the inner world of divinity, it becomes a mandala.

The mandala is a drawing of an archetypal self. It brings the inside to the outside. Emptiness is made visible by the mandala. Time is compressed in the mandala—from birth to death, the rise and the fall of sun and moon, and eternity.

However, the law of fabricated linear time is imposed on history, including my life. Some of the literary writings that emerge from the law of fabrication include manifestos, autobiographies, historical fiction, and poetry without poesy. These writings do not

Azalea

In the
Oxymoronic
World:
Kim
Hyesoon

vomit what the humans have eaten but strange dolls instead—dolls with their faces. They sell their souls to the linear fictionalization. Inside linear time, a butterfly that passes in front of my eyes can never be seen again. However, like the mandala, poetry does not exist inside such linear time. Several subjects exist equally, simultaneously. These things dream of conversing with each other, and the conversing becomes a subject in itself.

I am many inside poetry. "I" as a subject, the cognizant "I" is deconstructed. I have never once lived as a single "I" inside poetry. The confusion of the multiple "I" is what makes me write poetry. I am a mother, a young unmarried woman, an angel, a prostitute. I am an infant just born, an old woman near death. When I am a mother, "I" the young unmarried woman is ill, and when I am a young woman, the mother is ill. Like the children who defy school and run out the gate, multiple "I's" dangle from the open skirt of the Buddhist Goddess of Mercy. "You" inside poetry also dangle from the skirt.

My writing floats around the inside and the outside of me. Like a dog who has lost its owner, I follow the scent of this and that person, asking whether they are me. At such moments the poetic discourse is plural. The suffering multiple "I's" are merry. Their merriment rescues me from the forgetfulness of existence. Without merriment, poetry remains on a singular plane. In order to achieve polyphonic planes, my poetry needs to be merry—inside things, between things, inside the multiple "I's" and between the multiple "I's".

I sing, my skull sings, the world sings, the stars sing. The songs are all different but connected by merriment. The music is already within poetry.

As a woman, I observe the identity inside me that rises and falls, waxes and wanes, lives and dies like the moon. Therefore my body's form is infinitely fractal. I live according to the way that fractal form is read, feeling the path through which life flows in and out. I love, therefore I become myself. I see the "I" inside you.

As a woman I open my body not to men but to the context of eros. Such love has spilled out from my body before the beginning of time and it is from there that my voice of existence bursts forth. The essence of my existence does not have a fixed form; it has a moving form, always circulating but never repeating itself.

Therefore as woman, as poet, I dance and rescue the things that have fallen into the coil of magnificent silence; I wake the present, and let the dead things be dead.

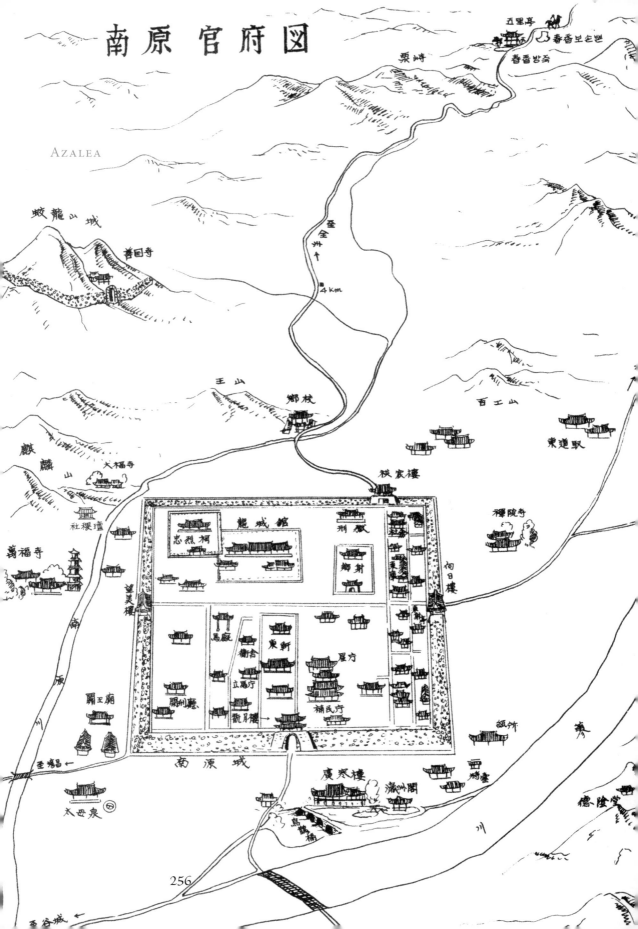

南原官府図

AZALEA

256

The Road to Ch'unhyang:
A Reading of the *Song of the Chaste Wife Ch'unhyang*

by Peter H. Lee

Another
Perspective

*Writing and reading are not separate, reading is a
part of writing. A real reader is a writer. A real
reader is already on the way to writing.*
—*Hélène Cixous,* Three Steps
on the Ladder of Writing

The story of Ch'unhyang 春香, known to all Koreans, is
the subject of narrative fiction for the eye or sung in a
p'ansori 판소리 version for the ear. It concerns Ch'unhyang, daughter
of a wealthy retired female entertainer and Second Minister Sŏng
成參判, who meets and marries Student Yi 李道令. When his father,
the magistrate of Namwŏn 南原, is transferred to a position at court,
Yi follows him to Seoul to prepare for his civil service examination.
Meanwhile, a new magistrate arrives and demands that Ch'unhyang
become his mistress. When she refuses because she is married, she
is tortured and put in prison. Yi then returns to Namwŏn as a secret
royal inspector and saves his beloved.

Background

There are some 120 different editions of the *Song of Ch'unhyang*,
short or long, in literary Chinese or in the vernacular, in narrative

---

*My trip to Namwŏn in April 2008 was made possible by an AAS Northeast
Asia Council small grant for a short-term trip to Korea. All Korean-language texts
were published in Seoul unless otherwise indicated. SPTK stands for the *Sibu
congkan* (1919-36) edition, a collection of Chinese classics.

257

fiction or in *p'ansori* to be performed by a professional singer (*kwangdae* 廣大), lasting from five to eight hours depending on which version has been compiled by which singer. The earliest extant version (1754), by Yu Chinhan 柳振漢 (1712-1791), is in literary Chinese[1] and consists of 200 heptasyllabic couplets. Chinese is the language of official tradition, authority, and power, indeed, the language of the symbolic father; vernacular is the language of the people. Chinese is a fixed language; vernacular, in a state of continual flux. In a hybrid culture that practiced written and oral circulation of stories and, as well, a bicultural society in which Chinese and vernacular literacies interacted with vernacular orality, it was inevitable that Yu's version, a memorial reconstruction of a version heard (or slightly misheard) on stage, must have effaced much that was distinctly oral. As a literatus, Yu was probably moved by the power of the human voice and the singer's competence and formal excellence. And the *Song of Ch'unhyang* he heard dealt with common material so that the broad outline of the plot was known in advance. *P'ansori* was a popular art form that joined the people in the immediacy of performance; but reception is a "unique, fleeting, irreversible act—no same performance experienced in an identical manner by any two audience members."[2]

"Textuality gave to utterance a materiality that memory does not have."[3] Traces of earlier oral productions may be seen in the frequency of parataxis, formulas, episodes, myths, and elements of literacy—orality and literacy merged and supported each other. We may speculate that the earliest version was composed orally in performance. The text was almost exclusively transmitted

---

1. For Yu Chinhan's version, see Hanguk kososŏl yŏnguhoe, ed. Ch'unhyang chŏn *ŭi chonghapchŏk koch'al* (Asea munhwasa, 1991), 469-504 (uncommon paging); Sŏl Sŏnggyŏng in ibid., 430-31.

2. A.N. Doane and Carol Braun Pasternack, eds., *Vox Intexta* (Madison: University of Wisconsin Press, 1991), 227. Paul Zumthor, *Oral Poetry: An Introduction*, trans. Kathryn Murphy-Judy (Minneapolis: University of Minnesota Press, 1990), 183.

3. Doane and Pasternack, 58.

in performances, which survived only in written versions.[4] By "oral" I mean, with Paul Zumthor, "any poetic communication where transmission and reception at least are carried by voice and hearing," and by "performance," "the complex action by which a poetic message is simultaneously transmitted and perceived in the here and now."[5] Among multiple retellings of some 120 versions, the one I have chosen is the Wanp'an wood-block edition, meant to be sung, titled *Yŏllyŏ Ch'unhyang sujŏl ka* 烈女春香守節歌 (Song of the Chaste Wife Ch'unhyang; 84 sheets, 168 pages). This version focuses on Ch'unhyang; it is the most well wrought, the richest in sound and sense, form and style, and probably the most literary and most readable.[6] Written from a pluralistic narrative perspective, with different voices and their corresponding value systems, it is polyphonic and heteroglossic, recognizing and exploiting to the fullest intralingual and interlingual features of the language. As an introduction, allow me to discuss for a moment the issues of orality and performance in Korean poetry, the oral narrative known as *p'ansori*, the female entertainer (*kisaeng* 妓生), and the professional singer (*kwangdae*).

Orality and Performance

> *E però sappia ciascuno che nulla cosa per legame musaico armonizzata si può de la sua loquela in altra transmutare sanza rompere tutta sua dolcezza e armonia.* ("Everyone knows that nothing which is harmonized by the bond of the Muses can be altered from its own to another language without destroying all its sweetness and harmony.")

> —*Dante*, Convivio[7]

---

4. Doane and Pasternack, 3.

5. Zumthor, *Oral Poetry*, 23, 22.

6. The version I have used is by Ku Chagyun, *Ch'unhyang chŏn*, Hanguk kojŏn munhak taegye 10 (Minjung sŏgwan, 1976), 2-215. Hereafter cited in the text with the page number, but without "p." According to Yu T'agil, "Wanp'an panggak sosŏl ŭi munhŏnhakchŏk yŏngu," this version is the oldest edition. Cited in Sŏng Hŏngyŏng, 'Ch'unhyang ŭi sinbun pyŏni kwajŏng yŏngu," in *Yangp'o Yi Sangt'aek kyosu hwallyŏk kinyŏm nonch'ong: Hanguk kojŏn sosŏl kwa sŏsa munhak*, 2 vols. (Chimmundang, 1998), 1:423 (n. 10). I have also consulted Kim Tonguk et al., eds., *Ch'unhyang chŏn pigyo y ngu* (Samyŏngsa, 1979).

7. Dante Alighieri, *Il Convivio*, ed. Maria Simonelli (Bologna: Riccardo Patron,

Le poème—cette hesitation prolongée entre le son et le sens. (The poem, this prolonged hesitation between sound and sense.)
—Valéry,"Rhumbs," Tel Quel [8]

La traduction n'est nullement destinée a faire disparaître la différence dont elle est au contraire le jeu: constamment elle y fait allusion, elle la dissimule, mais parfois en la révélant en souvent en l'accentuant, elle est la vie même de cette différence, elle y trouve son devoir auguste, sa fascination aussi, quand elle en vient à rapprocher orgueilleusement les deux langages par une puissance d'unification qui lui est propre et semblable à celle d'Hercule resserrant les deux rives de la mer.[9] ("Translation is the sheer play of difference: it constantly makes allusion to difference, dissimulates difference, but by occasionally revealing and often accentuating it, translation becomes the very life of this difference, and it is under the spell of this difference that translation discovers its august duty whenever it proudly sets out to bring the two languages closer together through its own power of unification, a power like that of Hercules drawing together the two shores of the sea.")[10]
—Blanchot,"Traduire," L'Amitié

Yi Hae-jo,
Okchunghwa,
1912.

In Korea all poems—more precisely, songs—were intended to be sung. Musical notations with lyrics dating from the early sixteenth century preserve both the musical settings and Middle Korean song words. Orality and performance were the salient characteristics of Korean poetry, and it was performance that helped to preserve classical vernacular poetry; for example, from the time of their emergence to their first transcription, Silla (Old Korean) songs were orally transmitted for about four hundred years and Middle Korean songs for about three hundred years. The postface to the Korean alphabet emphasizes the language's power to describe the "sound of the wind, the whoop of cranes, the crowing of cocks, and the barking of dogs."[11] This phonetic complexity, explored to the

---

1966), 15.

8. Paul Valéry, *Oeuvres*, ed. Jean Hytier (Paris: Gallimard, 1960), 2:637.

9. Maurice Blanchot, *L'Amitié* (Paris: Gallimard, 1971), 70-71.

10. Translation by Richard Sieburth in *Sulfur* 26 (1990), 83. Quoted in Lawrence Venuti, ed., *Rethinking Translation: Discourse, Subjectivity, Ideology* (London: Routledge, 1992), 13.

11. Chŏng Inji (1397-1478) says this in the postface (1446) to the *Hunmin chŏngŭm* 32a.

full by poets, known and unknown, makes translation into another language problematic. The translator must re-create not only the sense but also the sound, its structure and function, and convey how certain sounds suggest certain meanings—indeed, often the meaning depends on the intricate sound pattern. If fluency and transparency are essential for a successful translation, how does the translator make up for the loss of the sound—phonomimes, phenomimes, and nonsense sounds?

In the literary history of Korea, poetry written in literary Chinese and poetry in the vernacular are termed differently: *si* (poetry) was reserved almost exclusively for the former and *ka* (song) for the latter. This difference came from the ideological bias and cultural elitism of the literati, who espoused the Confucian and official Chinese literary canon and, through their alliance with the court and the ruling class, exercised power in Korea. The labeling of vernacular poetry as songs can, however, be interpreted not merely as pejorative but as suggesting other implications and may even indicate an understanding of orality and performance in their poetry.

The names of most native poetic genres in Korea (and Japan) contain the graph *ka* (song) or its cognates (*yo, cho,* and the like in Korean). Indeed, this designation of vernacular poetry as "song" does not merely distinguish it from poetry written in literary Chinese. Orality and performance had always been the distinguishing characteristics of vernacular poetry in Korea. While the performance aspect came to be less prominent in China and Japan, it became the most significant feature of vernacular poetry in traditional Korea.

Like all subsequent vernacular poetic forms in Korea, Silla songs known as *hyangga* 鄉歌 (sixth to tenth century) were sung. The forms and styles of Korean poetry therefore reflect its melodic origins. The basis of its prosody is a line consisting of metric segments of three or four syllables—the rhythm that is probably most natural to the language. In the ten-line *hyangga*, the ninth line usually begins with an interjection that not only indicates heightened emotions and a change in tempo and pitch but also presages the poem's conclusion. Musical notations indicate that the musical divisions of each popular Koryŏ song, signaled by an interjection followed by a refrain, are different from its poetic (stanzaic) divisions. Furthermore, the association of verbal and musical rhythms can be seen in the refrain of Koryŏ songs. Nonsense jingles or onomatopoetic representations of the sounds of the drum, for example, attest to the refrain's musical origins and function. Unlike other vernacular genres with extant musical notations, however, *hyangga* has no musical settings.

oda oda oda	We have come, have come, have come,
oda syŏrŏptara	How sad, we have come!
syŏrŏpta ŭinaeyŏ	Sad are living beings,
kongdŏk takkara oda	We have come to garner merits.

This is a popular song (ca. 635) sung during the construction of a sixteen-foot-high Buddha statue when men and women eagerly carried clay for the work. The compiler Iryŏn (1206-1289) adds that it was popular even in his day, almost six hundred years after its composition, and was sung when pounding rice or constructing buildings.[12] Beginning with a succession of spondees, the repetition of *oda* (come) and *syŏrŏpta* (sad), simple native words, leads to the fourth line with *kongdŏk,* a Sino-Korean Buddhist technical term. *Kongdŏk* (Skt: *guna*), usually translated as virtue or merit, refers to the merits a devotee's pious acts can accumulate; the repetition of the velar plosive /k/ provides a sharp awakening effect. The predominance of such bright vowels as *a* and *o* diminishes the influence of dark vowels (*u* and *ŏ*). The tone, therefore, is not sad: the devotees accept the fact that they are born as human beings to accumulate merits in whatever they do with devotion.

---

12. *Samguk yusa*, ed. Ch'oe Namsŏn (Minjung sŏgwan, 1954), 4:184-85.

The second stanza of "Che mangmae ka" (Requiem for the Dead Sister) by Master Wŏlmyŏng (ca. 742-765) recalls in simile and theme the words of Homer, who compared the generations of men to those of leaves (*Iliad* 6:146-50):

ŏNŭ kasal iRŭN paRaMae	n, s, l, r, n, p, m
ie chŏe ttŏdiL Niptai	ch, tt, l, n, p, t
haNan kajae Nago	h, n, k, j, n, g
kaNoNgot ModaoNdyŏ	k, n, n, g, m, d, n, d

Consisting of a group of native words, the stanza creates its effect by sound. The accumulation of appropriate sounds—euphonious soft bilabial nasal, alveo-dental nasal and liquid—creates a languid but sad effect, /d/ recalling an emotion that goes with such English words as "dread," "dead," and "darkness." The sound values of the original, which resonates with the lamenting voice, cannot be adequately re-created in translation:

We know not where we go,
Leaves blown, scattered,
Though fallen from the same tree,
By the early winds of autumn.

The characteristic songs of Koryŏ (918-1392) were all performed and transmitted orally until the early sixteenth century, when music books such as *Siyong hyangak po* 時用鄉樂譜 (Notations for Korean Music in Contemporary Use), the first systematic musical notation, providing both written music and written words, recorded them for the first time in the Korean alphabet then available. Whether Koryŏ songs were all orally composed is uncertain, but there was an interaction between oral and written forms and the high and the low as there was in medieval Japan, for example, where waterfront prostitutes and roaming actors and jugglers (*kugutsu*) played an important role in transmitting popular songs.[13]

Sijo 時調 (contemporary tune), the most popular of the classical poetic forms, consists of three lines in the original, with four metrical segments to a line, a caesura coming after the second segment:

3/4 4 3/4 4

3/4 4 3/4 4

3   5 4 3/4

The following example shows how the repetition of grammatical and syntactic elements enhances the intended tone and meaning:

Ch'ŏngsando *chŏllo chŏllo* (3/4)
> Green mountains are natural, natural

noksudo *chŏllo chŏllo* (3/4)
> Blue waters too, natural, natural.

san *chŏllo chŏllo* su *chŏllo chŏllo* (5/5)
> Between natural mountains and natural waters,

sansugane nado *chŏllo chŏllo* (4/2/4)
> I myself am natural, natural.

kŭjunge *chŏllo* charin momi (3/4/2)
> This body that grew naturally

nŭlkido *chŏllo chŏllo* nŭlgŭrira (3/4/4)
> Will no doubt naturally age.[14]

Except for *ch'ŏngsan* (green mountain) and *noksu* (blue water), the song draws its diction from native common words. In his philosophy of life, the author Kim Inhu (1510-1560) repeats the

---

13. Barbara Rush, "The Other Side of Culture in Medieval Japan," *The Cambridge History of Japan*, vol. 3, ed. Kozo Yamamura (Cambridge: Cambridge University Press, 1990), 500-43.

14. No. 2587 in Sim Chaewan, *Kyobon yŏktae sijo chŏnsŏ* (Sejong munhwasa, 1972).

264

adjective/adverb *chŏllo* thirteen times; the ideophone is charged with polysemy and musical property (melopoeia). The cognate of the Chinese *ziran* ("so-of-itself")—natural spontaneity, the Korean *chŏllo*, repeated for emphasis and metrical requirements—is associated with the Daoist view of life: detached, free, enlightened. A man fully awakened, the speaker has comprehended the relationship between the phenomenal world and ultimate truth and has taken transformation as his final abode.

In "Dispelling Gloom" (1618), Yun Sŏndo (1587-1671), generally considered the master of the *sijo* form, creates suspense by an emphatic repetition of verbs:

> Moehŭn *kilgo kilgo* (3/4)
> > A chain of mountains is long, long;
> murŭn *mŏlgo mŏlgo* (2/4)
> > Waters flow, far, far.
> ŏbŏi kŭrin ttŭdŭn (3/4)
> > Love for parents is endless,
> *mankŏ mankŏ hago hago* (4/4)
> > And my heart is heavy.
> ŏdŭisyŏ woegirŏginŭn (3/5)
> > Far off, crying sadly,
> *ulgo ulgo* kanŭni (4/3)
> > A lone wild goose flies by.[15]

The five adjectival verbs in the continuative form *ko* are among the simplest of Korean verbs, but tension builds as the poem moves steadily from one to the next. The long vowels in *kilgo*, *mŏlgo*, *mankŏ*, and *ulgo* (all repeated for emphasis) and the *l*'s in *kil*, *mŏl*, and *ul* provide a resonant tone. The fourth line literally means "much much vast vast" to underscore his longing for his parents in a place of exile in the cold northwest, but its music is lost in translation.

15. No. 1044 in Sim Chaewan.

The *Song of Ch'unhyang* explores to the maximum all the rhetorical devices known to the language. Simple repetition of verbs, adjectives, and adverbs fecundates the music of sound and sense. Here Ch'unhyang expresses longing for her husband after his departure:

> *Pogo chigo pogo chigo* (4/4)
>> I yearn to see him, yearn to see him,
> *Ime ŏlgul pogo chigo* (4/4)
>> Yearn to see my beloved's face.
> *Tŭtko chigo tŭtko chigo* (4/4)
>> I yearn to hear him, yearn to hear him,
> *Ime sori tŭtko chigo* (4/4)
>> Yearn to listen to his voice.

Again she attempts to describe in words the depth and height of her love:

> *Kŭnwŏn hŭllŏ muri toego* (4/4)
>> A spring grows into a stream,
> *Kipko kipko tasi kipko* (4/4)
>> Deep, deep, deep again—
> *Sarangmoe wa mega toeyŏ* (4/4)
>> Our love piled high like a mountain,
> *Nopko nopko tasi nopko* (4/4)
>> High, high, high again—
> *Kkŭnŏ chilchul morŭ kŏdŭn* (4/4)
>> Love does not know when to break;
> *Munŏ chilchul ŏi alli* (4/4)
>> Who would know when it might crumble?

Guards and servants rush to Ch'unhyang's home to take her to the new magistrate, and the head of female entertainers urges her on: "*ŏsŏ kaja pappi kaja*" (4/4)—"Let's go quickly, make haste."

266

Audience and jailers, after Ch'unhyang is beaten, exclaim:

Moji toda moji toda (4/4)
　　Oh, it's cruel, it's cruel,
Ch'unhyang chŏngjŏl *moji toda* (4/4)
　　Ch'unhyang's chastity is cruel—
Ch'ulch'ŏn yŏllyŏ roda (4/2)
　　A chaste woman sent from heaven!

Ch'unhyang speaks to her mother, who laments her lot with an implied criticism of the mother's preference for a son:

Mao mao sŭlp'ŏ *mao* (4/4)
　　Don't, don't, don't cry,
Oeson pongsa mot'arikka? (4/4)
　　Couldn't my children offer sacrifices after you die?

And note the parallel construction here:

Sonnŭni yuhyŏl iyo (3/4)
　　What rushes out is blood,
Hŭrŭnŭni nunmul ira (4/4)
　　What streams are tears.

In addition, the narrator often uses ideophones—phenomimes and phonomimes—to picture in sounds the state, mood, and acts of humans as well as phenomena of nature.

Phenomimes include, for example, *ajang ajang* (with toddling steps); *allong allong* (mottled); *chosok chosok* (drowsy); *hŏlttŏk hŏlttŏk* (panting); *hŭnŭl hŭnŭl* (swaying gently); *hwich'in hwich'in* (round and round); *kubi kubi* (at every turn); *nŏul nŏul* (sways, undulates); and *taerung taerung* (dingle-dangle). Phonomimes include, among others, *ch'ullŏng ch'ullŏng* (lapping); *kamul kamul* (flickering); *kurŏng chŏrŏng* (one way or another); *k'wang k'wang* (a dog's barking—bowwow); *pŏllŏng pŏllŏng* (quivering); *p'ŏl p'ŏl* (fluttering); *tongdong* (jumping up and down); and *tungdung* (boom-boom).[16] Most of these imitations of sounds and acts occur when Ch'unhyang is the object of focalization: her movements, surroundings, feelings, wishes, prayers, and what others do to her.

Enumeration is another device as, for example, in *sasŏl sijo*—Pangja lists fourteen scenic spots in the country; the narrator cites fourteen items of Yi's attire and nine items of Ch'unhyang's; nineteen dishes are served for Yi by Wŏlmae; the word "love" (*sarang*) is repeated twenty-eight times in "Song of Love"; words with the graph *chŏng* appear thirty-nine times ("Song of the Graph *Chŏng*"); words with the graph *kung* appear sixteen times ("Song of the Graph *Kung*"); the verb "to ride" (*t'ada*) appears sixteen times ("Song of the Graph *Sŭng*"); words with the graph *chŏl* appear seventeen times ("Song of Parting"); twenty-four entertainers are reviewed; each stop along the route is counted as Inspector Yi travels from Seoul to Namwŏn; and the blind fortune-teller appeals to some twenty mythological and historical persons.

We are often reminded of the fact that certain poems are untranslatable. John F. Nims comments: "There is no way, for example, to translate 'nostra vita' [*Inferno* 1:1] into English so that the two simplest words for the idea 'our life' preserve the cadence of the Italian."[17] Or, one might add, "L'amor che move il sole e l'altre stelle" (*Paradiso* 33:145) with its alliteration of *m*, assonance of *o*, and consonance of *l*; or Goethe's "Gretchen am Spinnrade" (Meine Ruh ist hin, / Mein Herz is schwer; / Ich finde sie nimmer / Und nimmermehr); or Verlaine's "Chanson d'automne."[18] If translation of Dante, Goethe, and Verlaine is difficult, what about translation

---

16. Ho-min Sohn, *Korean* (London: Routledge, 1994), 491, 495-96; see also section 4:1, ideophones (495-519) in *The Korean Language* (Cambridge: Cambridge University Press, 1999); and Samuel E. Martin, *A Reference Grammar of Korean* (Rutland: Tuttle, 1992), 340-47. The term "ideophone" was coined by Clement M. Doke in *Bantu Linguistic Terminology* (London: Longmans Green, 1935).

17. John F. Nims, "Poetry: Lost in Translation?" *Delos* 5 (1970), 113.

18. Donald Frame, "Pleasure and Problems of Translation," in *The Craft of Translation*, ed. John Biquent and Rainer Schulte (Chicago: University of Chicago Press, 1989), 71.

of an East Asian poem into a Western language, when the resources of East Asian languages differ from those of, say, English, and the field of association and allusion and the cultural context the poet/singer exploits are different? Is it possible to translate, transfer, reproduce, or approximate the materiality of language, its physical properties and recognizable qualities, words charged with musical property, and such sound-making devices as alliteration, assonance, consonance, and verbal synesthesia?

We are reminded too that to translate a poem well is harder than to write a new poem; that the translator should take nothing for granted; that no translation (which involves interpretation and creation) is ever finished; that translation is an approximation but must provide an experience comparable to the original; and that the translator of poetry must himself be a poet. Here I have attempted to point out the relations that exist between sound and meaning—a meaning embodied in the audible shape of words, mimetic expressiveness in sounds, and sound symbolism in all its diverse aspects. I have also tried to show how Korean poets, past and present, have skillfully explored the intrinsic expressive power of sound symbolism and exploited words of native origin—particularly the concrete, sensory words belonging to the common language. In the words of Paul Zumthor: "All poetry aspires to being made voice, to making itself heard one day."[19] Where orality and performance have been the characteristics of vernacular poetry, a poem in Korea has been an elaborate rhythmical structure that explores all the hidden possibilities of the language bequeathed to the poet by his tradition. Christopher Middleton comments that the translator "must extend his own linguistic resources beyond their normal limits so that he can reach out with both hands and touch the original, and modify, modulate, and transfigure his own linguistic resources and extend them."[20]

19. Zumthor, *Oral Poetry*, 127.
20. Edwin Honig, *The Poet's Other Voice: Conversations on Literary Translation* (Amherst: University of Massachusetts Press, 1985), 190. This applies as well to the translation of English poetry into East Asian languages. Sound symbolism in

Intertextuality:
Quotation and Allusion

Sukchong taewang chŭgwi ch'o e (4/4)

sŏngdŏgi nŏlbusisa (3/4)

sŏngja sŏngson ŭn / kyegye sŭngsŭng hasa (5/6)

kŭmgu okch'ok ŭn / Yo Sun sijŏl iyo (5/6)

ŭigwan munmul ŭn / U T'ang ŭi pŏgum ira (5/7)

The first five lines of the *Song* are intelligible to the listener because they invoke names known generally—Chinese sage lords Yao and Shun and culture heroes Yu and Tang. Yu controlled the flood and became the founder of the Xia; Tang the Completer is the mythical founder of the Shang—these names are widely known for their frequent appearances in the mirror literature and even in conversation. "*Kyegye sŭngsŭng*" are two reduplicatives for emphasis by repeating *kye* (continue) to convey the sense of "unbroken" and *sŭng* (inherit, continue what has gone before). "Royal sons and grandsons will succeed one another" (line 3) is somewhat ambiguous—it could be read as a prophecy or taken to imply that the reigning king, Sukchong, succeeded his father and grandfathers going back to the dynastic founder. I have chosen the future tense here considering line 2 ("Royal virtues are / vast,") because unbroken succession in the future is the product of his virtues guaranteeing continuity. The listener, especially one without the classics, encounters the first hurdle in the phrase, "*kŭmgu okch'ok*"— *kŭmgu* 金甌 (a golden bowl, or a flawless golden bowl), a metonymy for the perfect and secure national polity. *Okch'ok* 玉燭[21] refers to the harmony of the four seasons—spring should be warm; summer,

---

certain poems by Stevens, Williams, Moore, and Cummings would be difficult to reproduce. After reading an analysis of Cummings's "love is more thicker than forget," in Roman Jakobson and Linda R. Waugh, *The Sound Shape of Language* (Berlin: Mouton de Gruyter, 1987), 225-32, few will attempt a translation into Korean or Japanese.

21. *Erya* (SPTK) 2:6a.

hot; autumn, cool; and winter, cold. The difficulty of the phrase does not matter, though, because this segment is followed by another mention of Yao and Shun; so it can be understood as recalling the times of Yao and Shun, all the good qualities associated with them, and equating Sukchong's reign with a golden age. Other examples of repetition for emphasis occur in *kaga* (every house); *mijae mijae* (how beautiful, how admirable), and *ch'ŏch'ŏ* (everywhere). Englishing the rhythmic compactness of literary Chinese (and Korean) requires more words and syllables than in the original. Resonant Sino-Korean words, like Latinate expressions in English, echo canonical predecessors, force such terms into a position of emphasis, and delight the reader/listener upon recognition.

The text quotes from twenty-one Chinese—mostly Tang— poets in citing thirty-four heptasyllabic, nine pentasyllabic, and four tetrasyllabic lines. Some represent direct quotations to enhance a description of a given scene or object, while others are allusions to intensify a given mood or tone. Heptasyllabic lines harmonize well with the *p'ansori* meter (4/3, 3/4). Two lines (3-4) from Cen Shen's (715-770) "Song of the Bay Steed of Governor Wei,"[22] for example, are brought in to help describe how Yi's donkey is rigged out:

> *hongyŏng chagong sanhop'yŏn* (4/3)
> > Crimson reins, scarlet bridle, crop of coral,
> *ogan kŭmch'ŏn hwanggŭm nŭk* (4/3)
> > Jade saddle, embroidered blanket, and bit of gold.

The narrator recalls them from memory. The listener, however, will have trouble making them out in sounds alone. They constitute an example of direct quotation that might escape an inattentive audience without knowledge of the poem. They are more for the eye—the meaning of the four graphs with the radical 177 (or 227: "leather, hide") will help, if the reader has a printed version of the

---

22. Wu-chi Liu and Irving Yucheng Lo, eds., *Sunflower Splendor: Three Thousand Years of Chinese Poetry* (Garden City: Doubleday, 1975), 148-49.

text before his eyes. Some lines later, the narrator says the people turned to watch Student Yi, handsome as the Tang poet Du Mu (803-852) and the Wu musician Zhou Yu (174-218), then adds two lines from Cen's same poem:

> *hyangga chamaek ch'unsŏng nae* (4/3)
>> On the scented streets and purple paths of our Phoenix City,
> *mansŏng kyŏnja suburae* (4/3)
>> The wonder and envy of all who see him.

They repeat from a different angle the intent of the previously given lines: to praise Yi's appearance as a person of lofty bearing.

Next the narrator describes what Yi sees from Great Cold Tower as he scans the four directions and quotes lines 2-3 from Du Fu's (712-770) "On Yueyang Tower,"[23] comparing what he sees to the Chinese lake:

> *O Ch'o tongnamsu nŭn* (2/4)
>> East and south waters of Wu and Qu
> *Tongjŏngho ro hŭllo chigo* (4/4)
>> Flow into Grotto Court Lake.

Here the narrator has replaced the graph *t'ak* (split, cleave) with that for *su* (water), changing the original, which read: "Now today I've climbed up Yueyang Tower. / The lake cleaves the lands of Wu and Qu to east and south." He has also dropped the first two graphs that begin the original poem, "*sŏngmun*" (Long ago I heard). The lines now convey a dimension of vastness and offer parallels between the landscape around Namwŏn and those celebrated in Du's poem: Yueyang Tower and Great Cold Tower; Grotto

---

23. David Hawkes, *A Little Primer of Tu Fu* (Oxford: Clarendon, 1967), 209; *Dushi xiangzhu* (Peking: Zhonghua, 1985) 22:1946.

Court (Dongting) Lake and the artificial lake with Magpie Bridge spanning it—an instance of hyperbole.

When Yi playfully rewrites the meaning of the graph *suk*, he quotes line 36 from Wang Bo's (649-676) "Looking Down from the High Terrace,"[24] which becomes a whole line with a quotative particle –*ra*:

> *karyŏn kŭmya suk ch'angga ra* (4/4)
>> Wonderful to spend tonight (*suk*) at the singing girl's home
>
> *wŏnankŭmch'im e chal suk* (5/2)
>> Under a mandarin-duck embroidered coverlet and pillow—*suk*

When Yi says good-bye and mounts his horse, Ch'unhyang throws herself down on the ground outside the main gate, pounding the earth with her slender hands: "*Aego, aego,* my wretched lot!" In that single cry,

> *Hwangae sanman p'ungsosak* (4/3)
>> Brown dust spread in billows, howling was the wind, . . .
>
> *Chŏnggi mugwang ilsaekpak* (4/3)
>> The royal banners shed no light, the beams of sun were pale.

These two lines (43, 45) from Bo Juyi's (772-846) "Song of Lasting Regret" (807)[25] concern the enduring love and sorrow of the Tang emperor Xuanzong for the Precious Consort Yang, whose beauty shook an empire. The lines liken Ch'unhyang and Yi's sorrow to that of the emperor after Lady Yang was strangled at the Mawei post station on 15 July 756 to pacify the angry soldiers

---

24. *Quan Tangshi* 55:674-75. Stephen Owen, *The Poetry of the Early T'ang* (New Haven: Yale University Press, 1977), 115-18.

25. *Quan Tangshi* 435:4828-4830; Owen, *Anthology of Chinese Literature* (New York: Norton, 1996), 442-47 (lines 43 and 45).

accompanying the royal party in their escape from the An Lushan rebellion. Essentially, then, the lines try to capture the state of mind of the devastated Ch'unhyang. These poetical reminiscences ask us to look before and after, but only a tiny circle that has drunk deep of Chinese learning would have recognized them by bringing into play the intertextual resonance. Retroping Bo Juyi in this context makes us hear the hoofbeats of horses upon the young couple's hearts.

Lastly, in her dream journey to the shrine of chaste women celebrated in myth and literature, Ch'unhyang meets the spirit of Wang Jaojun (Brilliant Consort), who became a bride of the khan of the Xiongnu (Hun) in 33 B.C. In her speech to Ch'unhyang, Lady Wang quotes two lines (5-6) from Du Fu's poem, "Thoughts on Historical Sites 3: On Wang Jaojun" 王昭君:[26]

Uri tul chŏn ilmyŏng pyŏl Ch'unhyang chŏn, 1924.

> *hwado sŏngsik ch'unp'ung myŏn iyo* (4/5)
>> A painter might well have recognized a face lovely as the spring breeze;
> *hwanp'ae konggwi wŏryahon ira* (4/5)
>> Now, pendants jangling, her soul returns in vain on moonlit night.

The Korean particles –*iyo* (it is and . . .) and –*ira* (a quotative indicative assertive) have been added to connect the two lines. The quotation is more for the eye than for the ear: Ch'unhyang's circumstances are akin to those of Lady Wang, and the quotation stresses the former's grievance. All these quotations add a classical aura to the text, reminding the listener and reader that intertextuality is possible not only because literature is a system but also because "most allusions of subtlety and efficacy are likely to be related in some important way to inheritance."[27]

---

26. Liu and Lo,140.

27. Quoted in Eleanor Cook, *Against Coercion: Games Poets Play* (Stanford: Stanford University Press, 1998), 101 (the quotation is from Christopher Ricks without reference). See Christopher Ricks, *Allusions to the Poets* (Oxford: Clarendon, 2002), 86.

P'ansori

P'ansori (song sung in an arena) is a Korean oral narrative
sung by a professional singer, accompanied by a single drummer,
who narrates with mimetic and conventional body movements
and gestures, sings, and assumes the roles of his characters. The
singer dons no special costumes, wears no mask, and uses no props
except for a fan (although sometimes a screen is on the stage). As
in other vernacular poetic genres, performance helped to preserve
and maintain *p'ansori*. "As a product of serial composition by many
singers over a long period of time, *p'ansori* has four characteristics: it
is a solo oral technique, dramatic, musical, and in verse. It developed
its three aspects—music, drama, and literature—in response to the
demands of audiences; and it interpolates songs of various kinds
with a variety of modes and rhythms."[28] *P'ansori* emerged from the
narrative shaman songs in the southwestern part of Korea, Chŏlla
province, and the singer was from a hereditary shaman household;
in fact, he was the husband of a shaman, "who had served as
an accompanist or assistant to his wife, eventually emerging as
a professional actor and singer on his own." The shaman was a
spiritually empowered woman who acted as a medium for gods and
spirits, healed the sick, summoned the dead, and drove out demons.
A professional mnemonist, a ritual specialist, and a repository of
tales and songs, proverbs and riddles, in the community, she was
socially abject. A study of the stages of serial composition from
the original text or ur-form as it grew in size through accretions of
more episodes and interpolated songs raises the following questions:
How did the singer/redactor take advantage of the full resources of
language in all its representative power? A close textual analysis of
the language shows heteroglossia at its most exuberant; the diglossic
and dialogic imagination work to suggest experiential richness of
the luxuriant world. What is the relation between different modes
of cultural production at specific historical moments? The different

---

28. This and the next quotes are from Marshall Pihl, *The Korean Singer of Tales*
(Cambridge: Harvard University Press, 1994), 5-20 passim.

versions reflecting the fluidity of the oral tradition represent a collaborative re-creation involving singer/performers and redactors/ scribes. Here Zumthor's notion of "*mouvance*,"[29] an esthetic principle of transmission leading to changes that were intended and perceived as improvements to the received text, is useful. Successive singers and redactors went on to revise the *Song* for a new audience—a dialogue between the performer and tradition and the performer and the present audience, who played a role in shaping each oral performance. The ur-form is forever inaccessible and irrelevant, because each surviving redaction is ultimately authorized by the singer (or redactor). *P'ansori* is an anonymous collective oral work that lives through its variants in a state of perpetual re-creation.[30]

This study will focus on nineteen narrative songs that constitute the core of the *Song of Ch'unhyang*. Most versions contain all or some of them, and a close textual and cultural study will illuminate the organization and rhetoric of the *Song*. While authorizing a poetics of *mouvance*, these songs at crucial junctures represent repositories of themes, images, and episodes, highly intertextual and rhythmic. Formulaic style is a narrative strategy— effects of recurrence such as repetition of an identical syntactic/ lexical structure at fixed intervals; repeated lines that help retention in memory; the use of refrain and enumeration; wordplay; and multiple meanings in the sequence of sounds. These are the most efficacious means of verbalizing "a spatiotemporal experience and of bringing the audience to participate in it."[31]

---

29. Paul Zumthor, *Essai de poétique mediévale* (Paris: Seuil, 1972), 65-74; translated as *Towards a Medieval Poetics* (Minneapolis: University of Minnesota Press, 1992), 42-55. For *mouvance* see also Zumthor, "The Text and the Voice," *New Literary History* 41 (1984-5): 67-92; "Spoken Language and Oral Poetry in the Middle Ages," *Style* 19.20 (1985): 191-98; *Speaking of the Middle Ages* (Lincoln: University of Nebraska Press, 1986), 59-62, 85; and Mary B. Speer, "Wrestling with Change: Oral French Textual Criticism and *Mouvance*," *Olifant* 7.4 (1980): 311-26. Elizabeth Aubrey, in *The Music of the Troubadours* (Bloomington: Indiana University Press, 1996), renders "mouvance" as "fluidity," 28 and 289, n. 6.

30. Doane and Pasternack, 244; see also Bernard Cerquilini, *In Praise of the Variant: A Critical History of Philology* (Baltimore: Johns Hopkins University Press, 1999), 38.

31. Zumthor, *Oral Poetry*, 118. For a discussion of interpolated songs, see Chŏn Kyŏnguk, Ch'unhyang chŏn *ŭi sasŏl hyŏngsŏng wŏlli* (Koryŏ taehakkyo Minjok

The *Kisaeng*

The origin of the *kisaeng* (female entertainer)[32] is often traced to the wicker workers (*yangsuch'ŏk* 楊水尺 or *kori changi* 고리장이) who made round baskets or other utensils from wicker (*kori*) or poplar. The word for professional actor or singer—*kwangdae*—may come from *kwangjang*, one who makes baskets. If a wicker worker's son was talented, he became a *kwangdae*—one who possessed special skill; if not, a slave. If a wicker worker's daughter was talented and beautiful, she became a *kisaeng*; if not, a slave. The female entertainers came from the lowborn. Those registered with the central government (*kyŏnggi* 京妓) and those belonging to the local administration (*kwangi* 官妓) had different functions. They were trained by the state from a young age to develop such special skills as singing, playing musical instruments, dancing, composing poems in literary Chinese and the vernacular, painting, and engaging in polite and sometimes learned conversation with upper-class men. They were public performers commanded to entertain the king, the court, and foreign envoys in the capital and local magistrates in the provinces. History records a number of exceptional female entertainers known for their loyalty, filial piety, and literary and musical accomplishments. The important social and legal issue raised by the *Song* is whether Ch'unhyang, like her mother who was once an entertainer, is herself one.

Ch'unhyang's father, Second Minister Sŏng, is a member of the ruling class, but her mother is a retired entertainer belonging

---

munhwa yŏnguso, 1990). For *p'ansori*'s melodic modes (*cho*) and rhythmic patterns (*changdan*), determined by meter, accent, tempo, and phrase, see So Inhwa, *Theoretical Perspectives on Korean Traditional Music: An Introduction* (National Center for Korean Traditional Performing Arts, 2002), 103-22, and Chan E. Park, *Voices from the Straw Mat: Toward an Ethnography of Korean Story Singing* (Honolulu: University of Hawaii Press, 2003), 168-77.

32. *Koryŏsa* (Tongbanghak yŏnguso, Yonsei University, 1955-61) 129:22b6-8; *Koryŏsa chŏryo* (Asea munhwasa, 1972)14:36b; Yi Ik, *Sŏngho sasŏl* 23:7a-8a (translation in Kojŏn kugyŏk ch'ongsŏ 115; *Sŏngho sasŏl*, 9: 21-22); Chŏng Yagyong, *Aŏn kakpi*, in *Yŏyudang chŏnsŏ* (Kyŏngin munhwasa, 1982)1:43a; Kang Hŏngyu, "Kisaeng ŭi ŏwŏn," in *Kang Hŏngyu kyosu hwagap kinyŏm kugŏhak nonmunjip* (Kongju: Posŏng, 2000), 218-44; and Cho Kwangguk, *Kinyŏdam kinyŏ tŭngjang sosŏl yŏngu* (Wŏrin, 2000), 32-47.

AZALEA

The Road to
Ch'unhyang:
Peter H. Lee

(opposite)
From
Okchunghwa,
1929.

to the lowborn. It is very likely that either by petition or a purchase (100 *yang* cash) of freeborn status, Wŏlmae became a free woman and her name was removed from the roster of entertainers.

Ch'unhyang's father promised Wŏlmae to take his daughter to Seoul to rear as his own, even if he never saw her, but it is unclear whether he went through the necessary procedure to have her registered as a freeborn (*soksin* 贖身), as the *Kyŏngguk taejŏn* 經國大典 (State Code of Administration, 1485; 5:445-46) stipulated.[33] Ch'unhyang has been acknowledged as the daughter of a ruling-class member, but her legal status is ambiguous. In our text her age is given as sixteen, the latest age to have her status changed. As the daughter of a minister, as attested by Student Yi's servant boy and officials in Namwŏn, she grew up self-confident. She herself does not think she behaves like an entertainer. She was educated like a member of the literati class. When the servant boy, at Yi's request, comes to invite her, she throws insulting words at him; only at the third invitation does she consent. To the community she is known for her beauty, literary talent, and virtue; officials in Namwŏn know her as a freeborn, as they remind Magistrate Pyŏn on several occasions. Although the chief clerk and secretary assert that "Ch'unhyang is not an entertainer," Pyŏn nonetheless treats her like one. The class difference implied or suggested between Ch'unhyang and Student Yi has narrowed, however, since the first extant edition of the *Song* in 1754.

The *Kwangdae*

Until 1894, when the class system was abolished,[34] the *kwangdae*[35] was a hereditary lowborn social group who intermarried

33. Han Ugŭn et al., trans., *Yŏkchu Kyŏngguk taejŏn* (Sŏngnam: Hanguk chŏngsin munhwa yŏnguwŏn, 1992), 2 vols. Also consulted: *Sok Taejŏn* (Sŏul taehakkyo Kyujanggak, 1998) 5:28a-29a; and *Kugyŏk Taejŏn hoet'ong* (Koryŏ taehakkyo Minjok munhwa yŏnguso, 1982) 5:573-75.

34. *Kojong sillok* (T'amgudang, 1977), 32:1b.

35. On *Kwangdae* and his music I have relied on Son T'aedo, *Kwangdae ŭi kach'ang munhwa* (Chimmundang, 2003), 1-12 and 47-152; for *hwarang(i)*, *Sŏngho sasŏl* 23:7a-8a (translation in *Sŏngho sasŏl* 9:21-22); *Sŏngjong sillok* 20:5a.

御使道 本官 生日잔치에

御使道본관생일잔치에

드러가니 눈치잇는

운봉영장 기성

雲峯營將、벗짝 식혀술勸한다

279

among themselves and passed on their hereditary occupations.
They could not take the civil service examination, nor own
land,[36] but paid cloth tax (*mup'ose* 巫布稅) every year. They were
musicians who played musical instruments but also acted as public
performers and entertainers. In the south, they were drawn from
male relations (usually husbands) of the hereditary shamans, and
their origin is often traced to the *hwarang* 花郎—Silla's unique
social group who through communal life and rites learned military
arts, cultivated virtue, and toured famous mountains and rivers
to nurture love of their country. From the Koryŏ period, they
were mobilized to perform in national ceremonies: when *sandae*
山臺 plays (discontinued from 1694),[37] in conjunction with the
p'algwanhoe 八關會,[38] were staged to please the autochthonous gods
and spirits of the Korean people; when the tablet of the former
king was enshrined at the Royal Ancestral Shrine; at the reception
of Chinese envoys (discontinued from 1784);[39] when the king
attended certain functions outside the palace; and when a new
governor arrived at his appointed province.[40] They also performed
at the exorcism rite at year's end to expel evil spirits (*narye* 儺禮)[41]
at court and in the provinces, and during the festivities celebrating

36. *Koryŏsa* 73:3b and 78:41b.

37. See *Sejong sillok,* ed. Kuksa p'yŏnch'an wiwŏnhoe, 48 vols. (1955-58; all
Chosŏn king annals are quoted from this edition) 31:22a (60 feet high); *Munjong
sillok* 12:27a-b; *Yŏnsangun ilgi* 63: 22b; *Kwanghaegun ilgi* (Chŏngjoksan ed.) 144:7a;
and (T'aebaeksan ed.) 144:20c; Yi Saek, *Mogŭn chip,* in *Koryŏ myŏnhyŏn chip,* 5
vols. (Sŏnggyungwan taehakkyo Taedong munhwa yŏnguwŏn, 1973), vol. 3, 33:27a
(for his poem on "sandae chapkŭk"). *Sandae* was a mountain-shaped structure
with crevices and terraces for performers. Decorated with colored silk and
lanterns, man-made animals and birds, the mountain was supposed to symbolize
three magic seamounts, such as Mount Penglai, in the Yellow Sea, an abode of
transcendents, or the Diamond Mountain, Mounts Chiri or Halla in Korea. It
was about 60 feet high or as high as Kwanghwa Gate. Some *sandae* had wheels
to facilitate transport (*yesandae; Tanjong sillok* 11:38b). On the terraces actors
performed somersaults, tightrope walking, Ch'ŏyong dance, fireworks, songs, and
dances.

38. *Samguk sagi,* ed. Yi Pyŏngdo (Ŭryu, 1977) 4:40; *Koryŏsa* 69:33a-b.

39. *T'aejong sillok* 12:30b.

40. *Sejong sillok* 52:25b, 26a.

41. *Koryŏsa* 64:38a-40a; *Sukchong sillok* 5: 35a; *Yŏngjo sillok* 94:22b; Sŏng Hyŏn,
Yongjae ch'onghwa 1: 12 (Chōsen kosho kankōkai ed.), 17-18; Yi Saek, *Mogŭn chip*
21:9a-b for his poem, "Kuna haeng."

successful candidates in the civil service examinations—such as one performed at the palace (*ŭnyŏngyŏn* 恩榮宴)[42] and a procession through the streets of the capital and provincial towns for three to five days (*yuga* 遊街).[43] Similar festivities were also held in the administrative offices in the provinces (*yŏngch'inŭi* 榮親儀)[44] and at the candidate's own home (*munhŭiyŏn* 聞喜宴).[45]

The term *kwangdae* first referred to a mask or a masked performer;[46] later, to public entertainers and those belonging to the group. Early Koryŏ musicians attached to the palace were recruited from official slaves (*kwanno* 官奴) and were called *akkong* 樂工 (artisans of music), not *kwangdae*. Registered as performers of musical instruments, the *kwangdae* became a central group of performing artists serving the needs of the court and government and preserving Korean folk arts. They were both a status group and a skilled occupation group. The size of the group can be seen in the 1836 registry of Kyŏnggi province, which lists some 40,000 members.[47] In addition to being musicians and singers, some *kwangdae* also performed certain acrobatics, such as tightrope walking, dish spinning, somersaulting, spitting fire, throwing large round beads into the air and catching them, and tricks on horseback. *Kwangdae* also performed masked dance plays and puppet plays.

As male members of the shaman households, the *kwangdae*'s repertory included songs, incantatory and religious in nature, invoking the blessings of gods and spirits of houses and villages at the beginning of the new year (*kosa sori*)[48]—as Silla *hwarang* sang to entertain gods of famous mountains and rivers or to praise the dynasty and the reigning king; when the successful candidates

---

42. Son T'aedo, 356, 359-60; *Kyŏngguk taejŏn* 3:248.
43. *Koryŏsa* 74:5b; *Sejong sillok* 81:5b5; *Sŏngjong sillok* 100:11b.
44. *Koryŏsa* 68:29b-31a; *Kyŏngguk taejŏn* 3:248.
45. *Koryŏsa* 74:5b; 68:30a; *Kyŏngguk taejŏn* 3:248; Son, 223, 356-57, 387-407.
46. *Kwanghaegun ilgi* 106:29b.
47. Son, 50-51.
48. Son, 156-79; *T'aejo sillok* 2:5a: *Chŏngjong sillok* 6: 10b: *T'aejong sillok* 22:10b; *Sejong sillok* 52:42b.

offered sacrifices at the shrines of their ancestors (*sobun* 掃墳); when a monument was erected at the grave site; or when a building was completed. These *kosa* songs are extant only in Chŏlla and part of Ch'ungch'ŏng provinces.

T'aryŏng 打令, perhaps the most popular genre of song, etymologically derived from the words *t'aryŏng* 妥靈 written in different sinographs, means "to quiet the spirits,"[49] and, by extension, a song sung for that purpose by the shaman. It was used when an ancestor was placed in a family shrine or a scholar was enshrined in a private academy. Later it became a folk song for amusement, and the term was used as a synonym for "song."

Yŏngsan 靈山,[50] originating in Buddhist and shamanist rites to pray for the repose of the dead, refers to Vulture Peak, where Śākyamuni Buddha is said to have preached the *Lotus Scripture* to his disciples. This touching song concerning the transience of life reminds humans of the urgency of awakening from illusion and ignorance so that they can shuttle to paradise in order to take part in the Buddha's assembly. The singer developed it as a literary and musical work, and soon this kind of song began to be sung outside the ritual context.

Before the advent of *p'ansori*, entertainers in both the south and the north developed witty humorous chatter (*chaedam* 才談)[51]—hilarious jokes, ingenious witticisms, satire addressing physical defects, wordplay based on similar sounds with different meanings (*paronomasia*), and parody. Inspired by the shamanist narrative songs detailing the origin of gods and hardships in their career, the singer needed a long secular narrative song to entertain, for example, successful candidates at their festivities. The earlier term for *p'ansori* was *t'aryŏng*—especially narrative *t'aryŏng*.[52] In its earlier phase, the *p'ansori* repertory included humorous episodes as, for example, in *pyŏl Ch'unhyang ka* dating from the 1840s;

49. *Sŏnjo sillok* 187:41; *Hyŏnjong sillok* 10:40a; Son, 179-89.
50. Son, 189-218.
51. Son, 218-38.
52. Son, 239-41.

but the extant five pieces have dispensed with these, perhaps to cater to the taste of the educated. The four requisites of the singer, according to Sin Chaehyo (1811-1884), the first commoner teacher and redactor of the *p'ansori* repertory, include stage presence (*inmul* 人物), narrative art (*sasŏl* 辭說), vocal attainment (*tŭgŭm* 得音), and mimetic ability (dramatic gestures: *nŏrŭmsae* or *pallim*). *P'ansori* developed continuously as the singer won the affection of the audience with his narrative song and highly developed vocal art. What set the singer apart from other entertainers was that he could sing and sing. Sometimes he sang all night long—when he entertained at the feast in honor of the successful candidate, for example, or had the opportunity to sing before the king and the common people.

Namwŏn: Setting of the *Song*

The Korean city of Namwŏn,[53] in the southeastern part of Chŏlla province, is famed for its many historic and religious sites. Its current population is over 89,898 (2008 census); in the mid-fifteenth century, it had 1,300 households with 4,912 people. A noted tourist resort, Namwŏn is part of the national park of Mount Chiri 智異山, one of Korea's three sacred mountains, where main railroad lines meet and climbers begin their hiking. Known from the Three Kingdoms period, the city belonged to Paekche; in 1380 General Yi Sŏnggye, founder of the Chosŏn dynasty, repulsed a host of Japanese pirates at Mount Hwang 荒山 in Unbong 雲峯 (Cloud Peak).[54]

Above all, however, Namwŏn is known as the birthplace of Ch'unhyang—the most enduring female protagonist in classic Korean literature. The administration complex lies in the center of the walled town; a shrine to loyal officials is to the northwest, a jail to the northeast. The district school (*hyanggyo*) is north of the

---

53. *Sejong sillok* 151:16b-17a; *Sinjŭng Tongguk yŏji sŭngnam* 39:1a-12b.
54. Canto 50 of *Songs of Flying Dragons* (Cambridge: Harvard University Press, 1975), 203-205.

wall almost at the midpoint. Sŏnwŏn monastery is to the northeast, the shrine to Guan Yu (d. 219)[55] to the southwest. Southwest of the walled town are the precincts of a walled and gated park named Great Cold Tower Park 廣寒樓苑 (Kwanghallu Wŏn), considered an exceptionally pleasant place.[56] At the north corner there is a shrine to Ch'unhyang, with her full-length portrait in the midst of a bamboo grove, the bamboo representing fidelity and constancy. The shrine was built in 1931; its first sacrificial rite was offered on Double Five (Tano 端午), the day of purification. Some steps south is Great Cold Tower, the Palace on the Moon, and the Milky Way galaxy (the Silver or Han River), constructed by drawing water from Smartweed River (Yoch'ŏn) nearby, and Magpie Bridge 烏 鵲橋 (Ojakkyo) over it. The bridge figures prominently in the story of the star gods Herd Boy 牽牛 (Altair) and Weaver Maid 織 女 (Vega)—fated to be separated on the east and west sides of the Milky Way throughout the year but allowed by the god of heaven to meet once during the night of Double Seven when magpies build a bridge for them to cross.[57] The mythopoeic imagination has created earthly representations (or counterparts) of the celestial bodies and the galaxy. Great Cold Tower is where Ch'unhyang and Student Yi (Yi Toryŏng), the son of the magistrate of Namwŏn, meet for the first time. On the lake are three sacred seamounts from Chinese mythology—Yŏngju (Yingzhou; Mount Halla), Pongnae (Penglai; Diamond Mountain), and Pangjang (Fangjang; Mount Chiri).

Let the narrative's servant boy (*pangja*) describe the setting: "Now listen to what Namwŏn offers: if you go out East Gate, there is Sŏnwŏn monastery in the long forest; from West Gate you reach the temple of Guan Yu, where the commanding presence of the ancient hero seems to linger; out of South Gate you will see Great

55. *Sanguozhi* (Peking: Zhonghua, 1975) 36: 939-42. For his description see Moss Roberts, trans., *The Three Kingdoms: A Historical Novel* (Berkeley: University of California Press, 1991), 9.

56. Built 1419; Chŏng Inji named the building Kwanghallu in 1444. Kwanghan kung/lu/chŏn/pu is the name of a palace on the moon.

57. Anne Birrell, *Chinese Mythology: An Introduction* (Baltimore: Johns Hopkins University Press, 1993), 165-67, 206-207.

Cold Tower, Magpie Bridge, and Yŏngju Pavilion; out of North Gate you see sheer rocks like a golden lotus piercing the blue sky and the fortress of Mount Flood Dragon (Kyoryong) on a strange-shaped rock—let's go and see!"

The Story: Chronotope and Narrative

The *Song of the Chaste Wife Ch'unhyang* begins with the typical provision of the time of the story, an outgrowth of historiography indicating that history and fiction are branches of the same tree. In addition, the introduction offers an image of peace and prosperity enjoyed by the people, a gift of virtuous rule that guarantees order and harmony. Thus the song defines itself by means of the time and space relations (chronotope)—the "intrinsic connectedness of temporal and spatial relations artistically expressed in literature."[58]

> When Great King Sukchong ascended the throne, (4/4)
> His royal virtues were vast, (3/4)
> And royal sons and grandsons would succeed one another;
> (5/6)
> The nation was flawless, as in the days of Yao and Shun, (5/6)
> And civilization quite like the days of Yu and Tang. (5/7)[59]
> Advisers on left and right were pillars of state, (5/6)
> And brave generals prancing like dragons and guards racing
> like tigers[60]
> Were able to repulse the foe and protect the state. (5/6)
> Moral influences of the court (3/5)
> Reached remote districts and villages, (3/4)
> And security reigned within the four seas. (4/3)

58. M. M. Bakhtin, *The Dialogic Imagination,* ed. Michael Holquist (Austin: University of Texas Press, 1981), 84; Gary Saul Morson and Caryl Emerson, *Mikhail Bakhtin: Creation of a Prosaics* (Stanford: Stanford University Press, 1990), 366-432; John Bender and David E. Wellbery, eds., *Chronotope: The Construction of Time* (Stanford: Stanford University Press, 1991); and Hwang Hyejin, Ch'unhyang chŏn ŭi suyong munhwa (Wŏrin, 2007), 32-63.

59. For Yao, Birrell, 238-40; for Shun, ibid., 74-75, 104-105; for Yu, 146-59; and for Tang, 156, 256-57.

60. *Hanshu* 43:2127.

Loyal subjects filled the court (3/4)

As filial sons and virtuous daughters filled every house. (4/4)

How beautiful, how admirable! Rain and winds were
     seasonable, (5/6)

The people enjoyed a happy contented life; (4/4)

Everywhere, beating the ground to keep time,[61] they sang of
     peace.[62] (3/4)

*Man'go
chŏngyŏl
Ch'unhyang
chŏn, 1921.*

It was in the early years of King Sukchong (1674-1720), the nineteenth ruler of Chosŏn, and the place was the city of Namwŏn, a specific geographical space. In this introduction, the anonymous narrator (redactor) is conversant with the metrical scheme of vernacular poetry. Note how this narrated portion (*aniri*) scans, each line consisting generally of two metric segments, as the syllable count in parentheses shows. At the outset, one is made aware of the work's distinctive music, a marriage of sound and sense, its rhythms resembling the pulsing of the human heart, rich in echoes, as the narrator purloins a line or phrase, pirates an image or trope. Throbbing with felt life, the diction summons the sensory world in its inexhaustible richness to invite the fullness of response it creates in the reader.

The story time (*Erzählte Zeit*) covers about eighteen years; the discourse time (*Erzählzeit*) covers about two years: from Double Five when Ch'unhyang and Student Yi, both aged sixteen (fifteen by Western count), meet and marry, about "a year" passes (101) before Yi leaves in the fall for Seoul and returns as inspector the following autumn. Instances of an evocation of events that occurred before the present moment in narration (*analepses*; flashbacks) include when Wŏlmae recalls first her conception dream and later Ch'unhyang's education (57) and her dream of a blue dragon, the

---

61. "In the days of Ho Xu, /. . .Their mouths crammed with food, they were merry; drumming on their bellies, they passed the time." Burton Watson, *The Complete Works of Chuang Tzu* (New York: Columbia University Press, 1968), 106.

62. *Gushiyuan* (Sipu beiyao) 1:1a; Burton Watson, *The Columbia Book of Chinese Poetry* (New York: Columbia University Press, 1984), 70.

night before Student Yi, named Mongnyong (Dream Dragon), visits her home (27); and when Magistrate Yi recalls an event seven years before when his son was eight (47). Contrarily, for the evocation of events that will occur after the present moment, we may cite the blind diviner's prediction that Ch'unhyang's husband will return soon and her sorrow will end. While 214 pages of discourse time is allotted for two years, only the final seven lines (215) cover some sixty years of the couple's life.

Our narrator, omniscient and heterodiegetic,[63] knows everything about the situation and events recounted; he is overt, learned, and reliable. He also pretends to be an intradiegetic[64] narrator posing as an insider to imitate his individual characters. The story's center of action is Ch'unhyang, and the narrator has an agreement with his/her audience/reader that he will tell a story of a chaste wife who triumphed after a great ordeal. The place where the story unfolds is Namwŏn; the secondary space is Seoul, where Yi passes the civil service examinations and is appointed secret inspector by the king. Namwŏn functions structurally—it is where Ch'unhyang is born and has lived sixteen years of her life until she meets Student Yi. Her marriage takes place in Lotus Hall in her home, and that is where she awaits the return of her husband after his departure for Seoul. Yi, son of the town's magistrate, lives in one of the buildings in the administration complex. And it is there that the new magistrate Pyŏn tortures Ch'unhyang and throws her into prison and later, Inspector Yi dismisses him and saves his wife. Great Cold Tower Garden (with the Milky Way and Magpie Bridge), situated almost equidistant from the administration complex and commoners' houses, functions thematically—a mythopoeic representation of stars and the galaxy. When one cleanses one's mind/heart with waters of the Milky Way, crosses Magpie Bridge, and ascends Great Cold Tower on the moon, one

63. Gerard Prince, *A Dictionary of Narratology* (Lincoln: University of Nebraska Press, 1987), 40b.

64. Prince, 46a–b; Nancy Felson-Rubin, *Regarding Penelope: From Character to Poetics* (Princeton: Princeton University Press, 1994), 11 and 149 (n. 37).

may fancy riding the winds, pacing the void, and being among the heavenly bodies.

Temporal and spatial formations are expressed in the story's chronotope. Both Ch'unhyang and Yi exercise choice and are aware of the responsibilities that follow. The time/space relationship illuminates the sequence of events; socialized intersubjective time and the rhythms of inner time interact. Ch'unhyang learns from her decisions and becomes an individual with a sense of historical consciousness and inner time. She affirms the enduring self-identity. She is a reliable reporter of her own feelings, motives, and beliefs. Diverse social classes interact—the literati (ruling class), commoners, and slaves. Ch'unhyang affects and is affected by a society whose value systems are changing. The narrator's creativity is evinced from his responses to social and economic problems emerging in the late seventeenth century, when the story is set, and the late nineteenth century, when this wood-block edition came into being, reflecting the changing epistemic configurations and the view of the anonymous redactor and singer. Interaction among characters is dialogic, and the text is polyphonic, hopeful, and open. Both the listener and the reader of today should not, Bakhtin reminds us, suppress chronotopic differences.[65]

Wŏlmae 月梅, approaching forty, laments her lack of progeny and speaks to her husband: "I don't know what good deeds in my former life have brought us together as husband and wife. I have given up my career as entertainer, observed manners, and made efforts to do needlework. But what great sin have I committed that I have no child of my own? Since we have no relations, who will offer sacrifices and burn incense to our ancestors and bury us after death? If I pray at famous mountains and major temples in order

---

65. Morson and Emerson, 429.

to bear a child, male or female, then will I realize my desire. . . . We should try to offer prayers." Wŏlmae passes through hills and waters and reaches Prajna Peak on Mount Chiri where she builds an altar, sets out sacrificial offerings, prostrates herself beneath the altar, and prays. Then she has a dream: an auspicious pneuma (*ki*; Ch: *qi*) fills the place, in five brilliant colors; a transcendent lady riding on a blue crane comes, crowned with flowers and in iridescent robes, her pendants and bangles tinkling. She holds a branch of cassia flower, ascends to the hall, raises her hands with respect, and slowly makes a low bow.

> I am the lady of Luo River, Consort Fu. (3/4)[66]
> On my way to the Jade Capital to present immortal peaches,
>   (4/4)
> I happened to meet Master Red Pine[67] in Great Cold Palace;
>   (5/5)
> Our feelings were endless, and I dallied until it was dark. (4/4)
> I was late, though, and committed an offense; (4/4)
> The Jade Emperor in anger banished me to the world of dust.
>   (2/4//3/4)
> I did not know where to go, (3/4)
> But a spirit of Mount Turyu[68] directed me to you. (5/5/4)
> Please, take pity on me. (3/4)

"So saying, she enters Wŏlmae's bosom. The crane cries loudly because its neck is long. Its cry startles Wŏlmae awake—it was

---

66. Fufei is the daughter of the Luo River, Fuxi's daughter who drowned in the Luo; see Cao Zhi (192-232), "Rhymeprose on the Goddess of the Lo," Burton Watson, *Chinese Rhyme-Prose: Poems in the Fu Form from the Han and Six Dynasties Periods* (New York: Columbia University Press, 1971), 55-60; and Edward H. Schafer, *The Divine Woman: Dragon Ladies and Rain Maidens in T'ang Literature* (Berkeley: University of California Press, 1973),132-37.

67. The rainmaster under Shennong. See Kenneth DeWoskin and J. I. Crump, Jr., trans., *In Search of the Supernatural: The Written Record* (Stanford: Stanford University Press, 1966), 1-2.

68. Turyu is another name for Chiri.

*Man'go
chŏngyŏl
Yŏjunghwa,
1935.*

nothing but a dream."[69] She conceives, and after ten months she gives birth to a child. The narrator does not forget to arrange for fragrance to fill the room and colored clouds to hang resplendent—auspices accompanying the birth of heroes and heroines. It was a girl fine as jade. Wŏlmae wanted a son, but her desire for progeny was nonetheless realized. She called the baby Ch'unhyang and nurtured her like a jewel in the palm of her hand. Gentle and gracious as the unicorn, the child had no equal in filial devotion. When she reached the age of seven (six by Western count), she took to reading books and devoted herself to good manners and fidelity, and the whole town praised her filial devotion.

Ch'unhyang is born in answer to prayers, and the association of the birth of the heroine with the divine indicates that Ch'unhyang is the daughter of Consort Fu 宓妃, the Chinese culture hero Fuxi's 伏羲 daughter, who drowned in the Luo River and became a river goddess. She is incarnate, exiled to earth for the infraction of breaking a heavenly taboo against dallying with a male transcendent. Nature sends auspices, as in the case of heroes and saints, and as a child Ch'unhyang distinguishes herself with virtue, learning, and talent—qualities that define a class. The servant boy describes her as a "gentlewoman" and the "noblest woman in myriad years" (*mango yŏjung kunja* 萬古女中君子, 23). She is the joint handiwork of nature and heaven, a living embodiment of the ideal.

⤿

Stirred by spring, a "time to make merry," Yi, the magistrate's son, decides to go sightseeing. Yi is likened to Du Mu (803-852) for his fine presence,[70] his generosity like the emerald sea, and his

---

69. Li Gongzo's (ca. 778-848) tale; see Wang Mengou, *Tangren xiaoshuo yanjiu* (Taibei: Yiwen yinshuguan, 1971), 2 vols. 1:201-207; "An Account of the Governor of the Southern Branch," in Victor Mair, ed., *The Columbia Anthology of Traditional Chinese Literature* (New York: Columbia University Press, 1994), 861-71.

70. A handsome Tang poet.

magnanimous wisdom. His talent for poetry is that of Li Bo (701-762),[71] and his calligraphy is like that of Wang Xizhi (321-379).[72] When the servant boy reminds him that he should study rather than go out, Yi retorts to justify his planned outing:

LET'S GO SIGHTSEEING

Talented writers have ever sought
Places of superb scenic beauty
As sources of their poetry.
Even the transcendents travel around widely.
So how is my going out improper?
When Sima Qian[73] was traveling south by boat on the Yangzi
     and Huai rivers,
He was sailing against the river,
With raging waves and cold, howling winds—
From of old, it has been said,
Changes in all things in the universe
Are sometimes surprising, joyful, and lovely—
Always material for poetry.
Li Bo, king of poetry,
Went boating on Colored Stone River;[74]
Su Shi enjoyed autumn moonlight at the Red Cliff,[75]
Bo Juyi,[76] the bright moon on the Xinyang River;
And Great King Sejo,[77]

---

71. A Tang poet known for his poems on the moon and wine; *Jiu Tangshu* 140B: 5052-5054.

72. A famous calligrapher of the Jin.

73. His dates are ca. 145-85 B.C., the author of the *Shiji* (Records of the Historian).

74. Below Maan mountain in Dengtu, Anhwei; see *Jiu Tangshu* 140B: 5053.

75. Su's rhymeprose on the Red Cliff, where Cao Cao's (155-220) fleet was destroyed by the Wu admiral Zhou Yu (175-210) in A.D. 208.

76. A Tang poet whose dates are 772-846; his 128 poems and one short prose piece are translated in Burton Watson, *Po Chü-i: Selected Poems* (New York: Columbia University Press, 2000).

77. Sejo (r. 1455-68) is the seventh ruler of Chosŏn; Munjang Terrace is atop Mount Songni.

Munjang Terrace on Mount Songni in Poŭn.

So how can I not enjoy myself?

Reaching Great Cold Tower and Magpie Bridge, Yi ascends the tower and scans all four directions. The scenery is indeed splendid:

> "Purple halls and red towers shine sparkling everywhere,
>
> Jade-plaqued chambers, brocade halls, laid out like
>> latticework,"
>
> Says Wang Bo in "Looking Down from the High Terrace."[78]
>
> "Its marble railing and carved towers, tall in the sky,"
>
> Truly refers to the Great Cold Tower in Namwŏn.
>
> Yueyang Tower[79] and Gusu Terrace,[80]
>
> To east and south the waters of Wu and Qu
>
> Flow into Grotto Court Lake.
>
> At the northwest of Swallow Tower,[81] I can see Pengze Lake[82] . . .
>
> Among a riot of pink and white blossoms,
>
> Parrots and peacocks fly—
>
> In the landscape all around,
>
> Twisted pines and overcup oaks,
>
> Unable to withstand spring breezes, sway.
>
> Beside the tumbling stream,
>
> The stream-girding blossoms chuckle,
>
> And towering pines luxuriate.
>
> The season of green shade and fragrant grasses excels that of
>> flowers.

---

78. For Wang Bo's (649?-676?) poem, see *Quan Tangshi* 55:674, and "Looking Down from the High Terrace,"in Stephen Owen, *The Poetry of the Early T'ang* (New Haven: Yale University Press, 1977), 115-18.

79. At the northeast corner of Lake Dongting, a large lake in Hunan, and Du Fu's poem (760) on the tower reads: "The lake cleaves the lands of Wu and Qu to east and south." *Dushi xiangzhu* 22:1946. David Hawkes, *A Little Primer of Tu Fu* (Oxford: Clarendon, 1967), 209.

80. A pavilion in the state of Wu where the residence of Xishi was.

81. Northwest of Tongshan district in Kiangsu.

82. Shanyang Lake in Kiangsi.

Drunk by laurel trees, purple sandalwood, peonies, and blue
  peaches,
A hillscape sinks in the long Smartweed River with a splash.

Yi cannot view the Korean landscape without seeing at the
same time the scenery mentioned in Chinese poetry. This technique
of superimposition (which Yi uses to display his plumage) was
a means to show one's familiarity with the works of canonical
poets in China and Korea. The skillful use of written Chinese, the
supreme cultural creation, was a status symbol whose value was
seldom questioned. If a soldier, merchant, or slave is mentioned in
history, it is because of his or her ability to write poetry in literary
Chinese. During the Japanese invasion of Korea from 1592 to 1598,
Korean literati prisoners taken forcibly to Japan were set free when
at the captor's request they showed their ability to write poetry in
Chinese.[83] Educated men from different countries had a common
language. The educated reader would have at his fingertips a
grounding in the thirteen Confucian canonical texts, histories, and
canonical writers of verse and prose in Chinese.

⮌

Ch'unhyang on the Swing

Unable to resist the spring feeling
At the singing of birds,
A fair girl plucks a spray of azaleas
And puts them in her hair;
She picks a white peony

---

83. See Peter H. Lee, *The Record of the Black Dragon Year* (Seoul: Institute
of Korean Culture, Korea University, and Honolulu: Center for Korean Studies,
University of Hawaii, 2000), 37-48; "Athenian prisoners of war in Sicily [. . .] gained
their freedom from their captors by their ability to recite the choruses of Euripides,"
says Eric A. Havelock, *The Muse Learns to Write: Reflections on Orality and Literacy
from Antiquity to the Present* (New Haven: Yale University Press, 1986), 94.

And puts it in her mouth;

Lifting her unlined gauze garment,

She bends to rinse her hands

And takes a mouthful of water to cleanse her mouth

In the clear water of a flowing stream;

She picks up a pebble and

Throws it at the orioles in the willow.

Was this not "Striking the oriole to wake it up"?[84]

She strips the leaves off the willow

And scatters them on the water.

Snow-white butterflies and bees,

Holding the stamens,

Dance in pairs, swaying;

Golden orioles

Flit among the trees.

Great Cold Tower is beautiful,

But Magpie Bridge is better—

Truly the loveliest in all Chŏlla province.

If this is indeed Magpie Bridge,

Where are Herd Boy and Weaver Maid?

In such a beautiful place,

How can there be no poetry?

Yi then composes two couplets:

A boat, light and bright, left by magpies,

Jade steps to Great Cold Tower.

Who is Weaver Maid in the sky?

Today, what pleasure, I'll be Herd Boy.

The spring landscape, so insistently described in several
places, is a conventional opening for a love poem—as, for example,

---

84. Refers to Jin Changxu's poem, "Chunyuan," in *Quan Tangshi* 768:8813.

신판사투춘 향을텽문 치눈광경 리도령이광한 루에셔춘향 을부른다

From

Okchung

chŏldae kain,

1925.

in troubadour poetry and in *sijo*. Indeed the harmony of nature has a strong bearing upon Yi and Ch'unhyang: earth and sky strengthen the awakening of love. The space evoked, adorned by flowers, is one where amorous desire is felt and expressed. The tradition of the connection between desire in nature and the natural desires in human beings offers "a playfully eroticized version of the natural world."[85] The sighting of Ch'unhyang may be the beginning of Yi's poetic impulse. Spring also recalls a shared experience of the mutability of life and the transience of beauty. Can one halt the flux of time? It is better to accept time as it is and the impossibility of permanence in this world.

Ch'unhyang, versed in poetry, calligraphy, and music, surely knows the Tano festival. Accompanied by her maid Hyangdan, she comes out to play on a swing. Her hair, lovely as orchids, is combed over her ears, neatly plaited, and fixed with a golden hairpin shaped like a phoenix. Her waist in its gauze skirt seems as frail as the slender willow of Everlasting Palace.[86] With her lovely gait, at a

85. Simon Goldhill, *Foucault's Virginity: Ancient Erotic Fiction and the History of Sexuality* (Cambridge: Cambridge University Press, 1998), 5, 9.
86. Weiyang palace built by Xiao He (d. 193 B.C.) in Changan. *Hanshu* 1B:64; 4:122.

leisurely pace, treading lightly, she enters and walks through the long forest with its green shades, sweet grasses, and golden turf, and a pair of golden orioles flits hither and thither. A swing suspended from a thick, tall willow tree is a hundred feet high. She takes off her long coat of green brocade with pomegranate pattern, long hood, unlined trousers, and unlined indigo silk skirt and hangs them up. She then takes off her purple embroidered Chinese silk shoes. She pulls up her new white petticoat under her chin, grasps two thick hemp ropes in her slender hands, and mounts the swing in her white stocking feet, setting the swing in motion. With her body, slender as a thin willow, her jade hairpin in the back of her hair and the amber—and jade-encased knives in front, her silver bamboo hairpin, and her lined gauze blouse matching well with ribbons of the same color, she cries:

"Hyangdan, push me!"

One push, she goes higher; another push, she goes higher, fine dust underfoot flying to the winds, far forward and far back. The leaves above follow her body, hurtling downward, zooming upward. The hem of her red skirt billows in the green shade. Riding the wind, like a flash of lightning among the white clouds, she flies forward like a light swallow darting to seize a falling peach blossom and then backward like a butterfly that has lost its mate. Surprised by a sudden wind, she turns around like the female transcendent on Mount Shaman[87] riding the cloud and descending to the Sun Terrace. Ch'unhyang bites a spray of leaves and plucks a flower and sticks it in her hair.

"Oh Hyangdan, this strong wind is making me dizzy.
 Catch the rope for me."

The swing goes back and forth many times before they can stop it, and her jade hairpin falls on the rock by the tinkling stream.

"Oh my hairpin, my hairpin!"

---

87. In eastern Sichuan where the transcendent of the mountain, near the Yangzi Gorges, is believed to dwell. See Song Yu, "Gaotang fu" and Lois Fusek, "The 'Kao-T'ang Fu'" *Monumenta Serica* 30 (1972-73): 392-425.

Her voice is like a coral pin tapping a jade tray—her bearing and figure do not seem to belong to this world.

Yi feels lonely, imagining all sorts of things, and mumbles to himself. He wishes to identify this female transcendent on the swing.

Who Is She?

Xi Shi followed Fan Li[88]
On a skiff to Five Lake,
So she couldn't be here.
Lady Yu sang a sad song before she turned
To Xiang Yu in the moonlight at Kaixia,[89]
So she couldn't be here.
Lady Wang Zhaojun left Tanfeng Palace
And went to the desert
Where now she lies in her Green Tomb,[90]
So she couldn't be here.
Ban Jieyou shut herself in Changxin Palace
Where she sang her sad song,[91]
So she couldn't be here;
Zhao Feiyan left Shaoyang Palace
After attendance in the morning,[92]
So she couldn't be here.
Is this a transcendent of the Luo River,

---

88. Xishi, a famous beauty from Yue, followed Fan Li (ca. fifth cent. B.C.) on a skiff to the Five Lake(s). Five Lake refers to Lake Tai or five lakes nearby (including or not including Lake Tai).

89. Lady Yu parted from Xiang Yu (232-202 B.C.), hegemon of Qu, with a sad song on a moonlit night at Kaixia. See Burton Watson, *Records of the Grand Historian of China,* 2 vols. (New York: Columbia University Press, 1961), 1:70.

90. Wang Jiaojun (Brilliant Consort) became a bride of the khan of the Xiongnu in 33 B.C. Green Tomb is her tomb that is supposed to stay green throughout the year.

91. Favored Beauty (ca. 48-6 B.C.) served King Cheng of the Han but had to retire to Lasting Trust Palace (Changxin). *Hanshu* 97B:3983-3988.

92. "Flying Swallow" (d. 6 B.C.), a favorite of Han emperor Cheng who ousted Favored Beauty Ban.

A transcendent on Mount Shaman?
His soul flew away to heaven
Bearing his body weary—
Truly he was still single.

The usual moment of the onset of desire is sight.[93] The overpowering effect of her beauty makes Yi, smitten at first sight, identify her with an incarnation of a heavenly ideal. Everything disappears before her beauty. Love is a power that annihilates masculine pride. A victim of the power of love beyond his control, he has contracted the malady of love. Finally, the servant interjects and identifies her for him as "an entertainer Wŏlmae's daughter in this town." Yi orders the servant to go and fetch her, but he adds his own blazon—extended praise of the qualities of her body: "Her snow-white skin and flowerlike face are famous throughout the south. . . . She is beautiful as Lady Zhuang Jiang, wife of Duke Zhuang of Wei (d. 672 B.C.),[94] virtuous as Tairen, King Wen's mother, and Taisi, King Wen's wife, and chaste as the two consorts of Lord Shun, sage ruler Yao's two daughters who became Shun's two wives known for their humility, frugality, intelligence, and devotion—a woman of peerless beauty, the noble lady in myriad years." When the servant returns for the third time to say that Yi wishes to compliment her literary talent, she agrees to go to the tower and meet Yi with her mother's approval. ("When a gentleman sends for you, how can you refuse? Go and see him.") After a brief exchange, Yi promises to visit her at home in the evening. At the discovery of her identity, he succumbs to the eternal power of the feminine.

When birds do sing, hey ding a ding, ding;
Sweet lovers love the spring. (*As You Like It* 5.3:21-22)

---

93. Goldhill, 9.
94. Watson, *The Tso chuan: Selections from China's Oldest Narrative History* (New York: Columbia University Presss, 1989), 5-6.

In spring lovers consent / and the birds marry.
(*Vigil of Venus*)[95]

　　Ch'unhyang's social position has changed: from the daughter of a retired entertainer in the 30-sheet version, she has become a secondary daughter of Second Minister Sŏng, former magistrate of Namwŏn. Therefore, when Ch'unhyang meets Yi at the tower, she does so as a social equal, and when Yi visits her house, he treats her as an unmarried woman of a respectable family.

　　Unable to collect his thoughts, Yi goes to his room and spends hours in anguish as he waits until dusk. No books interest him: not the *Doctrine of the Mean, Great Learning, Analects, Mencius, Book of Songs, Book of Documents, Book of Changes, Treasury of Ancient Writings, Comprehensive Mirror for Aid in Government,* compendia of history, works of Li Bo and Du Fu—books every student must read and memorize for the civil service examinations. Finally he settles on the *Qianziwen* (Thousand-Sinograph Primer) by Zhou Xingsi (fl. 550), the first text of literary Chinese every four-year-old boy begins with. When his servant, who is eager to show off his broken phrases from the flotsam and jetsam of all he has overheard, tries to quote from the text, Yi then makes humorous puns on each graph:

SONG OF THE *THOUSAND SINOGRAPH PRIMER*

Heaven opened at the time of the Rat,[96]
The Great Ultimate[97] is vast—*ch'ŏn* 天.
Earth split open at the time of the Ox,[98]

---

95. George Steiner, ed., *The Penguin Book of Modern Verse Translation* (Harmondsworth: Penguin, 1966), 149.

96. *Zhuzi yulei* 45 (Peking: Zhonghua, 1994), 3: 1154-1155. The time of the Rat is 11 P.M. to 1 A.M.

97. Also translated as the Grand Culmen, the source of the yin and yang, which by their complementary action generates all things. Joseph Needham, *Science and Civilization in China* 2:46off. (the Supreme Pole).

98. 1 to 3 A.M. In scene 17, "Sorceress of Tao," "the old bawd's monologue consists essentially of ludicrously misapplied lines of the *Thousand Character Text*" (p. 80, n. 3). See Tang Xianzu, *The Peony Pavilion*, trans. Cyril Birch (Bloomington:

Five elements[99] and eight trigrams[100]—*chi* 地.

Thirty-three heavens[101] are empty and void,

The hearts of humans regard them as black—*hyŏn* 玄.

Twenty-eight lunar lodgings[102]—

Metal, wood, water, fire, and earth is yellow—*hwang* 黃.

The sun and moon in the universe are bright again and again,

The abode of the Jade Emperor is lofty—*u* 宇.

Rise, prosperity, and decline of a state's capital

From ancient times to the present—*chu* 宙.

Yu controlled the flood[103] and Viscount Ji's[104]

Great Plan[105] and its nine divisions are vast—*hong* 洪.

After the death of Three August Ones[106] and Five Lords,[107]

Rebels and thieves raged wild—*hwang* 荒.

East will be bright,

At the sky's edge the sun's red disk

Will rise—*il* 日.

Myriad people sing the "Ground Thumping Song,"

Indiana University Press, 1980). She uses line 171, then line 170, not line 1. See Kang Yŏngmae, "*Ch'unhyang ka* wa Chungguk *Moranjŏng* ŭi 'Ch'ŏnjamun' suyong yangsang pigyo," in Pak Chint'ae et al., eds., *Ch'unhyang yesul ŭi yangsikchŏk punhwa wa segyesŏng* (Pagijŏng, 2004), 233-53.

99. Or Five Agents: water, fire, wood, metal, and earth.

100. *Qian, dui, li, zhen, sun, kan, gen,* and *kun*. Needham 2, table 13 and Richard Wilhelm, *The I Ching or the Book of Changes* (New York: Pantheon, 1951), 1:305.

101. *Trayastrimsas*: the Indra Heaven, the second of the six heavens of form. Its capital is on the summit of Mount Sumeru, where Indra rules over his thirty-two devas, who reside on thirty-two peaks of the mountain, eight in each of the four directions.

102. Twenty-eight constellations divided into four mansions of seven each referring to east/spring, south/summer, west/autumn, and north/winter. Needham 3: Fig. 94; table 24 on 242-59.

103. Birrell, 157-59.

104. See Peter H. Lee, ed., *Sourcebook of Korean Civilization*, 2 vols. (New York: Columbia University Press, 1993-6), 1: 7, 19-20, 535-36.

105. On political, economic, moral, and religious principles to be observed by the people. *Zhou i* (SPTK) 7: 10a; *Shangshu* (SPTK) 7:1a-b; James Legge, *The Chinese Classics*, 5 vols. (Hong Kong: Hong Kong University Press, 1960), 3:320-44.

106. Fuxi, Shennong, Suiren or Zhurang.

107. Yellow Emperor, Zhuanxu, Di Ku, Di Yao, Di Shun. Bernhard Karlgren, "Legends and Cults in Ancient China," *Bulletin of the Museum of Far Eastern Antiquities* 18 (1946): 206-34.

The misty moonlight in the great highway[108]—*wŏl* 月.

Sad early moon that starts to wax

Will be full on the night of the fifteenth—*yŏng* 盈.

When I ponder the world's myriad affairs,

They are like the bright moon

About to wane from the sixteenth—*ch'ŭk* 昃.

Twenty-eight lunar lodgings, River Diagram and Luo

       Document[109]—

Sun, moon, and stars—*chin* 辰.

Wonderful to spend tonight at the singing girl's home—*suk* 宿.

Under a mandarin-duck embroidered coverlet and pillow,

An elegant pastime with a peerless beauty

Throughout spring and fall—*yŏl* 列.

At the third watch[110] under a soft waxing moon,

Express all that's in my heart—*chang* 張.

Today a cold wind comes soughing—*han* 寒.

Let's retire to the bedroom;

If your pillow is too high,

Then use my arm,

Come on, then, close to me—*nae* 來.

Holding you tight

And entwining our legs,

It's warm despite snow and gales—*sŏ* 暑.

If the bedroom gets hot,

Let's take the northern wind

And move around—*wang* 往.

When is the time neither hot nor cold?

Phoenix trees shed leaves—autumn (*ch'u* 秋).

White hair will come soon,

---

108. *Liezi* 4: A. C. Graham, *The Book of Lieh-tzu* (London: John Murray, 1960), 90.

109. "The scroll of the Luo River and the plan of the Yellow River": Heaven gave Yu the mysterious tortoise that made fifteen appearances in the Luo, bearing marks on its back. *Zhou i* 7:10a (Legge 5: 374); *Liji* 4: 9; Needham 3 (1959): 55-62; *Analects* 9:8 (Arthur Waley, *The Analects of Confucius* [London: Allen & Unwin, 1949], 140).

110. 11 P.M. to 1 A.M.

Gather the fruits of youth with an imposing presence—*su* 收.

Cold wind on the bare tree,

Snow on the rivers and hills—winter (*tong* 冬).

Sleeping or waking, I'll never forget

Our love hidden in the inner room—*chang* 藏.

Last night's drizzle brings

Lustrous sheen on the lotus—*yun* 閏.

Such beauty will endure

Even after a lifetime—*yŏ* 餘.

The solemn oath of the marriage bond,

Vast as myriad acres of azure waves, will be fulfilled (*sŏng* 成).

While we play this way and that,

We won't know the passing of years and months—*se* 歲.

The State Code[111]says—*yul* 律—

A wife who shared poverty with you[112]

Can't be cast away,

Nor be ill-treated.

Is she not a gentleman's fit mate?

When Ch'unhyang's lips are pressed ardently to mine,

Will that not be "two mouths together"[113]—*yŏ* 呂?

How I long to see her!

As soon as the yamen is closed and dusk announces night, Yi and his servant boy steal out, heading for Ch'unhyang's house. Helpless in the face of love and its transforming power, Yi's desire to be with her intensifies—from the graph *yŏl* Yi rewrites the text with Ch'unhyang in mind. Ch'unhyang's mother welcomes the surprise guest and regards her daughter's meeting with Yi as an ineluctable destiny based on her auspicious dream the night before.

---

111. State Code of Administration, a collection of statutes compiled first in 1470, revised in 1474, and 1485. Annotated translation in 2 vols., published by Hanguk chŏngsin munhwa yŏnguwŏn in 1985.

112. Literally "wife of dregs and husks," who accompanied a man through his days of youthful poverty.

113. The graph *yŏ* (*lü*: tube, musical note) looks like two graphs for "mouth" joined by a vertical stroke.

From Okchung chŏldae kain, 1925.

Yi then describes what he sees upon arrival at the house. Already Yu Chinhan has spent nine lines describing the house, garden, screens, furniture, utensils, dishes, wine, and meat. Unlike the Seoul editions, our text, following other Chŏnju editions, limits description to the garden:

SONG OF THE HOUSE AND GARDEN

After the main and middle gates,
Go round the rear garden—
An old thatched cottage
With candles alight inside.
A willow's drooping sprays
Hide the candlelight
Like the strands of a beaded blind.
To the right a parasol tree,
Dripping with clear dewdrops,
To startle the dream of cranes.
To the left a gnarled pine—
When the clear breeze blows,
It bends like the old dragon.
The plantain by the window,

Its tender leaves stand out
Like the phoenix's tail feathers.
The young lotus flowers—
Black pearls from the heart of the water—
Barely above the pond's surface,
Hold up the dewdrops of jade.
Sleek and plate-sized golden carp
Try to change into dragons,
Beat the water wriggling,
Slopping in their play—
The new lotus leaves
Open to receive them.
Three lofty peaks of the rock garden
Pile upon pile;
Cranes standing by the steps,
Startled by visitors, spread their wings,
Stride with their long legs,
And whoop.
A little shaggy dog barks under the laurel tree.
A pair of ducks in the pond
Afloat free and easy
Seem to welcome the guest.

The garden, private, enclosed, and in harmony with the surroundings, is cultivated for its beauty, inviting visitors to behold and contemplate its simple and symbolic scenes. As a system of signs, it is emblematic of those who inhabit it. It is a pleasant place (*locus amoenus*) that exists over time after people are gone. One might say it combines nature and nurture, utopian innocence and classical learning. Ch'unhyang, "beautiful as the shining moon emerging from the clouds," opens the screens and comes out. Her room in Lotus Hall, a "topographical middle ground between culture and nature,"[114] is like a place in fairyland.

114. Tony Tanner, *Adultery in the Novel: Contract and Transgression* (Baltimore:

Looking at the walls,

A number of implements—

Wardrobes carved with dragons and phoenixes,

Cabinets with many drawers,

Ornamented with paintings. . . .

Ch'unhyang is a maiden

But a studious girl,

So she won't have acquired these items,

But her mother, a famous entertainer,

Prepared them for her daughter.

Calligraphy by Korean writers of renown

And famous paintings in between—

A striking painting of eight transcendents

With a colophon:

The emperor gives audience

To holders of the red tally.

Li Bo, the retired gentleman from Qinglian,[115]

Reads the *Scripture of the Yellow Court*[116]

Kneeling at Yellow Crane Tower.[117]

Li He[118] invited to draft a report

When the ridge beam is raised

Upon completion of White Jade Tower for Jade Emperor.

On the eve of Double Seven

Herd Boy and Weaver Maid on Magpie Bridge.

Johns Hopkins University Press, 1979), 114.

115. In Sichuan, identified as the birthplace of the poet.

116. Isabelle Robinet, *Taoist Meditations: The Mao-shan Tradition of Great Purity*, trans. Julian F. Pass and Norman J. Girardot (Albany: State University of New York Press, 1993), 55-96; *Taoism: Growth of a Religion*, trans. Phyllis Brooks (Stanford: Stanford University Press, 1997), 114-98 (on the Shangqing school).

117. Refers to Cui Hao's poem, "Huangho lou," in *Quan Tangshi* 130:1329.

118. His dates are 790-816; he wrote poetry of allusion with Daoist and shamanist elements, which is compared to Mallarmé, in Victor H. Mair, ed., *The Columbia History of Chinese Literature* (New York: Columbia University Press, 2001), 310.

The moon goddess pounds magic herbs

At Great Cold Hall in the moonlight—

These arrayed paintings dazzled him.

Off to one side another painting:

Yan Guang on Mount Fuchun,[119]

Having declined the offer of Grand Master of Remonstrance,

White seagulls for friends,

Monkeys and cranes for neighbors,

Dressed in sheepskin

And casting his line

In the Seven League Brook at Chutong River.

The room is truly a fairyland,

Fit for the bride of a gentleman!

With a sincere heart,

Wishing to serve only one husband,

Ch'unhyang wrote a poem

And pasted it above her desk:

"Elegant bamboo rustles in the spring breeze,

Burning incense I read books at night."

Paintings are described according to the convention of ecphrasis, a narrative description of a work of art. Ch'unhyang has a room of her own, privacy, and leisure, but probably no economic independence. She leads a circumscribed existence in a tightly regimented culture—where accidents of birth determine her station not just ideologically but also architecturally, "since women occupied the inner, private quarters . . . in the culture marked by gender distinction and isolation."[120] Woman—docile, silenced, patient, and obedient—is consigned to a separate private sphere (if

---

119. His dates are 37 B.C. to A.D. 43, a contemporary of Emperor Guangwu; he retired to Mount Fuchun and spent his time fishing. *Hou Hanshu* (Peking: Zhonghua, 1963), 113: 2763-2764.

120. Anna Roberts, "Introduction," in *Violence Against Women in Medieval Texts* (Gainesville: University Press of Florida, 1998), 7.

her parents can afford it) and subjected to the three dependencies[121] (that she follow the wishes of her father, husband, and son) and the seven wifely faults[122] (failure to produce a son; adultery; extreme disobedience; extreme talkativeness; theft; jealousy; and grave illness).

Yi wants to marry her right then and there, without the formalities required of his class, and obtains Wŏlmae's consent. Both are sixteen years old (fifteen by Western count)—a nubile age in the *State Code of Administration* (3:241).[123] An informal wedding takes place, therefore, in Ch'unhyang's mother's house without an exchange of gifts, a nuptial procession, or the bridegroom's visit to the bride's home to present a wooden goose, symbol of conjugal fidelity. That is, the young bride's rite of passage is not made spatially—unlike the prevalent custom, she does not move to a new home to live with her husband and in-laws. The best dowry she can bring to Yi is her goodness and constancy: her moral center. After a feast, Wŏlmae calls Hyangdan to prepare the bedroom.

Theirs is a spontaneous and irrepressible love at first sight. Ch'unhyang and Student Yi, of the same age, valorize voluntary love and marriage. As opposed to the arranged union characteristic of the time, they exalt a relationship of mutual love. Although gender roles then were not equal, both share intelligence, refinement of taste, internalization of cultural codes and values, steadfastness of purpose, and loyalty to each other. Neither Ch'unhyang nor Yi, we should note, feels that their love has crossed class lines—there is no disparity in status.

At this point Yi learns from Wŏlmae that Magistrate Sŏng passed away in Seoul and Ch'unhyang was raised by a single mother. Thus Ch'unhyang never knew her biological father.

---

121. "Three dependencies" suggests T'ung-tsu Ch'ü, in *Law and Society in Traditional China* (Paris and La Haye: Mouton, 1961), 102-103, 140; *Kongzi jiayu* (SPTK) 6:12a-b. Women have to obey their father at home, their husband after marriage, and their eldest son after the husband's death.

122. T'ung-tsu Ch'ü, 118-23; *Kongzi jiayu* 6:13a.

123. Boys age 15 and girls age 14 may marry.

Courtship is brief—a romance convention to underscore that love at first sight is the most authentic and must be consummated on the first night. Nevertheless Yi goes through, as in troubadour poetry, the five phases of love—seeing, speaking, touching, kissing, and consummation. From this point on the narrator switches modes from the decorous to the erotic. After a second night, they renew their joys and lose their shyness; they begin to joke with each other, and jointly they compose an impromptu love song:

SONG OF LOVE

Love, love, my love,
Love high as Mount Shaman under the moon
Shining upon seven-hundred-tricent Grotto Court Lake,
Love deep as water at the horizon's end,
Deep like heaven and emerald sea,
Love high as the top of Mount Jade under the bright moon,
Enjoying it on myriad peaks of autumn mountain—
Love as she has spent her years for the study of dance
And asks for one who plays the pipe[124]—
Love that shines like the evening sun and moon
Upon the peach and plum blossoms seen through the screen—
Love that abounds in winsome smiles and graces
With a new moon powdered white,
Love that brings us together through three lives,
Bound by the Old Man of the Moonlight[125]—
Love between husband and wife without reproach—
Love like a well-rounded peony on the eastern hill
Amid the rain of blossoms—

---

124. Lu Jiaolin (635-84), "Changan gui," *Quan Tangshi* 41:522-53 (The text reverses lines 17 and 18 and gives only 4 graphs to fit the *p'ansori* meter): "Tell me of her who plays the pipes off into purple mist—/ she has spent her years of beauty in the study of dance," in Owen, *The Poetry of the Early T'ang*, 105-09.

125. See *Taiping guangji* (in the *Chingyin Siku quanshu* ed.) (Taiwan: Shangwu yinshuguan, 1983), 159:1a-3a.

Love entwined and bound

Like a net in the sea off Yŏnp'yŏng[126]—

Love joined on end like a brocade woven by

Weaver Maid in the Silver River—

Love sewn tightly

Like seams in the quilt of a singing girl,

Love drooping

Like fronds of weeping willow by the river—

Love piled up like grains

In the southern and northern granaries—

Love deeply etched in every corner

Like silver and jade inlays in the chest—

Love enjoyed by golden bees and white butterflies

As they hold pink flowers

And dance in spring breezes—

Love that floats like a pair of mandarin ducks

Bobbing on the clear green stream—

Love of Herd Boy and Weaver Maid

On the night of Double Seven—

Love of Sŏngjin, pupil of Master Liugwan,[127]

Frolicking with the eight fairies—

Love of Xiang Yu, whose strength can pluck up the hills,

Meeting with beautiful Lady Yu[128]—

Love of the Brilliant Emperor of Tang

For Precious Consort Yang[129]—

Love swaying gracefully

Like the sea roses on long Bright Sand Beach[130]—

---

126. On the southern shores of Hwanghae province, consisting of two islands, known for a fishing place.

127. The protagonist in *A Dream of Nine Clouds* (1687-88) by Kim Manjung (1637-92).

128. *Shiji* 7:295-339; and see Burton Watson, *Records of the Grand Historian of China*, 2 vols. (New York: Columbia University Press, 1961), 1:70.

129. Xuanzong (r. 713-56) with his undying love for Yang Gueifei (d. 15 July 756) is immortalized by Bo Juyi in his "Song of Everlasting Sorrow" (806); *Quan Tangshi* 435:4828-30.

130. Well-known beach in Wŏnsan, South Hamgyŏng.

You're indeed my love, all of you is love—
Ohwa tungdung, my love,
O my lovely one,

My love!

Yi emphasizes the power of love, which he attempts to re-create by the stock-in-trade of romantic rhetoric, enumerating love's charms and delights and celebrating the claims of physical passion. He runs through the repertory in similes and catalogs its manifestations. Love is high as a mountain, deep as the ocean, abounds in smiles and graces. Old Man of the Moonlight, a matchmaker who ties knots between a man and a woman by using red strings, brought them together through three lives—past, present, and future. Love is entwined and bound like a net, joined like a brocade sewn tightly—the lover's sense of interlacement becomes embodied in a net—a distinctly feminine discourse with its own diction emerging from a feminine body and experience. Catullus compared an amorous couple to a vine entwining a tree (Poem 61).[131] Yi's song also explores a feminine space of language together with images of water, immersion, and engulfment— passionate merging, the union of beloveds.

Poets in the past have defined love in various ways to probe its diverse responses, mystery, and power. Love is a fire that converts and melts and dissolves. Love is a sickness for which there is no remedy. Love is a violent gust that shakes the mountain oaks (Sappho). Love is death, involves the whole of existence. Love offers highest ecstasies and deepest torments. "Love is a smoke made with the fume of sighs; / Being purg'd, a fire sparkling in lovers' eyes; / Being vex'd, a sea nourished with [lovers'] tears; / What is it else? A madness most discreet, / A choking gall, and a preserving sweet" (*Romeo and Juliet* 1.1:196-200). Ch'unhyang possesses a fund of passion and laughter, and Yi wishes to commemorate love and the

131. Peter Green, trans., *The Poems of Catullus: A Bilingual Edition* (Berkeley: University of California Press, 2005), 107-23, esp. 109, lines 31-35.

310

beloved in monuments more lasting than bronze. The body is the source of language, yet language outlasts the body:

Life After Death

When you die, I'll tell you what you'll be:
You will be a sinograph—
Graphs for earth, for female (*ŭm* 陰),
For wife, and the radical for woman.
When I die, I'll become graphs
For heaven (*kŏn* 乾), husband (*pu* 夫), male (*nam* 男),
The body of the son (*cha* 子) attached to the woman radical
Making the graph for good (*ho* 好).
Love, love, my love!

When you die, I'll tell you what you'll be:
You'll become water—
Water in Silver River,
Water of waterfalls,
Of myriad acres of emerald seas,
Of clear valley brooks, of jade valley brooks,
Ending in a long river for the whole region.
Even during a seven-year drought,
You'll become the water of yin and yang
Overflowing always and sinking to the bottom.

When I die, I'll become a bird,
Not a cuckoo,
Nor a blue bird at Jasper Lake,
Nor a blue crane, white crane, or roc,
But a mandarin duck
That never leaves its mate,
Bobbing on the green waters—
Love, love,

Ŏhwa tungdung, that's me.

Love, love, my fascinating love!

"No, I don't want to be any such thing."

All right, then. I'll tell you what you'll be after death.

When you die, you won't be the great bell at Kyŏngju,

Nor that in Chŏnju, or Songdo,

But the one in Chongno in the capital.

When I die, I'll become the clapper of the bell,

In accordance with thirty-three heavens and twenty-eight

lunar lodgings.

After the beacon on Mount An[132] flares three times,

After the beacon on Mount South flares twice,

The first sound of the Chongno bell—

Every time it rings,

People will think,

Only the bell:

But inside ourselves we'll know

It's Ch'unhyang's clang, my clang.

Let the two of us conjoin,

Love, love, my fascinating love!

"No, I don't like that either."

Then, when you die, what will you be?

You will become a mortar,

I'll become a pestle when I die,

The mortar made by Jiang Taigong[133]

At the hour, day, month, year of the White Monkey . . .

And when I pound, clang clang,

You'll know it's me.

Love, love, my love,

132. In Imje county, Kangwŏn province.

133. Taigongwang (Lü Shang), a counselor to King Wen of Zhou who found him fishing in the Wei River. *Shiji* 32:1477-1481 and Sarah Allen, "The Identities of Taigongwang in Zhou and Han Literature," *Monumenta Serica* 30 (1972-73): 57-99.

My charming love!

"I don't like it, I don't want to be that either."
Why do you say that?
"Why must I be
At the bottom
In this life and the next?
It's no fun, it won't do."
Then, when you die, I'll put you on top.
You'll be the upper plate of a millstone,
And I the lower plate,
When slender hands of young handsome faces
Hold the millstone and turn,
Like round heaven and square earth together,
Then you'll know it's me.
"Still I don't like it and won't be that either.
When I was born, this top part was given only to me.
For what sort of grudge
Was I given an extra orifice?
I don't want anything."

Then when you die, I'll tell you what you'll be:
Be a sea rose on long Bright Sand Beach;
When I die, I'll be a butterfly
And nibble with antenna
And you brush it with pollen.
When spring winds blow,
We'll dance swaying—
Love, love, my love,
My charming love!
If I look here, you're my love;
If I look there, you're my love.
If all this is my love,
How can I live caught up in love?

Ohŏ tungdung, my love!
My beloved, my love!
When you smile sweetly,
The peony, king of flowers,
Seems half open
After a night's drizzle.
Wherever I look, I see my love!
My charming love!

The death and transfiguration of the lovers culminate in a
series of parallel metaphors that meet in the linked images (love-
death) and the lovers' metamorphosis as a sea rose and a butterfly
dancing in the spring breeze. First Yi equates Ch'unhyang with
earth, female, and wife, the radical for woman (radical 38), and
himself with heaven, husband, and male. He then brings in the
mandarin duck to underscore his devotion and conjugal fidelity,
clappers, pestle, the lower plate of millstone, and a butterfly;
Ch'unhyang is the Chongno bell, mortar, upper plate of a millstone;
and a sea rose. He is the subject; she is the other. When Ch'unhyang
cites female anatomy to point out their differences, those of a
Freudian cast of mind may call it penis envy (her lack of a phallus),
but the imposition of such theory on another culture, we know, is
at best problematic. In all likelihood, an image of woman in a male-
authored text (the object of a male gaze) is meant to provide the
male audience with voyeuristic titillation—a romance tendency; but
it may also be read as registering a male bias in favor of woman's
traditional place at the bottom of the socioeconomic hierarchy.
Earlier in the "Song of Love" she is associated with the sea, the
source of creativity and sublimity. Is she exploring a feminine
space of language with images of water—virtues associated with
the female in Daoism? Not a silenced subject, she interrogates the
accepted hierarchy where man holds power and prevails.

     We may recall that Ch'unhyang is a reincarnation of the
goddess of the Luo River, Consort Fu, and is at times also likened to

the Xiang goddesses, Yao's two daughters Fairy Radiance (Ehuang 娥皇) and Maiden Bloom (Nuying 女英), married to Shun long ago and far away. In her dream journey to the Temple of the Yellow Tumulus (Huangling Miao 黃陵廟), Ch'unhyang meets Nongae[134] the patriot, who drowned herself with an enemy captain, and the Xiang consorts mentioned earlier. More important, Ch'unhyang meets Yi in the Korean counterpart of Great Cold Tower on the moon. The moon is feminine in East Asia and represents "the female principle in the cosmos."[135] The moon is also the mother of waters—the genetrix of sublunar waters[136] (Irigaray's economy of fluids whose properties are "continuous, compressible, dilatable, viscous, conductible, diffusible"[137] may be cited as a modern example). Here the narrator seems to play on the feminine-moon-water association. In addition, the given name of Ch'unhyang's husband Yi is Mongnyong 夢龍 (Dream Dragon)—a dragon that resides in great rivers and marshes and brings down rain. In a conception dream, however, the dragon betokens a male child. It is also a thematic emblem of royalty in East Asia—the rulers of China and Korea wore dragon robes.

---

134. An entertainer in Chinju, she died on 6 August 1592. When the Japanese celebrated the fall of Chinju fortress on Ch'oksok tower, she enticed one drunken Japanese commander and threw herself with him into the South River. In 1722 her deed was recognized officially, and in 1740 a shrine was built for her spirit and sacrifice offered in the spring and fall.

135. Edward H. Schafer, *Pacing the Void: T'ang Approaches to the Stars* (Floating World Editions, 2005), 171-200.

136. Ibid., 174; and Schafer, *The Divine Woman*, 40.

137. Luce Irigaray, *This Sex Which Is Not One*, trans. Catherine Porter with Carolyn Burke (Ithaca: Cornell University Press, 1985) 111; Diana Fuss, *Essentially Speaking: Feminism, Nature and Difference* (New York: Routledge, 1989) 59. "Physiologically and psychologically, women are wet . . . The emotions of eros are especially liquid and liquefying," says Anne Carson, in "Putting Her in Her Place: Woman, Dirt, and Desire," in *Before Sexuality: The Construction of Erotic Experience in the Ancient Greek World*, ed. David Halperin et al. (Princeton: Princeton University Press, 1990), 137, 139, 142, 159, esp. 137-38. Elizabeth Robertson describes "the medieval belief that women were physiologically cold, wet, and incomplete" and the "pervasiveness of images of moisture in the medieval women's texts" in "Medieval Medical Views of Women and Female Spirituality in the *Ancrene Wisse* and Julian of Norwich's *Showings*," in *Feminist Approaches to the Body in Medieval Literature* (Philadelphia: University of Pennsylvania Press, 1993), 142-67, esp. 142 and 161.

Listen, my love,

You and I are in love,

So how can we not be loving?

Clean waters of a long river

Carry the traveler's sorrow[138]—kaek*chŏng*

I can't send you off at the bridge,

The trees on the riverside

Harbor a traveler's lonesome feelings[139]—ham*jŏng*

I send you off to South Cove,[140]

I can't overcome my sadness—pulsŭng*jŏng*

With no one to see my parting sorrow—a*jŏng*

The founder of the Han's Glad Rain Pavilion[141]—Hŭiu*jŏng*

Three terraces,[142] six ministries,[143] a hundred officials at
      court—cho*jŏng*

The clean and pure place of worship—ch'ong*jŏng*

Woman's natal home—ch'in*jŏng*

Friends sharing feelings—t'ong*jŏng*

Suppressing turbulence—p'yŏng*jŏng*

Our love that lasts a thousand years—in*jŏng*

The moon is bright and stars are few,

Xiao and Xiang rivers and Grotto Court Lake—Tong*jŏng*

All the creations fashioned by nature—chohwa*jŏng*

---

138. Wei Chengqing's (640-706) poem, "Nanxing bieti," line 2; *Quan Tangshi* 46:560.

139. Song Jiwen's (d. ca. 713) poem, "Song Du Shenyan," in *Quan Tangshi* 52: 640.

140. Reference to a poem, "Parting," by Chŏng Chisang (d. 1135); see *Tong munsŏn* (Hyŏpsŏng munhwasa, 1985) 19:19b, and Peter H. Lee, ed., *The Columbia Anthology of Traditional Korean Poetry* (New York: Columbia University Press, 2002), 206.

141. Built by Su Shi (1037-1101) in northeastern Fengxiang district in Shensi in 1061. The completion of the pavilion is said to have brought rain after a drought. *Dongpo quanji* 35:2a-3a.

142. Refers to three communication agencies: imperial secretariat, the censorate, and tribunal of reception. See Charles O. Hucker, *A Dictionary of Official Titles in Imperial China* (Stanford: Stanford University Press, 1985), 403.

143. Personnel, Punishments, Rites, Taxation, War, and Works.

Cares—kŏk*chŏng*

Petitions and pleas for grievance—wŏn*jŏng*

Sharing love—in*jŏng*

Grumbling about food—t'u*jŏng*

Unfortunate frivolity—pang*jŏng*

Law court and palace courtyard—song*jŏng*/kung*jŏng*

Internal conditions—nae*jŏng*

External affairs—oe*jŏng*

Loving Pine Arbor—Aesong*jŏng*

Archery Arbor—Ch'ŏmyang*jŏng*

Fragrance Sinking Arbor and Precious Consort Yang[144]—
　　Ch'imhyang*jŏng*

Lord Shun's two consorts' Xiao-Xiang Arbor—Sosang*jŏng*

Cold Pine Arbor—Hansong*jŏng*

Spring Delight Arbor when a hundred flowers bloom—
　　Hoch'un*jŏng*

The moon above Giraffe Peak over White Cloud Arbor—
　　Paegun*jŏng*

The joyous meetings—mannan*jŏng*

If we speak of eight feelings—p'al*chŏng*

My mind encompasses *qian*'s virtues—

Fundamentality (*yuan*), prevalence (*heng*), fitness (*li*), and
　　constancy (*zhen/chŏng*),[145]

Your mind is what appeals to my feelings—t'ak*chŏng*

But if in all this affection—ta*jŏng*

If ever we should grow cool—p'a*jŏng*

How it hurts inside to sever ties—chŏl*chŏng*

And that in truth (chin*jŏng*)

Is how I protest my original feelings—wŏn*jŏng*.

---

144. Built by Yang Guozhong, where Xuanzong and his Precious Consort Yang enjoyed viewing the peonies and had Li Bo write a poem.

145. Richard John Lynn, *The Classic of Changes: A New Translation of the* I Ching *as Interpreted by Wang Bi* (New York: Columbia University Press, 1994), 129-42.

The meanings of the graph *chŏng* 情 (*qing*) include affection, love, passion. The song also brings in homonyms in Sino-Korean (but not in Chinese) pronunciation: *chŏng* 亭 (*ting*: pavilion); *chŏng* 定 (*ding*: decide, fixed); *chŏng* 庭 (*ting*: courtyard, law court); *chŏng* 淨 (*jing*: clean); and *chŏng* 貞 (*zhen*: loyal, faithful, chaste). The rhapsodic and sonorous enumeration of words ending in *chŏng* evinces an overflowing playfulness with language.

Song of the Graph *Kung*

Open Way Palace in the narrow universe,

Majestic Heaven's Gate Palace,

Shined by the auspicious air of the sun, moon, and stars

Amid wind and rain with thunder and lightning,

Where the king ruled the people wisely with august virtue—

Great Court Palace of the King of Yin who, in full flourish,

Welcomed guests to the lake of wine[146]—

Ebang Palace of the First Qin Emperor,[147]

Manifest Yang Palace of the founder of the Han

Who asked how he had won the world,[148]

Enduring Joy Palace[149] beside it,

Lasting Trust Palace of Favored Beauty Ban,[150]

Enjoying Spring Palace of the Brilliant Tang Emperor,

The detached palace here,

The separate palace up there,

Crystal Palace in the Dragon King's palace,

Great Cold Palace in the moon,

You and I become one body (*hapkung*),

Our life will be without limit.

---

146. *Shiji* 3:105.

147. Built by the first Qin emperor in the Shanglin Park; *Shiji* 6:256.

148. *Shiji* 8:380-81.

149. Changle Palace was erected by Liu Bang out of an old Qin palace in 200 B.C. and became his residence. *Shiji* 8:385; *Hanshu* 1B:58.

150. The palace where Favored Beauty Ban retired after losing favor with Emperor Cheng.

Let's stop talking of these palaces—
A water dragon palace between your legs
I'll make my way there
With my powerful cudgel.

Here is a similar catalog of words ending in *kung* 宮 (*gong*: palace, temple, womb, a note of the ancient Chinese pentatonic scale), culminating in a sexual union (*hapkung* 合宮), two becoming one body. The narrator leads us to the bedroom door and invites our covert gaze through peepholes drilled in the paper screen.

Song of the Piggyback Ride

Listen, I'll tell you nice things—
As if I'm carrying on my back Fu Yue,[151]
Lü Shang (Taigong),
He has great plans in his heart
And will be known throughout the land.
A pillar of state, a loyal minister who builds up the kingdom.
As if I am carrying Six Martyred Ministers,[152]
Six Loyal Subjects,[153]
Master Sun, Master Moon,
Koun Ch'oe Ch'iwŏn,[154]
Chebong Ko Kyŏngmyŏng,[155]
Kim Ŭngha, count of Liaodong,[156]

151. Minister of Wuding of Shang; *Mencius* 6B:15.
152. Those murdered by the usurper Sejo include Yi Kae (1417-56); Ha Wiji (1387-1456); Yu Sŏngwŏn (d. 1456); Yu Ŭngbu (d. 1456); Sŏng Samnun (1418-56); and Pak P'aengnyŏn (1417-56).
153. Six ministers who refused to serve the usurper Sejo include Yi Maengjŏn (fl. 1427); Cho Yŏ (1420-89); Wŏn Ho (fl. 1423); Kim Sisŭp (1435-93); Sŏng Tamsu (d. 1456); and Nam Hyoon (1454-92).
154. Ch'oe Ch'iwŏn (b. 857), the most famous Silla writer of poetry and prose.
155. Ko Kyŏngmyŏng (1533-92), leader of 6,000 troops at Kŭmsan; died in a battle against the Japanese invaders.
156. Kim Ŭngha (1580-1619), a military official who lost a battle against the Manchu.

Songgang Chŏng Ch'ŏl,[157]

Lord Ch'ungmu, Admiral Yi Sunsin,[158]

Uam Song Siyŏl,[159] T'oegye Yi Hwang,[160]

Sagye Kim Changsaeng,[161] Myŏngjae Yun Chŭng[162]—

You're my husband, my husband,

The husband I love forever.

Passing the literary examination,

You'll be recorder at the Royal Secretariat,

Learned doctor of the Office of Royal Decrees,

Then Third, Second,

And First Royal Secretary—

After serving as governor of eight provinces,

You'll be called to court

As an official of the Royal Library,

Second Diarist of the Office of Royal Decrees,

Official to choose a state counselor,

Director of the Office of Special Advisers,

Assistant Master of the Confucian Academy,

Minister of six boards,

Third, Second, and Chief State Counselor,

And head of the Royal Library,

You'll fill three thousand court and eight hundred external

     posts,

A pillar of the state, my husband,

My husband I love forever.

Not only is her knowledge of government offices and positions
of the Chosŏn dynasty impressive, but she understands that the civil

---

157. Chŏng Ch'ŏl (1537-94), a Chosŏn poet and politician.
158. Yi Sunsin (1545-98), the most famous Korean admiral, who never lost a sea
battle against the Japanese navy.
159. Song Siyŏl (1607-89), Chosŏn scholar and politician.
160. Yi Hwang (1501-71), the most famous Neo-Confucian philosopher in
Korea.
161. Kim Changsaeng (1548-1631), Chosŏn scholar.
162. Yun Chŭng (1629-1714), Chosŏn scholar and politician.

service examination is the only path to success. From childhood virtually all aspirants for public service were trained in the same (primarily Chinese) works. Upon passing the examinations, the successful candidate received a political appointment that carried immense social prestige—the highest recognition a man of letters could achieve. Official titles stand for power and authority, and at every turn one needs the help of those holding them. Ch'unhyang wants her husband to be a class individualized, the best in officialdom, with exemplary character. The only valid test of being the king's man lies in his ability to right wrongs and to care for powerless people subjected to unspeakable cruel treatment. The narrator's list reminds us of the importance of ranks and titles for the literati class. They would study a chart listing all the coveted positions at court and would play a dice game on a board with these titles written on it[163]—all to whet their ambition. Soon Ch'unhyang will, she hopes, have a chance to use her own life as evidence to appeal to the court.

Song of the Graph *Sŭng*

Let's play riding—
Like the Yellow Lord who drilled his men and made clouds
    and fog,
Caught Chiyou in the Zhuolu wilderness,[164]
Beating the drums of victory
On the leading chariot—
Like Great Yu of Xia in his land-roaring chariot
When he tamed the nine-year flood,
Like Master Red Pine riding on the cloud,
Like Lü Tongbin[165] on his egret,
Li Bo, banished transcendent, on the whale,

---

163. See Peter H. Lee, *A Korean Storyteller's Miscellany: The* P'aegwan Chapki *of* Ŏ Sukkwŏn (Princeton: Princeton University Press, 1989), 180-82.

164. *Shiji* 1:3-4; Birrell, 132-34.

165. Lü Tongbin (755-805), Chinese alchemist; see Needham 2:159.

Meng Haojan[166] on the donkey,

Transcendent Great Unique[167] on the crane,

A Chinese emperor on the elephant,

Our king on the carriage,

Three state counselors on sedan chairs,

Six ministers on carriages,

A general of military drill on his war carriage,

Magistrates on their palanquin,

Magistrate of Namwŏn on a special carriage—

Old fishermen on their leafy boat at sunset

But I've nothing to ride on.

This night at the third watch,

I'll ride on Ch'unhyang's belly,

Hoisting the quilt for a sail,

My member as an oar,

Enter into her sunken spring—

As without effort I cross

The waters of yin and yang,

If I take you as horse to ride,

Your pace may vary—

I'll be the groom

Gently holding your reins.

You may trot and canter,

Go rough and hard

Gallop like a piebald horse.

Yi offers lessons to his new wife, hitherto innocent of amorous experience, serving as the agent of initiation to erotic love with various moves and caresses. Both "Song of the Piggyback Ride" and "Song on the Graph *Sŭng*" become more erotic and verge on sexual blazon with the diction of attack and penetration: "I'll ride on

166. Meng Haojan (689-740), Tang poet.

167. Taii (Great One or Unique) is the supreme sky god in Chinese mythology who resides in the palace at the center of heaven, marked by the pole star. Needham 3:260.

Ch'unhyang's belly, / Hoisting the quilt for a sail, / My member as
an oar, / Enter into her sunken spring"; and "If I take you as horse
to ride, / Your pace may vary— / I'll be the groom / Gently holding
your reins." That is, Ch'unhyang can either trot, canter, or gallop
to guide and control Yi's movements. Just as there is a homology
between hunting and sexuality in early Greek poetry, there is a
homology between combat and sexual intercourse in Chinese and
Korean fiction.[168] Nineteenth-century Koreans are not the prudes
we might take them for.

Propertius (2:15) describes the lovemaking of a pair: "O that
tangle of arms clasping, O the kisses / when you held me with
your lips and wouldn't let go."[169] Sydney fell in love with Penelope
Devereux, then twelve, the daughter of the Earl of Essex, who
became the Stella of his sonnets: "I on my horse, and Love on me
doth trye / Our horsemanships" (sonnet 49). Carew (1594/5-1640),
in "A Rapture,"[170] refers to Aretino's (1492-1556) sixteen sonnets on
coital posture:

> . . . Till a soft murmure, sent
>
> From soules entranc'd in amorous languishment
>
> Rowze us, and shoot into our veins fresh fire,
>
> Till we, in their sweet extasie expire . . ." (51-55)

> Now in more subtile wreathes I will entwine
>
> My sinowie thighs, my legs and armes with thine
>
> Thou like a sea of milke shalt lye display'd,
>
> While I the smooth, calme Ocean, invade
>
> With such a tempest . . . (79-83)

---

168. Charlotte Furth, "Rethinking van Gulik: Sexuality and Reproduction in
Traditional Chinese Medicine," in *Engendering China: Women, Culture, and the State*,
ed. Christina K. Gilmartin et al. (Cambridge: Harvard University Press, 1994), 135.

169. John Warden, trans., *The Poems of Propertius* (Indianapolis: Bobbs-Merrill,
1972), 82.

170. Sidney's sonnet is cited from *Astrophil and Stella*, ed. Max Putzel (Garden
City: Doubleday, 1967), 49. Carew is quoted from Rhodes Dunlap, ed., *The Poems
of Thomas Carew with His Masque* Coelum Britannicum (Oxford: Clarendon,
1949), 49-53.

My Rudder, with thy bold hand, like a tryde,

And skilfull Pilot, thou shalt steere, and guide

My Bark into Loves channel, where it shall

Dance, as the bounding waves doe rise or fall. (87-90)

Culture intrudes on life, and intertextuality defines the song's playfulness, festiveness, and fun, and functions to serve the interests of Yi's class.

In a Confucian hierarchical society, there was patriarchal oppression and subordination of women. They were restricted to the private domestic sphere with a sociosexual division of labor— pregnancy, child care, and household management. Marginalization of women in the patriarchal, patrilocal, and patrilineal kinship system increased from the seventeenth century as Confucian moral discourse became repetitive and repressive. A uniform portrait of the premodern Korean woman has been constructed by recent studies that present her as powerless, dependent, passive, and denied opportunity for education, inheritance, and participation in family ritual. Girls could no longer associate or eat with boys and men from the age of seven and were segregated in separate living quarters. Mothers and elderly women in the family would teach them how to move, talk, eat, and dress. Girls also learned how the female body became sexualized, how different parts of the body became associated with sexuality, and how heterosexual sex is governed by the institution of marriage. Sexuality, "that social process which creates, organizes, expresses, and directs desire, creating the social beings we know as women and men,"[171] was controlled by an ideal of chastity, limited by virginity cults, and upheld with a sanction against adultery. Thus sexuality, culturally variable, is an essential dimension of identity.

According to Wŏlmae, Ch'unhyang studied the *Xiaoxue* 小 學 (Elementary Learning; preface dated 1187) at seven, and she

---

171. Catharine A. MacKinnon, "Feminism, Marxism, Method and State: An Agenda for Theory," *Signs: Journal of Women in Culture and Society* 7.3 (1982): 516.

probably taught her daughter the importance of educational capital to advance in society. An educational manual for parents and teachers, this six-chapter text is organized around three main subjects: the foundation of moral teaching, the basic human relations (parent/child, ruler/minister, husband/wife, old/young, and friend/friend),[172] and the cultivation of self. The section on parent/child relations discusses the parental role in education, obedience to parents, and ritual duties after their death. The section on husband/wife discusses separate functions between the sexes, especially the subordinate position of women to men, female chastity, and nonremarriage of widows. The section on cultivation of self discusses mind cultivation, comportment, dress, and food. Then follow examples of sages, worthies, and the virtuous—such as self-sacrificing sons, wives, brothers, and officials—drawing apothegms culled from thirty-two classical and medieval texts from the Han to the Song. After a thorough study, the young student would have achieved a strong sense of self-discipline, order, and degree, a responsiveness to others, and unselfishness.

Ch'unhyang probably read other conduct books such as *Naehun* (Instructions for the Inner Quarters; 1574, 1611) by Queen Sohye (1437-1504),[173] *Samgang haengsil to* (Illustrated Conduct of the Three Bonds; 1431), and *Sok samgang haengsil to* (Illustrated Conduct of the Three Bonds Continued; 1514), which presents twenty-eight examples of faithful women to suggest the cult of chaste wife or widow. *Instructions for the Inner Quarters*, made up of selections from four basic Confucian texts, comprises seven chapters: speech and comportment; filial piety; marriage; husband and wife; motherhood; amiability; and thrift. History presents cultural models

---

172. M. Theresa Kelleher, "Back to Basics: Chu Hsi's *Elementary Learning* (*Hsiao-hsüeh*)" in *Neo-Confucian Education: The Formative Stage*, ed. Wm Theodore de Bary and John W. Chaffee (Berkeley: University of California Press, 1987), 219-51. King Yŏngjo translated the text into Korean (1744). See Yves Hervouet, ed., *A Sung Bibliography* (Hong Kong: Chinese University Press, 1978), 233-235.

173. John Duncan, "The *Naehun* and the Politics of Gender in 15th-Century Korea," in *Creative Women of Korea: The Fifteenth Through the Twentieth Centuries*, ed. Young-Key Kim-Renaud (Armonk, N.Y.: M. E. Sharpe, 2004), 26-57.

of acceptable femininity, which helped Ch'unhyang to construct her own conception of sexuality. Ch'unhyang has internalized behavioral patterns from exemplary women in mythology, romance, and history. Her understanding of her body, desire, and pleasure, as well as her ability to express emotional intimacy, seems to indicate that she exercised some agency within the limits of asymmetry in sex roles and gender relations and made interiority the source of her emotional spontaneity and daily conduct.

⤴

Meanwhile, Yi's father, the current magistrate of Namwŏn, is appointed Sixth Royal Secretary (*Tongbu sŭngji*; 3a) in Seoul and orders his son to depart the following day ahead of him. Yi tells his mother about Ch'unhyang only to be scolded, then goes to her house. At first Ch'unhyang suggests that he go first and she will follow. But Yi tells her that they have to part, because if their love becomes known at court, he will not be accepted. At this, Ch'unhyang loses her temper, wails, and protests. Yi tries to devise a futile means to smuggle her into the palanquin with the ancestral tablets. Resigning herself to the inevitable, she offers her beloved a cup of wine before he mounts his horse. She then sings the "Song of Parting," each word ending in *chŏl* 絶 (*jue*: break off, cut off) and another homonym, *chŏl* 節 (*jie*: chastity, moral integrity). After joy comes sorrow; after the bitter, the sweet, an adage says. Ch'unhyang spends her time praying and grieving.

SONG OF PARTING

Love,
Tell me, when are you coming back?
Cut off without news for four seasons—*sajŏl*
I send you off for a long farewell—*yŏngjŏl*
Green bamboo and pine, the lasting loyalty of Bo Yi and Shu

Qi[174]—*ch'ungjŏl*

No bird flies over a thousand hills[175]—*chobijŏl*

Lying in sickness cut off from others—*insajŏl*

Joints of bamboo—*chukchŏl;* joints of pine trunk—*songjŏl*

Spring, summer, autumn, and winter—four seasons—*sajŏl*

Severance—*tanjŏl*

Division—*punjŏl*

Forgoing my integrity—*hwejŏl*

My love leaves me and ruthlessly departs—*pakchŏl*

My hopeless chastity—*chŏngjŏl*

When I sleep alone in an empty room—*sujŏl*

Shall I ever think of forgoing my integrity—*p'ajŏl*

Details of my grievance, my sad unswerving loyalty—*kojŏl*

Night and day my thoughts never cease—*mijŏl*

I beg you not to leave me without news—*tonjŏl.*

❧

After some months, a new magistrate, Pyŏn Hakto, is appointed. The narrator enumerates his faults: he behaves irresponsibly, forgets his morals, makes errors of judgment. At the first staff meeting, Pyŏn inquires about Ch'unhyang. His curiosity has been kindled by rumors about her beauty. The first item on his official agenda is to inspect all entertainers registered in his town. Each is called to present herself for his review. After a survey of eighteen girls, Pyŏn notices that Ch'unhyang's name is not on the list and asks her whereabouts.

The head of slaves answers: "Ch'unhyang's mother was a female entertainer, but Ch'unhyang herself is not. She is so virtuous and beautiful that when the literati from powerful clans, talented writers, and officials visit here, they ask to see her; but mother and

---

174. They disapproved of the Zhou conquest of their overlord the Shang king and retired to Shouyang mountain where they died of starvation. *Shiji*, 61:2121-2129 and Birrell, 58-59, 220-221.

175. Liu Zongyuan, "Jiangxue," *Quan Tangshi* 352:3961.

daughter refuse. Not only the literati but even those who live in her neighborhood may see her only once in ten years, much less speak to her. . . . It seems that through heaven's predestined bond, your predecessor's son met her and pledged a hundred years' love to her. When he left Namwŏn, he said he would come to fetch her after he had been appointed to office, and Ch'unhyang believes him and remains faithful to him."

Then the chief clerk in the personnel section speaks: "Not only is Ch'unhyang not an entertainer, but her betrothal to the former magistrate's son is a serious matter. Although your ages are different, please summon her as one of the same social class as yourself. Otherwise we fear you may damage your honor as an official."

Ch'unhyang's reputation as a faithful and cloistered wife of Yi Mongnyong is known to the public; but Pyŏn orders his men to cut the chatter and fetch her at once. While soldiers are on their way to Ch'unhyang's house, she sings the "Song of Mutual Love."

SONG OF MUTUAL LOVE

I want to go, I want to go,
I want to follow my love,
I'll go a thousand tricents,
Ten thousand tricents,
I'll brave storm and rain,
Scale the high peaks,
Where even wild falcons, tamed falcons,
Peregrine falcons, trained falcons rest
Beyond Tongsŏn Pass.
If he'll come and look for me,
I'll take off my shoes,
Carry them in my hands,
Race to him without pause.
My husband in Seoul,

Does he think of me?

Has he forgotten me utterly?

Has he taken another love?

Her song includes a well-known *sasŏl sijo*,[176] a form of *sijo* in which more than two metric segments are added in each line, except for the first in the third line:

Pass where the winds pause before they cross,

Pass where the clouds pause before they cross,

The pass of Changsŏng Ridge

Where wild-born falcons,

Tamed falcons,

Peregrine falcons,

And yearling falcons pause before they cross—

If they said my love was over the pass,

I would cross it without a pause.

Another *sasŏl sijo:*

I take off my shoes to

Clutch in my hand,

My socks in my arms, then helter-skelter

Scurrying, hurrying,

Without a moment's rest,

I struggle up. . . .

When the soldiers arrive, Ch'unhyang serves them wine and gives them some money before going to the yamen. Pyŏn orders her to come up on the dais and then tells her to "attend on [him] in the yamen," a euphemism. His banter with the treasurer whom he

---

176. No. 1113 in Sim Chaewan, which has Changsŏng Pass; see Peter H. Lee, *The Columbia Anthology of Traditional Korean Poetry*, 152; for part of another *sijo* (no. 752) cited, see 156.

asks to serve as his matchmaker infuriates her. Pyŏn even goes to the length of pointing out the generational gap between himself— worldly and experienced—and Ch'unhyang's husband, a "mere boy" (*tongja nom*), thus placing himself in a different chronotope from that of Ch'unhyang and Yi. Ch'unhyang answers that she is married and would rather die than serve him. Now let us examine how she defends her decision.

To the magistrate: "Your commands overwhelm me, but since I wish to have only one husband, I cannot carry out your order. A loyal subject cannot serve two kings, and a chaste wife cannot have two husbands[177]—that is my principle. I would rather die than live on, however many times you ask me. Please deal with me as you see fit."

A pipsqueak official chimes in: "What do you singing girls know about fidelity and chastity? What have loyalty and chastity to do with a lowly person like you?" (The words simply steel her resolve and determination.)

To the official: "Loyalty, filial piety, and chastity are the same for both high and low. Please, listen, I will explain. Let's speak of female entertainers. There are no virtuous ones, you say; but I will cite them to you one by one. Nongsŏn 弄仙 of Hwanghae province died at Tongsŏn Pass; an entertainer of Sŏnch'ŏn, a mere girl, learned all about the seven wifely conditions; Nongae 論介 of Chinju is known as a patriot, and a memorial gate was erected to her where sacrifices are offered forever. Hwawŏl 花月 of Ch'ŏngju had a three-story tower raised in her memory; Wŏlsŏn 月仙 of P'yŏngyang has a memorial gate for her patriotism; Ilchihong 一枝 紅 of Andong had a memorial gate erected in her lifetime and was ennobled. So please don't belittle female entertainers."

To Pyŏn: "Even a mighty man like Meng Ben[178] could not wrest from me my resolve, high as Mount Tai and deep as the Yellow Sea, that I made to my young master Yi. The eloquence of

177. *Shiji* 82:2457.
178. A warrior of Qi who is said to have plucked the horns of an ox.

331

Su Qin and Zhang Yi[179] could not move my heart; Zhuge Liang's tactic[180] could summon the southeast wind to turn the tide of battle, but he could not make me bow to authority. Xu You[181] would not bend his will to Yao; Bo Yi and Shu Qi on Mount Shouyang would not eat the grain of Zhou. Were it not for Xu You, there would be no one to transcend the mundane world. Were it not for Bo Yi and Shu Qi, there would be many more traitors and outlaws. I may be of humble birth, but how could I not know these examples? If I betray my husband and become your concubine, it would be treason just as if a minister were to forget the state and betray his king. Please, deal with me as you see fit."

Again to Pyŏn: "If the rape of a married woman is not a crime, what is?"

When the fawning treasurer asks, "What have loyalty and faithfulness to do with a lowly person like you?" he is putting the Confucian virtue of chastity on trial. Is it a privilege for women of certain classes or for all women? Moral values transcend social status. All human beings, regardless of gender, have moral autonomy. At this affront, Ch'unhyang cites names from history as evidence that no force, eloquence, or strategy will work. Ch'unhyang is a woman who talks back—she resists the designs Pyŏn has on her body through direct defiance. She wishes to die rather than dishonor her husband. Note her unabashed directness of speech: "If the rape of a married woman is not a crime, what is?"

A magistrate rules not by law and punishment but by virtue, and guides by personal example. Having internalized social virtues expounded in the Confucian canon, which he must have studied for the civil service examinations, he is to develop such

179. Su Qin (d. 317 B.C.) and Zhang Yi (d. 309 B.C.) are renowned traveling persuaders during the Warring States period (403-221 B.C.). For Su see *Shiji* 69:2241-77, and for Zhang, *Shiji* 70:2279-2305.

180. Zhuge Liang (181-234), the counselor and a commander of military campaigns for Liu Bei, considered the greatest strategist of China. *Sanguozhi* 35: 911-937.

181. When Emperor Yao wished to make Xu his successor, he went into hiding. At the emperor's second offer, he went to the Ying River to cleanse his ears.

virtues in his people. The health of a community depends on the moral health of its magistrate, and the cultivation of moral standards, especially *ren* (benevolence, goodness, love), "to love human beings" (*Analects* 12:22), is the basis of human relations. A magistrate has the opportunity to inspire and guide his people to the good by his moral example. Unselfish magnanimity and the impartial administration of justice are the sine qua non of a humane government. But instead of providing protection and safety to his people, Pyŏn's deeds and passions poison them. He looks at Ch'unhyang with a predatory gaze of masculine domination and reduces her identity to the eroticized body alone. By ordering an excessively disproportionate punishment, not sanctioned by the state code, for what he labels "her disobedience and humiliation of an official," he threatens to contravene the stability of Namwŏn society. He attempts to transform a wife into an adulteress but realizes that he cannot budge her fidelity, not even "with a team of horses."[182] No longer the central symbol of order in his community, he becomes the source of disruption and injustice: he violates the three bonds and five relations, especially the centrality of marriage, the sanctity of the family, and the stability of society. Only the king's secret agent can punish this man's corrupt use of power and restore order and harmony to society.

Keep in mind that Ch'unhyang cannot temporize before a magistrate who stands for authority and whose mind is focused only on his aggressive desire. She is at a great disadvantage given the constraints intrinsic to this kind of interrogation. Penelope, by contrast, during her husband's twenty-year absence invents such ruses as the deceit of the loom and the contest of the bow and axehead to forestall her 108 suitors; Lucretia has at least two days before her decision to stab herself; Tomi's wife over several months' time inventively avoids the royal advance. Ch'unhyang's refusal,

---

182. Virginia Woolf, *To the Lighthouse*, ed. Margaret Drabble (Oxford: Clarendon, 1992), 231.

termed "suicidal"[183] by one reader, turns the interrogation into a public spectacle, and her voice dominates the scene.

"If the rape of a married woman is not a crime, what is?" The meanings of the original *kŏpt'al* 劫奪, here translated as "rape,"[184] include plunder, robbery, seizing a person by force, abduction by violence, and rape. Ch'unhyang here reminds Pyŏn, a member of the corrupt bureaucracy, of the consequences of the cross-class forced coitus committed by the upper-class male against the female slave or entertainer: the only extramarital relation allowed for men of the upper class in the Chosŏn dynasty was with a slave or entertainer. As chattel, slaves were bought and sold, bequeathed and exchanged, and their status by law was hereditary. They had no surnames. As the hands and feet of the ruling class, slaves were crucial to the economy and lifestyle of the elite. Forced coitus was systemic, as long as the upper-class male retained hegemony, and the relationship was that between oppressor and victim. Reduced to the status of an object, slaves were prey for the appetite of their masters. The damage done to these women by the prevailing gender and status hierarchy is unimaginable. No study thus far has scrutinized the double standard of sexual morality (adultery is permissible for men, forbidden for women) as a prevailing gender system with embedded assumptions. Indeed, violence against the rapable body pervaded Korean society until the end of the nineteenth century.

The slave population—both official (governmental) and private—declined from 30 percent in the early seventeenth century to below 10 percent by 1780. In 1801 the government manumitted almost all official slaves; in 1886 hereditary slavery was abolished; finally, in 1894, the institution of private slavery came to an end. From

---

183. Kim Tonguk, Ch'unhyang chŏn *yŏngu* (Yondae ch'ulp'anbu, 1965), 42.
184. I have borrowed some terms from Elizabeth Robertson and Christine M. Rose, eds., *Representing Rape in Medieval and Early Modern Literature* (New York: Palgrave, 2001); and Kathryn Gravdal, *Ravishing Maidens: Writing Rape in Medieval French Literature and Law* (Philadelphia: University of Pennsylvania Press, 1991).

the seventeenth century such enlightened scholars as Yu Hyŏngwŏn (1622-1673), Yi Ik (1681-1763), and Yu Suwŏn (1694-1775) indicted the evils of hereditary slavery,[185] including starvation, hardship, unremitting labor, and harassment.[186] In a mixed slave/commoner marriage, children followed the status of their mother (matrilineal succession law of 1039) or their fathers of noble or commoner status. After numerous changes between the matrilineal and patrilineal succession laws, depending on the increase or decrease of tax revenues (slaves did not pay taxes), the matrilineal succession was reinstated in 1731. Hundreds of thousands of female slaves were culturally invisible and voiceless, unless their offspring became known as the subject of history (Sin Ton, d. 1371), romance (Hwang Chini, ca. 1506-1544), or contemporary TV drama series (King Sejong's consort, née Kim, and King Chŏngjo's consort, née Song).

Discrimination against the sons and daughters from such alliances—the illegitimate or secondary children—was harsh and relentless.[187] Secondary sons were barred from the higher civil service examinations and prohibited from using their talents in the service of the state. They had to accept inferior social status before a legitimate half-brother and could not address their father as "Father," as the eponymous hero in the "Tale of Hong Kiltong" illustrates (he was the offspring of Minister Hong and his maidservant Ch'unsŏm). Some secondary daughters became renowned entertainers, for example Hwang Chini and Yi Okpong in the late sixteenth century.[188] Institutionalized inequality, a

185. For slavery see Yi Sŏngmu, *Chosŏn yangban sahoe yŏngu* (Ilchogak, 1995), 306-365; Yŏksa hakhoe, ed., *Nobi, noye—yesongmin ŭi pigyosa* (Ilchogak, 1998); Ellen J. Kim, "The Enduring Institution: A Case Study of Slavery in Traditional Korea," B.A. thesis, Harvard College, 1991; James B. Palais, "Slave Society," in *Views on Korean Social History* (Institute for Modern Korean Studies, Yonsei University, 1998), 23-47; *Hanguk minjok taepaekkwa sajŏn*, 27 vols. (Sŏngnam: 1991), 5:679c-688c; and Lee, *Sourcebook of Korean Civilization*, 1:326-28; 2:178-192.

186. *Sourcebook of Korean Civilization*, 2:182.

187. Lee, *Sourcebook of Korean Civilization*, 1:565-56; 2:192-207.

188. A secondary daughter is said to have exchanged poems with Chŏng Ch'ŏl (1536-93) and Yi Hangbok (1556-1618). *Karim sego* contains thirty-five poems. Kang-I Sun Chang and Haun Saussy, eds., *Women Writers of Traditional China: An Anthology of Poetry and Criticism* (Stanford: Stanford University Press, 1999), 215-217.

form of domination, can be maintained only by the exercise of force. Legitimacy is an ideology created by the oppressors. Again Yi Suwŏn laments the restrictions on the sons of concubines: "A person's capabilities should be determined more by his own efforts than by his bloodline." In 1568, Sin Yu and sixteen hundred other secondary sons presented a written complaint seeking redress for the restrictions imposed against them; in 1695, Nam Kŭkchŏng and nearly a thousand others from the southeastern part of the country did the same;[189] and in 1769 Yi Sudŭk (1697-1775) memorialized the throne on behalf of secondary sons.[190] This social injustice lasted until 1894 when the status system was finally repealed. Ch'unhyang is herself a secondary daughter of Minister Sŏng and Wŏlmae, a former female entertainer.

⸺

The soldiers drag Ch'unhyang down to the courtyard and throw her on the ground. Pyŏn orders them to "bind her to the chair, break her shinbones, and submit a report of her execution." That is, he wishes not only to leave permanent marks of torture on her body but also to club her to death (*mulgo* 物故).[191] Her crime is to have disobeyed and humiliated an official. His act of retaliation, however, is not commensurate with the situation. Torture is something that a public authority does or condones.[192] Here the torment is inflicted by a public authority for personal gratification. The jailor begins to flog her with the club (a thorn branch, gnarls and joints removed). At each stroke, she shouts out her response, punning on each count—one for *one* sincere firm heart; a chaste wife does not serve *two* husbands; *three* bonds; *four* classes/limbs; *five* relations/elements; and the like:

---

189. *Sourcebook of Korean Civilization*, 2:202.
190. Lee, *Sourcebook of Korean Civilization*, 2:204-207.
191. *Kyŏngguk taejŏn*, 2:167 and n. 374.
192. Edward Peters, *Torture* (New York: Blackwell, 1985), 3.

SONG OF TEN STROKES

One sincere and firm heart
Is to follow *one* husband.
One punishment
Before *one* year's over,
But not for a moment will I change.

A chaste wife does not serve *two* husbands—
Hence there can't be *two* husbands.
Though beaten and left for dead,
I'll never forget Master Yi.

"*Three* Dependencies" is a heavy law;
I know *three* bonds and five relations.
Though I am punished and exiled *three* times,
I'll never forget my husband—
Master Yi of Samch'ŏng Street.

A magistrate, a king's official,

Disregards the affairs of *four* classes;

He rules exercising his power,

Doesn't know the people

In forty-eight wards of Namwŏn resent him.

Even if you sever my *four* limbs,

I'll live and die with my husband,

Whom I cannot forget in life or death.

The *five* relations remain unbroken;

Husband and wife have separate duties.

Our tie, sealed by the *five* elements,

Cannot be torn apart.

Sleeping or waking,

I cannot forget my husband.

The autumn moon on the phoenix tree

Is watching over my love.

Will a letter come today?

Will news come tomorrow?

My innocent body

Does not deserve death.

Don't convict me unjustly—

Aego, aego, my lot!

Six times *six* is thirty-*six*—

Investigate every detail and

Kill me *six*ty thousand times;

Six thousand joints in my body

Are all tied by love—

My heart cannot be changed.

Have I committed the *seven* wifely faults?

Why should I receive *seven* punishments?

With a *seven*-foot sword,

Cut me up

And kill me quickly.

Bureau of Punishment,

Don't hesitate when you strike,

I, all *seven* jewels of my face, die!

This fortunate Ch'unhyang's body

Met a renowned official

Among magistrates of *eight* provinces.

Governors and magistrates of *eight* provinces—

You're sent to rule the people,

Not to inflict cruel punishments.

In the *nine* bends of my bowels and innards,

My tears will make a *nine*-year flood.

With tall pines on the *nine* hills[193]

I'll build a boat for a clear river,

Go quickly to Seoul,

Lay my case before the king

In the *nine*fold palace;

I'll then step down *nine* steps,

Go to Samch'ŏng Street,

Meet my love joyfully

And vent my grudge

Tied in knots.

Though I live *ten* times,

After escaping death nine times,

My mind is made up for eighty years—

A hundred thousand deaths

Won't change it,

193. *Book of Songs* 184:1 (Arthur Waley, *The Book of Songs* [London: Allen & Unwin, 1954], 158).

Will never change it.

Young Ch'unhyang, just sixteen,

How sad the wronged wretch beaten to death!

The full moon

(opposite)   Is hidden in the clouds,

From   My husband in Seoul

Okchunghwa,   Has withdrawn to Samch'ŏng Street—

n.p, n.d.   Moon, moon, do you see him?

Why can I not see where he is?

Playing the zither of *twenty-five* strings in the moonlight,[194]

I cannot restrain my sorrow.

Wild goose, where are you going?

On your way to Seoul,

Take a message to my beloved

Who lives in Samch'ŏng Street.

Note every detail of how I look now,

Do not, by any means, forget.

Note the public exposure of her body and the violence against her—as if a chaste wife deserves torture. One of the effects of torture is to disable language in the victim,[195] but Ch'unhyang interrupts the scene of violence with words addressed to her torturers and spectators. Although Pyŏn conspires to deny her any capacity for agency, Ch'unhyang refuses to be a passive victim of

---

194. Qian Qi, "Gueiyan," *Quan Tangshi* 239:2680. Guillaume de Machaut (ca. 1300-77) compares his lady's *gent corps* to "the 25 strings that a harp has" (17). Bruce W. Holsinger, in *Music, Body, and Desire in Medieval Culture: Hildegard of Bingen to Chaucer* (Stanford: Stanford University Press, 2001), comments on "pain's fundamental audibility . . . that produce[s] sounds that can be heard and felt" (192-94), "a commonplace association between torture and song" (198), and "devotional writers [who] imagined . . . the unique propensity of musical sonority to embody and channel extreme somatic experience, particularly pain" (208). Here one can say that unremittant percussive beatings felt by Ch'unhyang's body in pain produce her song.

195. Elaine Scarry, *The Body in Pain: The Making and Unmaking of the World* (New York: Oxford University Press, 1985), 3-5 and 35.

patriarchal violence and resists objectification through language. She presents herself as a moral agent accountable for her actions. How beautiful is death, she cries, when earned by virtue. She calls upon heaven to testify to her fidelity. The body in pain is the seat of resistance on which multiple meanings can be inscribed. Her sheer strength, stamina, and endurance are remarkable; her resistant female voice makes every spectator weep. She is beaten twenty-five times—her white body is covered with blood, and she faints. Blood could serve as a sign of innocence or culpability: here she must bleed for love to uphold fidelity. The narrator allows her to enjoy sympathy and affirmation from those outside—the *p'ansori* audience. No listener will want to forgive Pyŏn his perverse pleasure in inflicting pain on a frail body.

Pyŏn orders soldiers to put Ch'unhyang in a cangue and take her to prison. Violence against women is "represented not as it is suffered by women but as it is recognized by men. . . . The language of suffering is masculine."[196] Chastity is a virtue defined by men as well, constructed by male upholders of Confucian ideology and morality. The narrator can cause Ch'unhyang to perish in order to be sanctified and compensated by a moral reward—her gate marked and included in a conduct book illustrating the three bonds. As virgin martyrs endure torture for the faith, so Ch'unhyang prizes her chastity so highly, "a dearer thing than life" (*The Rape of Lucrece* 687), that she is willing to die for it. The threat to her body and her fidelity opens a space for female heroism. She is bound to be interpellated by Confucian ideology. Her chastity, a cultural construct, is a product of her classical upbringing.

"In what voice do female virgin martyrs speak—their own, those of their authors or readers, or voices continuous with the language of their oppressors?" asks Robert Mills in his article "Can the Virgin Martyrs Speak?"[197] Ch'unhyang, according to her mother,

196. Anna Roberts, ed., *Violence Against Women in Medieval Texts* (Gainesville: University of Florida Press, 1998), 10, 11.
197. Robert Mills, "Can the Virgin Martyrs Speak?" in *Medieval Virginities*, ed. Anke Bernau et al. (Cardiff: University of Wales Press, 2003), 179.

studied *Elementary Learning* at seven, which suggests that she began her studies at four or at the latest five—she had to start with the *Thousand-Sinograph Primer* and two or three other didactic texts. When Princess Hyegyŏng (1735-1815), at age nine, was chosen to marry the crown prince, her future father-in-law King Yŏngjo told her: "We'll send you a copy of *Elementary Learning*. Study it with your father and be happy until you return again to us."[198] On the walls of Ch'unhyang's room, we recall, Yi finds her composition, a pentasyllabic couplet in Chinese: "Elegant bamboo rustles in the spring breeze, / Burning incense, I read books at night." Yi reads these two lines as her credo showing the constancy of a girl who will serve only one husband. Her ability to make allusions to classical writers and understand them indicates her reading, including perhaps some chrestomathies: anthologies of passages in verse and prose for literary and moral studies. Her four walls are covered with paintings illustrating Li Bo (701-762), known as a banished transcendent delighting in the moon and wine; Li He (790-816), who is sometimes compared to Keats and Mallarmé for his precocity; and Yan Guang, who renounced the world to live in harmony with nature. She contemplates and appreciates them as capable of illustrating certain moral and esthetic principles, as she applies herself diligently to cultivating herself. Thus Ch'unhyang is capable of composing impromptu responses to every stroke she receives in order to demonstrate her conviction to the magistrate, his staff, and the community.

Or is this simply the strategy of the literate redactor to reaffirm the importance of benevolent and just rule for the maintenance of society and culture; to advocate chastity and containment for women; or to glamorize suffering and make it seem like a privilege? This anonymous redactor, most likely male, must have spent many years at study and passed or failed the civil

---

198. For Princess Hyegyŏng (later Queen Kyŏngŭi), see Peter H. Lee, ed., *Anthology of Korean Literature: From Early Times to the Nineteenth Century* (Honolulu: University of Hawaii Press, 1990), 142.

service examinations; but in nineteenth-century Korea perhaps he could not find a job and as a member of the lumpen intelligentsia wished to vent his frustrations against the court and society. If he was not starving, this song was composed as a pastime; if he was starving, it was a potboiler. Whatever the circumstances, he did write a work that is read and reread and studied.

Let us dwell a bit longer on this crucial scene that made Ch'unhyang the first Korean woman character who values love and virtue more than life. Magistrate Pyŏn, who says he has heard her name—then only a sign and absent figure of his fantasy—thinks that she is an entertainer like her mother and therefore must serve him. He insults her as "a willow spray or a roadside flower that any passerby can pluck" and demands that she abandon her integrity. Portrayed as a typical bureaucrat who indulges in extortion and plunder (the text explores the impoverished ethos of the ruling class and indicts the corrupt system—the organized brutality of the status quo), he tramples upon human rights. He is portrayed as a conflicted lover/torturer—torn between desire and dominance.

Ch'unhyang's resistance, by contrast, is against one who hinders her enduring love for her husband. She wishes to preserve the dignity of a married woman. Not to marry twice, or not to serve two husbands, was a general norm of Confucian morality—indeed, Confucian discourse emphasized it for several centuries. Even a lowborn has the freedom to maintain human dignity.

Literature offers examples of similar attempts at rape—beautiful married women who refuse a powerful man's attempt to seduce them. Tomi's wife defends her chastity with her life.[199] When King Kaeru (128-166) of Paekche cannot have her, he has Tomi's eyes gouged out and sets him adrift on the river. After putting off the king one last time, the wife escapes and finds her husband. In the story of Peach Blossom Girl and King Chinji (576-579) of

---

199. *Samguk sagi* 48:446-447.

Silla,[200] the girl says to the king: "It is not a woman's way to serve two husbands. To have a husband of my own and to accept yet another, this even a king with all his majesty cannot force upon me." Only after the death of her own husband and the king does she allow the king's spirit to enter her bedroom.

Pyŏn's violence against Ch'unhyang makes her the utter model of chastity, a paragon of womanly perfection. In this extreme situation she confronts his tyranny and testifies to her authenticity. With her virtue publicly recognized by the community and later by her own husband, spectators try to identify themselves with her, especially because they cannot imitate her deed. Eventually her status and virtue are recognized by the king, who confers on her the title of *chŏngnyŏl puin*, "a lady who is ready to die to preserve her chastity."[201] Indeed, Ch'unhyang single-handedly invented the discourse of chastity in Korean literature, especially in *p'ansori*. She answers the audience's emotional needs—sing me a song about a woman with defiant devotion to the claims of love. In the prologue to *Tristan*, Gottfried von Strassburg (died ca. 1210) comments that his work "will make love lovable, ennoble the mind, fortify constancy, and enrich their lives."[202] In her thirty-eight-line speech, Francesca da Rimini in Circle 2 (lust) utters a moving verse, "Love, which absolves no one beloved from loving" ("Amor, che a nullo amato amar perdona") (*Inferno* 5:103),[203] whose deep meaning Ch'unhyang would have understood.

In prison Ch'unhyang sings:

---

200. *Samguk yusa*, ed. Ch'oe Namsŏn (Minjung sŏgwan, 154), 1:56.

201. The 1754 version says, "She offers worship at the Yi clan's ancestral shrine (180b) and becomes a sister-in-law of the noble women (that is, whose husbands serve as royal secretaries or special advisors; 181a-b) of the Yi household." See Sŏng Hyŏngyŏng, "Ch'unhyang ŭi sinbun pyŏni kwajŏng yŏngu," in *Hanguk Kojŏn sosŏl kwa sŏsa munhak*, 1:417-430.

202. Stephen C. Jaeger, *Ennobling Love: In Search of a Lost Sensibility* (Philadelphia: University of Pennsylvania Press, 1999), 192.

203. Robert and Jean Hollander, *Dante Alighieri: Inferno* (New York: Doubleday, 2000), 89.

What Was My Crime?

AZALEA

The Road to
Ch'unhyang:
Peter H. Lee

What was my crime?

I've not stolen government grain.

Why was I beaten so savagely?

I've not killed anyone.

Why was I put in a yoke and fettered?

I've not plotted a rebellion,

Why was I bound hand and foot?

I've not committed adultery.

What is this punishment for?

The waters of three rivers for ink,

The blue sky for paper,

I'll protest my sorrow

And petition the Jade Emperor.

My heart burns with longing for my husband.

My sigh becomes a wind

That blows those flames;

I shall die in vain.

That single chrysanthemum,

Its constancy is great!

The green pine in the snow

Has kept faith for myriad years.

The green pine is like me,

The yellow chrysanthemum like my husband.

My sad thoughts—

What I shed are tears,

What soak me are sighs.

My sighs as a wind,

My tears as a drizzle,

The wind will drive the mizzling rain,

Blowing and splashing

To wake my beloved.

Herd Boy and Weaver Maid,

Meeting on the seventh night,

Never broke a promise

Even when the Silver River blocked them.

What water then divides me

From where my husband is?

I never hear news from him.

Rather than live in longing,

It's better to die and forget him—

Better to die

And become a cuckoo in the empty hills,

At the third watch when

The pear blossoms are white beneath the moon,

To sing sadly in my husband's ears;

Or become a mandarin duck on the clear river,

Calling in search of its mate,

And show him

My love and tender feelings;

Or become a butterfly in spring

With two scented wings,

Glorying in the spring sun,

And settle on his clothes;

Or become a bright moon in the sky,

Rising when night comes

And shedding my bright light

On my beloved's face.

With stagnant blood from my innards

I'd draw his likeness,

Hang it as a scroll on my door

To see it when I go in and out.

A peerless beauty, chaste and faithful,

Has been treated cruelly.

Like white jade of Mount Jing[204]

204. *Han Feizi* 4:13-14; Burton Watson, *Han Fei Tzu: Basic Writings* (New York: Columbia University Press, 1964), 80-83.

Buried in dirt,

Like a fragrant herb of Mount Shang[205]

Buried in weeds,

Like a phoenix that played in the pawlonia

Making its nest in the thorn patch . . .

From olden days sages and worthies

Died innocent—

Benevolent rulers Yao, Shun, Yu, Tang

Were imprisoned

By evil Jie and Zhou[206]

But were set free and became holy lords.

King Wen of Zhou,

Who ruled the people with bright virtue,

Was imprisoned in Yuli by Zhou of Shang.[207]

Confucius, greatest of all the sages,

Because he looked like Yang Huo,

Was imprisoned in Kongye,[208]

But he became a great sage—

When I think of these things,

Will my innocent body

Live to see the world again?

Stifling sorrow!

Who will come to rescue me?

Would my husband in Seoul

Come here as an official

And save me

Close to death?

Summer clouds on strange peaks[209]—

---

205. Four white beards retired to Shangshan at the end of the Qin. *Shiji* 55:2044-2045.

206. Jie is the bad last ruler of Xia; Zhou is the bad last ruler of Shang.

207. Birrell, 110-12, 239-60.

208. Yanghuo seized power in Lu (505 B.C.) and the people of Kuang mistook Confucius for Yang. *Shiji* 47: 1930; *Analects* 9:5 (Waley 139, 244-45).

209. "Summer clouds," supposed to be by Tao Qian in Ding Tinghu, *Tao Yuanming shijianzhu* (Taibei: Yiwen yinshuguan, 1960), 3:25.

Do the high hills block his way?

Will he come only when the highest peaks

Of the Diamond Mountains are flat?

Will he come only when at the fourth watch

A yellow crane painted on the screen

Stretches its wings

And caws at dawn?

Aego, *aego*, my wretched fate!

She is not a thief, rebel, or adulteress, but a victim of arbitrary
outrage. She compares herself to the green pine, an emblem of
integrity and constancy, and her husband to the chrysanthemum,
one of the four gentleman flowers known for the same qualities.
Her lot is worse than that of Herd Boy and Weaver Maid. Her
diction here recalls that of Chŏng Ch'ŏl (1537-1593) in his two
hymns to constancy[210] and that of Hŏ Nansŏrhŏn (1563-1585), the
author of "A Woman's Sorrow," a dramatic narrative in the *kasa*
form and a museum of topics.[211] She wishes for metamorphosis
in a dream or after death, then wishes to draw a portrait of her
husband with blood drawn from her innards. She likens herself to
white jade buried in dirt, a fragrant herb engulfed by weeds—no
one knows the difference because it is a world turned upside down,
where the phoenix makes its nest in the thorn patch rather than
in the paulownia, its tree of choice. She then cites examples from
history: the sage rulers Yao, Shun, and Tang (founder of the Shang),
imprisoned by the evil Jie and Zhou; King Wen, founder of the Zhou,
thrown in jail by the last evil king Zhou of the Shang; Confucius,
jailed after being mistaken for Yanghuo who had once created a
disturbance. Her only hope is her husband, who should come as
an official, for only such a person has the power to chastise the evil
magistrate Pyŏn. Her song ends with the topic of impossibility: the

210. Peter H. Lee, *Pine River and Lone Peak* (Honolulu: University of Hawaii
Press, 1991), 53-59.
211. Lee, *Anthology of Korean Literature*, 116-68.

Diamond Mountains becoming flat and a painted yellow crane, another symbol of the nobility of mind, crowing at dawn.

Chastity in women was valued in most times and cultures in the past, and women who violated it were threatened with death or shame. Penelope, the patient and devoted wife of Odysseus, is not convinced that the Cretan beggar is her husband until he can explain the secret of their bed—an olive tree whose trunk is used as a bedpost (*Odyssey* 23:188-204). In the *Heriodes* (The Heroines), Ovid's Penelope, however, is angry ("I'm stuck here in pseudo-widowhood / Forever") (105) and bitter ("Must I suppose you tell your beautiful / Mistresses what a frump your dutiful / wife is" (106) and ends the letter, "a girl the day you sailed away / You'd find a crone if you returned today" (107).[212] In Boccaccio's *De mulieribus claris* (Concerning Famous Women; ca. 1355-1359), Penelope is a "woman of untarnished honor and inviolate chastity and a holy and eternal example for women."[213] Christine de Pisan (1365-ca. 1431), in the *Livre de la Cité des Dames* (Book of the City of Ladies; ca. 1405), praises her as "wise, prudent, and devoted to the gods and to living virtuously."[214] Concerning Lucretia's wifely virtue and exemplary suicide after being raped, Laura speaks with her mother about her in Petrarch's *Canzoniere* 262:

> There never were,
>
> Mother, things dear or lovely without virtue,
>
> And anyone who lets herself lose honor
>
> Is not a woman and is not alive;
>
> Though she may look the same, her life's a death,
>
> Or worse than that, made bitter by her sorrow. (3-8)[215]

212. Daryl Hines, *Ovid's Heriodes: A Verse Translation of the* Heroides (New Haven: Yale University Press, 1991), 105-07.

213. Guido A. Guarino, trans., *Concerning Famous Women* (London: Allen & Unwin, 1964), 81.

214. Earl Jeffrey Richards, trans., *The Book of the City of Ladies* (New York: Persea Books, 1982), 158. For a study of this work see Maureen Quilligan, *The Allegory of Female Authority: Christine de Pisan's* Cité des Dames (Ithaca: Cornell University Press, 1991).

215. David Young, trans., *The Poetry of Petrarch* (New York: Farrar, Straus, &

Boccaccio calls her "the outstanding model of Roman chastity and sacred glory of ancient virtue, who cleansed her shame harshly, and for this reason she should be exalted with worthy praise for her chastity, which can never be sufficiently lauded."[216] Lady Rectitude speaks with de Pisan's persona about sexual violence: "Chaste ladies who live honestly take absolutely no pleasure in being raped. Indeed rape is the greatest possible sorrow for them."[217] She adds: "Many women are loved for their virtues more than other women for their prettiness."[218] In *The Legend of Good Women* (1386), Chaucer comments: "For the praise and the remembered glory / Of that true wife Lucrece, whose faithfulness / To vows of wifehood and great steadfastness / Won praise not just from pagans for her deed / But also from the one called in our creed / Augustine."[219]

⏝

While dozing in prison, Ch'unhyang has a dream of flying myriad tricents to the south. In a quiet bamboo grove among beautiful hills and waters, she sees a temple with a plaque in golden letters, "Temple of the Yellow Tumulus: Shrine of All Faithful Women." There she meets Lu Zhu, favorite wife of Shi Chong (249-300); Nongae, the Chinju entertainer who, during the Japanese invasion in 1592, threw herself into the river with a Japanese captain in her arms;[220] and Wŏlsŏn, the P'yongyang entertainer who sacrificed herself to help a Korean general kill an enemy commander.[221] They lead her to the inner sanctum of the temple where two women in white robes take her hands and ask her to

Giroux, 2004), 186.

216. Guarino, 101. See Ian Donaldson, *The Rape of Lucrece: A Myth and Its Transformation* (Oxford: Clarendon, 1982).

217. Richards, 161.

218. Richards, 206.

219. Ann McMillan, *Legends of Good Women* (Houston: Rice University Press, 1987), 120.

220. See n. 133.

221. Kim Ŭngsŏ kills her from fear of being discovered by Japanese soldiers. See Lee, *The Record of the Black Dragon Year*, 22-23, 74-78.

the dais, which she twice declines. At the third urging, Ch'unhyang goes up and takes a seat. The two ladies tell her that when they attended the heavenly court by Jasper Lake, they heard so much about Ch'unhyang that they wished to see her. Ch'unhyang bows and replies: "Although I am ignorant, I have read in old books that after death I might meet you." Still she is puzzled why she is there. Two Shang queens, Fairy Radiance and Maiden Bloom, Lord Shun's consorts, know and commend Ch'unhyang's constancy—she is equal to these ladies canonized in mythology and literature. Ch'unhyang also meets the spirits of Nongyu 弄玉, the daughter of Duke Mu of Qin (r. 659-21 B.C.), Brilliant Consort Wang and Lady Qi 戚夫人 (d. 194 B.C.), Han Kaozu's favorite. Then Fairy Radiance sends her away, and Ch'unhyang wakes up with a start. Was it a vision, or a waking dream? This episode resonates with allusions to antiquity's exemplary women.

When a blind man passes by the prison, Ch'unhyang asks him to divine her fortune:

SONG OF A BLIND MAN'S DIVINATION

To the constant and worthy Diviner,
I express my respect and pray.
What would heaven say?
What would earth say?
But you'll respond if I knock,
Spirit is wondrous,
Please feel and let me communicate.
Because we won't know good and bad luck
And can't resolve our doubts,
You spirits, I hope, will bestow clear guidance.
Please tell us whether it is right or wrong,
And respond at once when I knock.
Fuxi, King Wen, King Wu, Duke of Shao,[222]

---

222. Duke of Shao (fl. 841 B.C.), King Wen's secondary son.

Duke of Zhou,[223] Confucius, five great sages,[224]

Seventy-two worthies,[225]

Yan Hui,[226] Tsengcan,[227] Zisi,[228] Mencius,

Ten worthy disciples of Confucius,

Zhuge Liang, Li Shunfeng,[229]

Cheng Hao[230] and Cheng Yi,[231]

Shao Yung,[232] Zhou Dunyi,[233]

Zhu Xi,[234] Yan Junping,[235]

Sima Guang,[236] Master Gueigu,[237]

Sun Bin,[238] Su Qin, Zhang Yi,

Wang Bi,[239] Zhu Yuanzhang,[240] Liu Bei,[241]

Hemp-robed Master of Dao, dark daughters of nine heavens,

Divine generals Liuding and Liujia,[242]

You know intuitively, so together help us.

---

223. Duke of Zhou (d. 1094 B.C.) helped the founders of Zhou.

224. Probably refers to Yellow Emperor (Birrell 130-37); Yao (Birrell 238-40); Shun; Yu; and King Tang.

225. Refers to disciples of Confucius (551-479 B.C.), the most influential thinker of China. *Shiji* 47:1905-47.

226. Yan Hui (514-483 B.C.), Confucius's favorite disciple.

227. Tsengcan (505-ca. 436 B.C.), a pupil of Confucius's, noted for filial piety, to whom are ascribed the *Great Learning* and the *Book of Filial Piety*.

228. Zisi (492-431 B.C.), Confucius's grandson.

229. Li Shunfeng (602-70), Tang mathematician.

230. Cheng Hao (1032-85) built his philosophy on the concept of the principle (*li*) of nature; Wing-tsit Chan, *A Sourcebook in Chinese Philosophy* (Princeton: Princeton University Press, 1963), 518-43.

231. Cheng Yi (1033-1107) believed that the way cannot be found outside of material force; Chan, 544-71.

232. Shao Yung (1011-77) believed that the supreme principles governing the universe can be discerned in terms of numbers; Chan, 481-94.

233. Zhou Dunyi (1017-73), the pioneer of Song Neo-Confucian metaphysics and ethics; Chan, 460-80.

234. Zhu Xi (1130-1200), Song synthesizer of Neo-Confucianism.

235. Yan Junping (fl. ca. 34 B.C.), Han Daoist who made a living by telling fortunes at Chengdu; *Hanshu* 72: 3056-3057.

236. Sima Guang (1019-86), the author of *Zizhi tongjian* (Comprehensive mirror for aid in government).

237. Devil Valley Master (Needham 2:206), a leader of the vertical alliance against Qin. *Shiji* 67:2241, 2279.

238. Sun Bin (?378-301 B.C.) learned military arts from Gueigu and helped Wei; *Shiji* 69:2241.

239. Wang Bi (226-49), commentator of the *Book of Changes*.

240. Zhu Yuanzhang (1328-98; r. 1368-98), founder of the Ming.

241. Liu Bei (162-223), founder of the Shu kingdom (221-63).

242. Daoist deities.

The lad who arranges and throws divine sticks,

You who perceive without senses, . . .

Please descend!

The faithful wife Sŏng Ch'unhyang,

Born in the *imja* year,

Lives by a streamside

In Namwŏn, Chŏlla province.

In what month and on what day

Will she be released from prison?

And Yi Mongnyong

Who resides in Samch'ŏng Street in Seoul,

In what month and at what hour

Will he return here?

I humbly beg the spirits to explain clearly.

Now let's see: one, two, three, four, five, six, seven.

Good, it's a lucky number:

Ken, seventh diagram, keeping still, mountain.

The fish plays in the water but avoids a net.

Many a mickle makes a muckle.

Long ago, when King Wen of Zhou was in office,

He drew this diagram

And went home in glory.

Isn't it a good omen?

Knowing they're a thousand tricents apart,

Friends will see each other.

This means your husband

Will come back in the near future

And your sorrow will be over.

Don't worry, all is well.

The blind diviner draws lots from eight thin sticks made of
bamboo or bone and from the numbers etched on them makes
his prediction based on a trigram (or hexagram) in the *Book of*

Changes.[243] He invokes the spirits of sage lords, Confucius and his disciples, a mathematician, diviners, philosophers, traveling persuaders, famous generals, and others to ask when Yi will return. His list of names is random, both Confucian and Daoist, and invoked to impress his client that he is a professional versed in the art. He then draws the lucky number seven and declares that Yi will soon return. Then the blind man becomes an oneiromancer to interpret Ch'unhyang's dream. His diction is heavily Chinese and formal, and smacks of a technical language used in prayers and divination.

CH'UNHYANG'S DREAM

Your dream is a good one.
When the flower falls, the fruit can form;
When the mirror breaks, the sound is loud.
Only when it bears fruit
Will the flower fall.
If the mirror breaks,
Should there not be a sound?
A scarecrow over the door
Makes everyone look up;
When the sea runs dry,
You can see the dragon's face.
When the mountain crumbles, the earth becomes flat.
Good! It's a dream that foretells
You'll ride on a sedan chair drawn by two horses.
[Ch'unhyang sees a crow cawing twice overhead;
She raises her hands to shoo it away.]
Just a moment!
Doesn't the crow caw *kaok kaok*?
That's good.

---

243. For divination by blind people see Murayama Chijun, *Chōsen no senboku to yogen* (Chōsen sōtokufu, 1933), 436-41.

Ka is a graph for good;
Ok for a house.
A beautiful joyful event will come;
Your lifelong sorrow will end.
Don't worry at all.
Even if you were to pay me a thousand *yang*,
I wouldn't take it.
Wait and see.
When you gain riches and honor,
Don't pass me over.
Now I'll take my leave.

What is the origin of her dream? Is it heaven-sent or a message from the unconscious? Is its origin outside or inside the mind? In Penelope's dream of the twenty geese slaughtered by an eagle, the eagle returns and offers its symbolic interpretation:

> But [the eagle] came back again and perched on the jut of
> the gabled roof. He now had a human voice and spoke aloud
>   to me:
> "Do not fear, O daughter of far-famed Ikarios.
> This is no dream, but a blessing real as day. You will see it
> done. The geese are the suitors, and I, the eagle, have been
> a bird of portent, but now I am your own husband come home
> and I shall inflict shameless destruction on all the suitors."
>   (19:544-50)[244]

Just as Penelope's dream is the product of her unconscious thoughts, Ch'unhyang's dream—subjective, symbolic, and foreboding—is coming from inside her mind.

To Jean Paul (1763-1825), a dream is involuntary poetry;[245]

244. Richmond Lattimore, *The Odyssey of Homer* (New York: Harper & Row, 1967), 296.
245. Charles Rycroft, *The Innocence of Dreams* (New York: Pantheon, 1979), 40; and Bert O. States, *The Rhetoric of Dreams* (Ithaca: Cornell University Press, 1988), 77.

to Jung, a mysterious message from our night-aspect;[246] to Bert O. States, one kind of nocturnal thinking;[247] to Charles Rycroft, a private self-to-self communication;[248] to Christopher Evans, based on decades of neurophysiological research, a momentary interception by the conscious mind (while asleep) of material being sorted, scanned, sifted, during REM (rapid eye movement) sleep.[249] Dreaming is a form taken by the imagination during sleep[250]—an activity independent of will, occurring during sleep that is healthy and normal, not pathological.[251] Dreaming occurs during the paradoxical phase of sleep associated with REM.[252]

Ch'unhyang's dream as remembered constitutes its manifest content. She breaks it down into single items instead of apprehending them as a whole. She refrains from making free associations concerning the details of her dream and realizes that its images are oddly combined, hyperbolic, opaque, and cryptic. Her psychic experience does not disguise her emotions and feelings—her emotion precedes the images and can call them into being. The five dissimilar images and the dream plot seem to indicate a combination of fears, physical and psychological pain, and anguish. Coming at the moment of her great extremity, her dream, without beginning and ending, transforms mental excitation into its imagistic equivalents. It is a traumatic dream based on her experience of torture, as well as an anxiety dream evoked by the prospect of her imminent separation from loved ones—her husband and mother. Is it a lucid dream[253]—a quasi-lucid state of consciousness in which she is aware of dreaming? (Experimental research has demonstrated that lucidity is accompanied by normal

246. Rycroft, 53.
247. States, 38.
248. Rycroft, 72, 164.
249. States, 17.
250. Rycroft, 153, 163.
251. Rycroft, 39.
252. Rycroft, 131.
253. David Shulman and Guy G. Stroumsa, eds., *Dream Cultures: Explorations in the Comparative History of Dreaming* (New York: Oxford University Press, 1999), 94, 84-88.

REM.)[254] To qualify as a dream, the report of an awakened sleeper must be visually imagistic.[255]

The basic unit of the dream, States suggests, "is the image, because dream unfolds in the mode of action. It is constantly evolving, never a still picture."[256] The brain, "the tropological machine," thinks images out of feelings and then converts these images to other images along paths of likelihood. "The sequence never follows experience or logic."[257] In the dream state, we "produce images similar to our feelings, we dream like what we feel like."[258] "Every dream image is bitemporal: its present is a collusion of past and future in which [my] attention is trapped between 'something is happening that is going to happen' and 'something is going to happen to what has just happened.'"[259] A dream, Gaston Bachelard says, is hungry for images.[260] It "has no discretion, has a penchant for trivialities, is artless, seems to carry things to extremes,[261] and in it hypothetical and real are identical."[262]

In Korean myths, the mirror of stone, bronze, or silver symbolizes the ruler. A merchant returning from Tang China bought a mirror in the market. When hung on the wall, it revealed a prophecy in sinographs: Wang Kŏn (918-943), the founder of Koryŏ and the son of the heavenly deity, would conquer Silla and the territory of his new kingdom would extend to the Yalu River in the north. Canto 46 of *Songs of Flying Dragons* reads: "Wishing to display his august power, / Heaven induced him to have a game / And caused him to place / Ten silver mirrors." The poem's background is that King Kongmin (1351-1374) of Koryŏ asked the contestants to shoot ten small silver mirrors from eighty paces. General Yi Sŏnggye (1392-1398), the future founder of Chosŏn, hit

---

254. Shulman and Stroumsa, 105.
255. Shulman and Stroumsa, 94.
256. States, 95.
257. States, 93.
258. States, 115-16.
259. States, 145.
260. States, 151-52.
261. States, 145.
262. States, 157, 209.

them with ten arrows. The compilers claim that Heaven caused
the king to hold such a contest in order to display Yi's divine
skill. Moreover, the mirror (*myŏngdo*) is used by the shaman as
a guardian spirit with divine power derived from the sun's bright
light. In folklore and romance, the divided half of the mirror serves
as a token of pledge by lovers and friends. In other versions of
the *Song*, Ch'unhyang and her husband exchange a mirror and a
jade ring. A number of interdictions related to the mirror exist as
proverbs: If you break a mirror, it will bring disaster. If you look at
a broken mirror, you are out of luck. If a woman looks at a mirror
at night, she will be mistreated or deserted. The broken mirror
symbolizes breaking of an engagement, desertion, and death.[263] The
falling of flowers is a recurrent symbol of mutability. A scarecrow,
more likely a straw effigy, hanging over the door is commonly used
in exorcism. The crumbling of Mount Tai and the sea running
dry are conventional images for a cataclysmic change in nature,
world upside down, or end of the world. They are used in vows
and pledges (*When* the roasted chestnuts sprout, *then* . . .), and as a
rhetorical device in the poetry of praise and love. What goes on in
Ch'unhyang's dream, then, is a transformation of feelings, emotions,
and thoughts into their imagistic equivalents.

A dream's meaning is "always outside the text."[264]
Interpretation is "the translation of non-discursive pictorial
statements into words arranged into sentences." [265] The blind
man's oneiric hermeneutic is derived from what he knows about
Ch'unhyang's circumstances outside the dream—her identity and
existential situation. Evoking the discrepancy between surface
and deeper meanings,[266] like Artemidorus (2nd cent. A.D.) in his
Oneirocritica (Taxonomy of Dreams),[267] he reads Ch'unhyang's

263. *Hanguk munhwa sangjing sajŏn* (Dictionary of Korean Myths and
Symbols) (Tonga ch'ulp'ansa, 1992), 43-48.
264. States, 184.
265. Rycroft, 47.
266. Shulman and Stroumsa, 132.
267. Patricia Cox Miller, *Dreams in Late Antiquity*: *Studies in the Imagination of
a Culture* (Princeton: Princeton University Press, 1994), 80.

dream as a semiotic code to predict the future: her dream images are a disguised expression of her real-life situation, but in the different context of the waking world. The blind man finds connections between oneiric image and existential outcome by radical intervention.

The flowers fall—the fruit can form.
The mirror cracks—there is a sound.
A scarecrow hangs over the door—everyone looks up.
The mountain crumbles—you will ride on a sedan chair.
The sea runs dry—you can see the dragon's face.

These are recurrent symbols with culture-specific meaning. All this manifest content of her dream foretells that she will have a happy conjugal life and enjoy riches and honor. (The situation is about to take a sudden turn in Ch'unhyang's favor, but she does not know it.) Dreams lead *into the future*, not into the past. Of course, the anonymous narrator is compelled to offer a happy reading consistent with the ending of the *Song*. The blind man works within a tradition that placed value on dreams. Both Ch'unhyang and Wŏlmae, we recall, believe in the reality of dreams, visions, and supernatural beings. The dream is a cultural discourse shared by all Koreans regardless of social class or religious practices.

Meanwhile, Yi in Seoul studies day and night and passes the civil service examinations with flying colors. The king compliments him and appoints him a secret royal inspector (*amhaeng ŏsa* 暗行御史)[268] of Chŏlla province, the post he has wanted. Then he directs his agents and soldiers to meet at Namwŏn on such and such a day.

---

268. *Hanguk minjok munhwa taebaekkwa sajŏn* 14:581a-82c.

The secret royal inspector was a temporary post during the middle and late Chosŏn dynasty. Under the king's direct control, he was dispatched to provinces to inspect provincial administration, official misrule such as the exaction of illegal taxes and misappropriation of public funds, and the condition of the people. His appointment and duties were kept secret. Before this institution, officials in the Office of the Inspector-General (Sahŏnbu) or the king's close associates conducted their mission in secret. In the mid-seventeenth century, the number of such appointees increased. The king either selected a trustworthy young official or picked one from a list of qualified persons compiled by high ministers. The king then chose the place to be inspected by drawing a stick from a bamboo cylinder containing the names of the country's 360 districts (ch'usaeng 抽栍). If a person received a sealed envelope—his appointment letter—from the king, he was expected to depart immediately and open the envelope only after he had passed through the South or East Gate. If he opened it within the capital's walls or visited his family, he was punished.[269]

The inspector carried with him a document detailing his duties: a horse warrant (map'ae 馬牌)—usually with the image of two horses engraved on one side—that confirmed his authority to mobilize soldiers and servants and use horses kept at the stations. He also carried two brass rulers (yuch'ŏk 鍮尺) to inspect the careless manufacture of implements of punishment and to hold an inquest over a corpse. The death of his parents (or even death of the king) could not stop him from carrying out his job, nor could he return to Seoul without completing his mission. Accompanied by one or two lower-ranking officials, he walked around in disguise, wearing tattered clothes and a crushed cap. He was not expected to inconvenience the village chief and often carried dried cooked rice and camped outside. When necessary he would display the horse

269. The text has, "Yi said good-bye to his parents and left for Chŏlla province," which may be a scribal error. Another lapse is that Ch'unhyang says her mother's age is 60 (31, 105), but Wŏlmae says she is going to be 70 (103).

warrant to disclose his identity. If he found a corrupt magistrate, he would confiscate his official seal and dismiss him from office. Upon returning to Seoul, he submitted a detailed account of his findings (*sŏgye* 書啓)—mistakes of a magistrate, the state of civil and military administration, hidden deeds of a filial son or a chaste woman (*pyŏltan* 別單). The king then ordered the Border Defense Council (Pibyŏnsa) to act on his recommendations. The last inspector was appointed in 1892 by King Kojong (r. 1864-1907), the twenty-sixth ruler of Chosŏn.

Yi's disguise has a narrative function in the economy of the *Song.* The incognito guise of a beggar not only implies the low social status that guarantees anonymity and freedom of movement but also carries a set of literary and extraliterary associations. His disguise conceals his social person, status, education, and speech. It represents his calculated effort to investigate administrative and social problems and realize his goals by manipulating his identity. Since Yi can preserve the secret of his identity from all save his own wife, her maid, and his mother-in-law, the narrative's disguise episodes generate comic, ironic, or dramatic effect, depending on whom he encounters.

On the way to Namwŏn, Yi listens to farmers singing near Kuhwattol, Imsil:

FARMERS' SONG

Ŏyŏro sangsadiya
At the time of peace between heaven and earth,
High is the virtue of our king—
Children sing on the thoroughfare
As they once praised Lord Yao's virtue.

Ŏyŏro sangsadiya
Lord Shun's eminent virtues gave us the tool

And now we plow the field on Mount Li.[270]

Ŏyŏro sangsadiya
Divine Husbandman made the hoe
That has lasted myriad generations.
Wasn't that a noble invention?

Ŏyŏro sangsadiya
Yu of Xia, benevolent ruler,
Controlled nine years' floods.

Ŏyŏro sangsadiya
Tang the Completer of Yin[271]
Suffered seven years of drought.

Ŏyŏro sangsadiya
After tilling the soil
And paying our tax,
Keep what's left
To serve our parents
And feed wife and children.

Ŏyŏro sangsadiya
We plant the hundred plants
That tell the four seasons—
How trustworthy the hundred plants.

Ŏyŏro sangsadiya
High rank and name
Can't be compared to our work.

Ŏyŏro sangsadiya

---

270. Shun is said to have tilled on this mountain; *Shiji* 1:31-39.
271. See Birrell, 128-29, 256-58.

Till the southern fields, plow northern paddies,
Fill our bellies and take it easy.
Ŏnŏlnŏl sangsadiya!

Political rhetoric celebrates farmers as the foundation of the state in China and Korea. Among many regional variations, the farmers' song from Chŏlla is widely known. It is a means of keeping rhythm as farmers work together. The three aspects of such songs are music, function, and verse, and they allow farmers to mesh their efforts and work smoothly and more efficiently together. The lead singer sings alone and the group chorus repeats the same refrain.

At another place on Yi's journey, old farmers wearing bamboo hats and carrying rakes sing a song protesting gray hair:

LET'S PRESENT A PETITION

Let's present a petition! A petition!
If we submit a petition to a heavenly god,
    What should he say?
Let the old not die,
    Let the young never age.
Let's send a petition to a heavenly god.
It's hateful, how hateful!
Gray hair is our enemy.
We try to stop it
With an axe in the right hand,
With thorns in the left.
Strike down the oncoming gray hair,
Pull the ruddy face back,
Bind gray hair in blue threads,
Bind it tight; but
The ruddy face goes on its own,
Gray hairs come back,
Making wrinkles under our ears

Turning black hairs white.
This morning, blue-black strands of silk,
By evening turned to snow.
O heartless time!
Youth's pleasures may be many,
But the days run swiftly by.
Is this not time's nature?
I want to ride a fleet steed,
Ride the highway to Seoul.
I wish to see
Scenic beauty again;
With a beautiful lady beside me,
I wish to enjoy her airs and graces.
Morning flowers and moonlit evening—
All the glories of the seasons.
I cannot see or hear—
Eyes are dim and ears fail,
There is no remedy,
How sad, my friends!
Where are you now?
Like the falling maple leaves
You fall slowly soughing;
Like the dawn stars at daybreak,
You fade away thinly.
What path are you taking?
Ŏyŏro, our work of plowing—
Our life is nothing but
A spring dream!

This inserted song appears mostly in the Wanp'an editions
of the *Song of Ch'unhyang* and concerns capricious time and its
alliance with mortality and death. Change is the witness of human
follies and virtues. Ovidian time devours all things ("Tempus
edax rerum"; *Metamorphoses* 15:234)—constant inconsistency

365

characterizes his world. Time's daunting quality is its undeviating motion, the pervasiveness of change:

> So passeth, in the passing of a day,
> Of mortall life, the leafe, the bud, the flower. (*Faerie Queene*
>> II:12; 75)

Winter functions as "a metaphorical mirror of the speaker's state of mind, a link between his own condition and that of nature."[272] The winter of old age prefigures death's eternal cold. Seasons seem to lead relentlessly to death in winter—the devastation observed gives him the subject of meditation (*ubi sunt*). All things are in perpetual flux—hence his urgent desire to visit scenic spots and enjoy a beauty's graces, but these activities are not outside of time. He even attempts to block the assault of white hair, alluding to U T'ak's (1262-1342) *sijo*:

> Sticks in one hand,
>> Branches in the other,
> I try to block old age with thorn bushes,
>> And white hair with sticks.
> But white hair came by a shortcut,
>> Having seen through my devices.[273]

But he cannot prevail, because time's weapon is change and oblivion. Life lived according to nature yields death, as Tao Qian (365-427), for example, exclaims: "So I manage to accept my lot until the ultimate homecoming" ("The Return").[274] Western pastoral and East Asian nature poetry demand a commitment to the finality of death. The speaker declares at the end, "Life is a spring

---

272. Alan T. Bradford, "Mirror of Mutability: Winter Landscape in Tudor Poetry," *English Literary Renaissance* 4.1 (1974): 3-39, esp. 3, 33.

273. No. 3177 in Sim Chaewan.

274. James R. Hightower, *The Poetry of T'ao Ch'ien* (Oxford: Clarendon, 1970), 270.

dream"—a rehearsal of topos. A human's passing is likened to the falling of leaves and hiding of dawn stars. "Born into the midst of dream-illusion / Why should I submit to dusty bonds? (Tao Qian, "Twenty Poems After Drinking Wine," 8:9-10);[275] "Life in the world is a big dream" (Li Bo, "Waking from Drunkenness on a Spring Day");[276] and, "Man's life is like a dream" (Su Shi [1037-1101], "Recalling Antiquity at Red Cliff").[277] The images of insubstantiality and mutability are summarized in the *Diamond Scripture*:

> As stars, a fault of vision, as a lamp,
> A mock show, dew drops, or a bubble,
> A dream, a lightning flash, or cloud,
> So should one view what is conditioned.[278]

∽

Then Yi meets a youth on the way to Seoul, carrying Ch'unhyang's letter written in blood.

It reads: "I have had no news of you since we parted and pray that you and your parents are in good health. Your lowly wife Ch'unhyang has been beaten and put in the rack. I am at the brink of death. My soul flew to the Temple of the Yellow Tumulus and frequented the demons' quarters. Even if I were to die myriad times, I only know that a chaste wife cannot serve two husbands. Whether I live or die, I don't know what will become of my old mother. Please be kind to her." A heptasyllabic quatrain at the end reads:

> When did you part from me last year?
> Winter has gone, autumn has returned.

---

275. Hightower, 136.

276. Arthur Waley, *Translations from the Chinese* (New York: Vintage, 1971), 122.

277. James J. Y. Liu, *Major Lyricists of the Northern Sung* (Princeton: Princeton University Press, 1974), 139.

278. Edward Conze, *Buddhist Wisdom Books Containing the Diamond Sutra and the Heart Sutra* (London: Allen & Unwin, 1958), 68.

Midnight gales, rain like snow—
Why am I a prisoner in Namwŏn?

The letter is intercepted by the addressee on his way to Namwŏn. He cajoles the carrier into showing it to him and upon reading it sheds tears. He tells the boy that the addressee is a friend who will meet him at Namwŏn tomorrow. The purloined letter is unequivocal and austere. Ch'unhyang's voice seeks to transcend the confines of prison—the unlawful confinement of her body and freedom. What other meanings does the letter evoke that exceed or disrupt her intention? The letter of blood and love reveals her needs and fears. Words are made of flesh and bone, blood and tears. Every sentence conveys unbearable pain and despair. "Your lowly wife Ch'unhyang"—using a humility formula to observe decorum, she refers to herself in the third person.

She is inconsolable. She speaks of the impossibility of speaking of her torture. A primary characteristic of traumatic recollection is the lack of integration into conscious understanding. Her delayed response to emotional and physical trauma, "a blow to the tissues of the body and those of the mind,"[279] takes the form of "repeated intrusive hallucinations, dreams, thoughts, or behavior stemming from the torture, indicating the limits of representation and human understanding."[280] To render her trauma as narrative, she must present a coherent flow of the inconceivable event with death at its center. She thinks, therefore, she is near her death ("I am at the brink of death") and sees the advance of wailing ghosts and demons.

A group of girls washing clothes under Magpie Bridge chatter about Ch'unhyang's sorry state. Yi spots the willow tree where her swing once hung and reaches Ch'unhyang's dilapidated house toward dusk. He then announces himself to Wŏlmae, who

279. Cathy Caruth, ed., *Trauma: Explorations in Memory* (Baltimore: Johns Hopkins University Press, 1995), 183.
280. Caruth, 4.

is shocked to see her son-in-law in ragged clothes, suggesting that he is in trouble or ruined.With Wŏlmae, Yi visits Ch'unhyang in prison.

⌒

Half dreaming and half awake, Ch'unhyang thinks her husband has come, with a gilded cap on his head and a black-rimmed red court robe. They embrace each other and begin to talk of myriad dear memories. When she hears him calling, she asks: "Is that voice real or in a dream? It's a strange voice."

To Wŏlmae: "What are you talking about? You say my husband has come. Can I see him in reality?" [She grasps his hand between the bars and immerses herself in memories and grief.]

To her husband: "*Aego, aego*! Is it really you? I must be dreaming. Now I can easily see the one I have longed for. I have no regrets even if I should die. Why were you so heartless? Mother and I are wretched. Since you left, I have passed days and nights thinking of you; for days and months my heart has been burning. I have been beaten till I was almost dead. Have you come to save me? I don't care whether I live or die, but what has happened to you?"

To her mother: "I longed for my husband in Seoul as people long for rain after seven years' drought. Did he long for me? A tree planted gets rotten, the stupa built with labor collapses. Alas, there is no help for my lot. Mother, please let me feel no regret after I'm gone. The silk coat I used to wear is in the inlaid wardrobe. Please, take it out and exchange it for the best ramie cloth from Hansan and make him a decent coat. Sell my white silk skirt and buy him a horsehair hat, headband, and shoes. My silver hairpin shaped like a rice cake with imprinted flower patterns, my encased ceremonial knife with amber handle, my jade ring in the box—sell them too and make him an unlined inner jacket and short pants. Sell the contents in the drawers of wardrobes with dragon and phoenix designs for what you can get and use the money to buy him dainty side dishes. After I am dead, look after him as though I were still alive."

To her husband: "Listen, my beloved husband. Tomorrow is the magistrate's birthday. If he gets drunk, he will probably summon me and beat me. Unkempt hair tied up on my head, I will stagger along to the yamen and be beaten to death. Then pick up my body like a hired man and take it to Lotus Hall where we spent our first nights, lay me out with your own hands in a quiet place, dress me for burial, and comfort my soul. Please don't remove my clothes but bury me as I am in a sunny place. Then, after you have achieved high office, come back and rebury me in a fine linen shroud. Have me borne in a simple but elegant bier, not to the front or back of Mount South but straight to Seoul, and bury me near your ancestral plot. On my epitaph carve eight graphs: "Grave of Ch'unhyang, Chaste Wife, Unjustly Killed." It will serve as a legendary stone by which a constant wife awaited her husband, perished, and finally turned to stone. The sun that sets behind the western hills will rise again tomorrow; but poor Ch'unhyang, once gone, will never return. Requite my wrongs. *Aego, aego*! My wretched lot! My poor mother will lose me and, destitute, become a beggar, asking for food from house to house, and doze off here and there beneath the hill. When her strength fails and dies, the jackdaws from Mount Chiri, flapping their wings and cawing, will peck out her eyes, with no offspring standing by to scare them away. *Aego, aego*!"

Ch'unhyang blames him for his silence and can only register a skeptical expression of disbelief, "What has happened to you?" But she reveals a great deal about herself when she pleads with her mother to take care of him after her death. Yi arrives in Namwŏn on the day before Magistrate Pyŏn's birthday—the "nick-of-time" motif associated with hopes of his return. The narrator does not wish Ch'unhyang to die. But the only way to keep her alive is through an intervention from someone, such as a royal inspector, with more power and authority than the current brutal magistrate. The convergence of husband and beggar attests to the capacity of

여스가춘향
을옥에가
찻다

From
Okchunghwa,
n.p., n.d.

disguise to misrepresent reality, but Ch'unhyang's faithfulness to Yi does not diminish. She does not know the telos toward which the narrative rushes forward—her husband's identity is withheld from her. The audience/reader knows more about Ch'unhyang's situation, foreseeing an outcome contrary to her expectations.

Similarly, knowledge held by the audience/reader is withheld from other characters. When Yi is appointed royal inspector, the audience/reader knows that Magistrate Pyŏn will be dismissed, but Pyŏn himself does not know. Before his identity is revealed, Yi meets with farmers (who blame Yi for his long absence while his wife is suffering from Pyŏn's tyranny), a letter carrier, Wŏlmae, Ch'unhyang's maid, jailors and other minor officials. When Yi appears as a beggar to Wŏlmae, she cries out in disappointment, but the audience/reader chuckles. Finally, Yi pretends to be another evil magistrate asking Ch'unhyang to be his mistress while she lays bare her heart, uttering her fidelity to Yi. All these instances of dramatic irony provoke the audience/reader to observe the true mind of a given character and experience a heightened response. Ch'unhyang does not despair even if her husband is a ruined gentleman. She is more concerned about those who will live on: she prays that Yi will become a renowned official and take care of her mother. The audience/reader finds her last injunctions heroic. She thinks that she will die the following day, beaten by Pyŏn, but the audience/reader knows that she will be saved.

At Pyŏn's birthday party, Yi is given a seat and proposes that everyone compose a verse on a given rhyme. His heptasyllabic quatrain goes:

Fine wine in a golden cup is a thousand people's blood,
Viands on jade dishes are a thousand people's flesh.
When the grease of the candles drips, the people's tears are
    falling;
When the noise of music is loud, the people's grudges grow
    louder.

Pyŏn and his officials fail to fathom the intent of the verse. Yi then collects his troops who shout, "The Royal Inspector comes." Yi removes Pyŏn from office and suspends the administration. Ch'unhyang, together with others wrongly jailed, is brought in. Yi then puts his wife to the test ("Will you refuse to be my mistress?"), and she makes the last public declaration of her fidelity: "All you officials who come here are indeed *notorious*. Please, listen to me, inspector in embroidered robes! Can the wind break the layered rocks of a cliff? Can the snow change the verdure of the pine and bamboo? Do not ask such a thing. Have me killed quickly!" Only then does the inspector say: "Raise your eyes and look at me!" When she sees that the new inspector on the dais is none other than her own husband, she half laughs and half cries. There is no limit to her joy—this is the recognition (*anagnorisis*) scene for which the narrative has prepared the reader, an instant reversal of fortune (*peripeteia*), the most dramatic scene in the *Song*.[281]

What's in a Name?

The name Ch'unhyang literally means "spring fragrance." We may conjecture all the wonderful qualities associated with spring—rebirth of nature, awakening of love, birth of song, harmony between nature and humankind. The second graph, *hyang,* means fragrance, sweet-smelling, savory, perfume, and incense. Probaby no literati family would name their daughter so, because it is traditionally given as a professional name for

---

281. Terence Cave, *Recognitions: A Study in Poetics* (Oxford: Clarendon, 1988), 27-54.

an entertainer or public performer. The two graphs—*ch'un* and *hyang*—have few homonyms and little chance for paronomasia—no play on the sounds of her name. The name does not hint at a social identification by paternity or genealogical reference. Is it adequate for the heroine of the *Song of Ch'unhyang*? She plays the most vital role in the narrative, the central character with the greatest positive agency in the plot, but her name does not in fact display her full dimensionality. Even with the extratextual clue provided in the title of the work, *yŏllyŏ* (a woman who prefers to die rather than remarry or take another lover) and *sujŏl* (to remain chaste, not remarry), does it fix her heroic character and destiny? She is a woman with stout heart and steadfast mind and her own prodigious virtue, a heroine who has made the hard choice that no one else can, capable of enduring the most arduous and severe ordeal. A mere woman with the name Ch'unhyang is allowed to act like a mighty hero, and the fame of her fidelity shall never die—indeed, Ch'unhyang in Korean literature is synonymous with a woman "who maintains chastity even unto death" for the sake of her love. Is the secret of her name a mystery? Remember what it literally says, suggests Wŏlmae: spring fragrance comes from flowers. She is a goddess of spring, a mistress of flowers, a messenger of love, a symbol of youth and joy, and Yi's beloved.

⤴

P'ansori, a multivoiced genre before the arrival of the Western polyphonic "novel" in Korea, has been a "means of joining people in the immediacy of performance."[282] It is a supreme form of projecting emotional energy. "With its fluidity, dynamism, connectedness, and particularity," *p'ansori* answers the audience's emotional needs. It combines the literati culture of the classical tradition and the language spoken by everyday people, "superior to those that are

---

282. Doane and Pasternack, 139.

merely written and not intimately connected with speech."[283] The spoken language is "a mediator between humanity, nature, power, ideas, and god."[284] Every version may "displace, excise, add, but can never touch what gives the song life and meaning."[285]

Ch'unhyang was invented by a male author who created a feminine voice to speak for him and for other men and women. Working within a particular cultural and ideological climate, this anonymous male author, a protofeminist, presents a feminocentric song that sings the primacy of female experience. Composing within the antecedent canon of *p'ansori*, he manages the feat of pleasing both the lettered and the unlettered—one audience who can listen to a performance but cannot read, and another who can enjoy both a performed version and the text. He is able to internalize a female subject's position to present it and valorize certain qualities cherished by culture. In the eyes of Yi Mongnyong and the reigning king, for example, Ch'unhyang represents an ideal preexisting in their minds. Our author has textual authority but no political authority. The social consensus embodied in the narrative enables a participating response shared by his fellow human beings. He understands the complexities of a bicultural society in which literary Chinese and the vernacular interacted with vernacular orality. Exploring to the fullest the Korean luxurious indulgence in consonants and vowels, and with a passion for the concrete sensory world, he has an enviable lexical range and verbal ability and his marriage of sound and sense conveys exhilarating wonder at the world's plenitude.

Why are the characters in the *Song of Ch'unhyang* so real? Is it because they are so individual? Certainly the main characters are true to their kind and environment.[286] That is, for example, there is

---

283. Maria Rosa Menacol, *Shards of Love: Exiles and the Origins of the Lyric* (Durham: Duke University Press, 1994), 101.

284. Zumthor, *Towards a Medieval Poetics*, 20.

285. Zumthor, *Towards a Medieval Poetics*, 191.

286. Among Northrop Frye's five literary modes—myth, romance, high mimetic, low mimetic, and ironic—our song is a work in the low mimetic mode. See *Anatomy of Criticism: Four Essays* (New York: Atheneum, 1968), 33-66, esp.

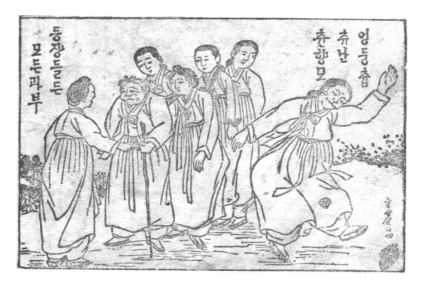

no machinery (*deus ex machina*)—supernatural beings who take
part in the action of a *p'ansori* as in the *Song of Sim Ch'ŏng* and the
Song of Hŭngbo. In the former, the Jade Emperor orders the dragon
kings of the four seas to save the filial daughter Sim Ch'ŏng who,
in order for her blind father to regain his eyesight, volunteers to be
cast away as a human sacrifice to appease the gods of the Yellow Sea.
In the latter, a grateful swallow brings the poor but good Hŭngbo
a magic gourd seed that yields worldly treasures. Ch'unhyang in a
written version rises off the printed page and comes fully alive. She
is a whole human being, a whole woman—virtuous, passionate,
intelligent, capable, dynamic, and genuine, attributes that make her
exemplary. "Personal autonomy is a way of living in harmony with
one's true self."[287] Secondary studies mention popular narratives
that may have inspired the *Song*: a tale of redressing a grievance—a
female entertainer named Ch'unhyang dies of unrequited love for
a son of the upper class; a tale of famous royal inspectors—No
Chin (1518-1578), Cho Sik (1501-1572), Sŏng Isŏng (1595-1664), Kim
Uhang (1649-1723), Pak Munsu (1691-1756); a love story between an

---

34, and Robert D. Denham, *Northrop Frye and Critical Method* (University Park:
Pennsylvania State University Press, 1978), 3 passim.

287. Diana T. Meyers, *Self, Society and Personal Choice* (New York: Columbia
University Press, 1989), 20.

upper-class man and an entertainer; and a tale of a faithful woman, especially a faithful female entertainer. Whatever the kernel, our song acquired artistic quality by combining colloquial and literary styles suitable to contemporary sensibility. Some have tried to identify a historical person behind each character; others complain that Yi could not have become an inspector in such a short period of time; some have even ventured to propose a historical person as the real author, such as Cho Kyŏngnam (1570-1641), which has created a rumpus among students of the *Song*.[288]

Ch'unhyang has been commemorated with a shrine, a grave, a theme park, a culture center, and a monument erected to honor the good administration of Sŏng Anŭi (1561-1629), who served as magistrate of Namwŏn in 1607. She has become a contemporary myth. A traditional folk festival is held in Namwŏn to commemorate her birthday on Double Eight (eighth day of the fourth lunar month), rather than on Double Five, the day she meets Student Yi. Her shrine was erected in 1931, and the festival in her honor has been held by the citizens of Namwŏn since 1986, with some 200,000 people in attendance to view dancing, musical performances, games such as archery contests, *sijo* singing, and choosing a young girl thought to embody Ch'unhyang's character and spirit as a twenty-first-century clone. On every Saturday of April 2008, for example, the Ch'unhyang Culture and Art Center and National Center for Folk Performing Arts presented a film and drama version, a *p'ansori* version sung by a professional singer (An Suksŏn, an intangible cultural asset), and a dance, "Echo of Love," to commemorate the late singer and intangible cultural asset Kim Sohŭi (1917-1995), who recorded the song. The *Song of Ch'unhyang* is not only a work of *p'ansori*, fully imagined, but also a lisible text, one that with each reading yields more pleasure. The fullness of response it creates in the reader is the measure of its success, and its literary quality will ensure its lasting permanence in cultural memory.

---

288. Sŏl Sŏnggyŏng's proposal in *Ch'unhyang chŏn ŭi pimil* (Sŏuldae ch'ulp'anbu, 2001), 19-20.

Atta Kim

The Portrait 1990-1991   (images are 90 × 113 cm, 30 × 40 cm)

The Portrait 002, 1991, chromogenic print 8

The Portrait 003, 1991, chromogenic print 68

The Portrait 004, 1990, chromogenic print 134

The Portrait 007, 1990, chromogenic print 170

The Portrait 009, 1991, chromogenic print 250

Deconstruction 1991-1995   (images are 115 × 155 cm, 50 × 60 cm)

Deconstruction 022, 1993, chromogenic print 116

Deconstruction 030, 1992, chromogenic print 34

Deconstruction 037, 1993, chromogenic print 64

Deconstruction 038, 1993, chromogenic print 78

The Museum Project 1995-2002   (images are 122 × 162 cm, 56 × 66 cm)

The Museum Project #001, The Field Series, 1995, chromogenic print 200

The Museum Project #011, The Field Series, 1995, chromogenic print 200

The Museum Project #002, The Field Series, 1995, chromogenic print 201

The Museum Project #079, The War Veteran Series, 1999, chromogenic print 202

The Museum Project #046, The People Series, 1998, chromogenic print 203

The Museum Project #050, The People Series, 1998, chromogenic print 204

The Museum Project #022, The Holocaust Series, 1997, chromogenic print 205

The Museum Project #022, The Holocaust Series, 1997, chromogenic print 206

ON-AIR Project 2002-Present

ON-AIR Project 16-8, The India Series, Chandini Chowk in Old Delhi, eight-hour exposure, 2007, chromogenic print, 188 × 248 cm, 96 × 126 cm 191

ON-AIR Project 150-4, The China Series, Tiananmen Square in Beijing, eight-hour exposure, 2007, chromogenic print, 191 × 312 cm, 106 × 172 cm 192

ON-AIR Project 150-28, The China Series, Nanjing Road in Shanghai, eight-hour exposure, 2007, chromogenic print, 158 × 312 cm, 106 × 209 cm 192

ON-AIR Project 150-35, The China Series, Nanjing Road in Shanghai, eight-hour exposure, 2007, chromogenic print, 158 × 312 cm, 106 × 209 cm 193

ON-AIR Project 110-1, The New York Series, Times Square, eight-hour exposure, 2005, chromogenic print, 188 × 248 cm, 96 × 126 cm 194

ON-AIR Project 110-2, The New York Series, Times Square, eight-hour exposure, 2005, chromogenic print, 188 × 248 cm, 96 × 126 cm 195

ON-AIR Project 051, Couples, Fifteen Couples, 2004, chromogenic print, 188 × 233 cm, 96 × 118 cm 196

ON-AIR Project 08, Reclining Woman, Fifteen Women, 2005, chromogenic print, 188 × 233 cm, 96 × 118 cm 197

ON-AIR Project 0043-1, Suwolgwaneum, Fifteen Women, 2004, chromogenic print, 188 × 233 cm, 96 × 118 cm 198

ON-AIR Project 082, Maria, Fifteen Couples, 2005, chromogenic print, 188 × 233 cm, 96 × 118 cm 198

ON-AIR Project 043, Bangasayu, Fifteen Men, 2004, chromogenic print, 188 × 233 cm, 96 × 118 cm 199

"Map of Namwŏn," in Kim Sayŏp, *Kyoju haeje Ch'unhyang chŏn: Yŏllyŏ Ch'unhyang sujŏl ka,* Hagwŏnsa, 1962. Courtesy of Peter Lee. 256

Images Courtesy of Adan mungo*

Yi Hae-jo, *Okchunghwa,* Pangmun sŏgwan, 1912. 260

Okchunghwa, n.p., n.d. 264

Hyŏnt'o hanmun Ch'unhyang chŏn, Tongch'ang sŏok, 1917. 270

Uri tul chŏn, Sinmyŏng sŏrim, 1924. 274

Okchunghwa, Pangmun sŏgwan, 1929. 279

Ŏnmun Ch'unhyang chŏn, Taegu: Chaejŏndang sŏp'o, n.d. 282

Man'go chŏngyŏl Ch'unhyang chŏn, Pangmun sŏgwan, 1921. 286

Man'go chŏngyŏl Yŏjunghwa, Sammunsa, 1935. 290

Okchung chŏldae kain, Yŏch'ang sŏgwan, 1925. 295

Okchung chŏldae kain, Yŏch'ang sŏgwan, 1925. 303

Kim Sayŏp, *Ch'unhyang chŏn,* Taeyang ch'ulp'ansa, 1952. 316

Okchung chŏldae kain, Yŏch'ang sŏgwan, 1925. 327

Man'go chŏngyŏl Yŏjunghwa, Sammunsa, 1935. 337

Okchunghwa, n.p., n.d. 340

Okchunghwa, n.p., n.d. 371

Okchung chŏldae kain, Yŏch'ang sŏgwan, 1925. 375

* *Books were published in Seoul unless otherwise noted.*

378

*AZALEA generally adheres to the McCune-Reischauer system in transcribing Korean into English. However, many Korean contributors have not followed this convention, and we respect their way of writing their names in English. Names are alphabetically ordered by last name.

Cindy Chen is a graduate of the University of British Columbia and attends Boston University Law School. Her translations of Pyun Hye-Young's stories appear in *Acta Koreana,* June 2009.

Don Mee Choi lives and works in Seattle. She is the translator of *When the Plug Gets Unplugged* (Tinfish, 2005), *Anxiety of Words* (Zephyr, 2006), and *Mommy Must Be a Fountain of Feathers* (Action Books, 2008). She is currently translating Kim Hyesoon's *Tangsin ŭi ch'ŏt.*

Jean-Marie Gustave Le Clézio (J. M. G. Le Clézio), a French novelist, poet, and philosopher, was awarded the Nobel Prize for Literature in 2008. A world traveler and student of early cultures, he was described by the Swedish Academy as an "author of new departures, poetic adventure and sensual ecstasy, explorer of a humanity beyond and below the reigning civilization." His daring novel *Le Procès-Verbal* won the 1963 Prix Renaudot, launching his distinguished literary career. A frequent visitor to South Korea, Le Clézio has taught French language and literature at Ewha Womans University in Seoul since 2007.

K.E. Duffin is an artist and writer living in Somerville, Massachusetts. She studied at the School of the Museum of Fine Arts, Boston, where she learned printmaking. Her work has been exhibited internationally and is in the collections of the Boston Athenaeum, the Boston Public Library, and the DeCordova Museum. She received a Massachusetts Cultural Council Artist Grant in 2005 and a Berkshire Taconic A.R.T. grant in 2007. Her first book of poems, *King Vulture*, was published by the University of Arkansas Press.

Bruce Fulton and **Ju-Chan Fulton** are the translators of several volumes of modern Korean fiction, most recently *The Red Room: Stories of Trauma in Contemporary Korea* (University of Hawai'i Press, 2009). Bruce Fulton is the inaugural holder of the Young-Bin Min Chair in Korean Literature and Literary Translation, Department of Asian Studies, University of British Columbia.

Gong Sun Ok is from Koksŏng, in South Chŏlla Province. She studied Korean literature at Chŏnnam National University. She debuted as a writer in 1991 when her first novella, "Seed Fire" was published. Since then, she has had many works of fiction published including several collections of short stories, novels, and children's stories. Her works have been recognized by many literary awards, including the Manhae Literary Award, the Shin Tong-yŏp Literary Fund Prize for This Year's Young Artist, and the O Yŏng-su Literary Prize.

Haïlji, born at Kyŏngju in 1955, studied creative writing at Chung-ang University in Seoul and earned a doctoral degree in France. Currently he is a professor at Dongduk Women's University where he teaches creative writing. His fiction published in Korea consists of ten novels, the first five constituting the provocative *Kyŏngmajang* (*Racetrack*) series. Several of his works have been made into movies or plays, including the film *The Road to the Racetrack*. He has written poetry in English and French and published *Blue Meditation of the Clocks* (Pine Press, 1994) and *Les Hirondelles dans mon tiroir* (Editions Librairie-Galerie Racine, 2003).

Han Kang was born in Kwangju, Korea, in 1960 and studied Korean literature at Yonsei University. She began her writing career when one of her poems was featured in the winter issue of the quarterly *Literature and Society*. She made her official literary debut in the following year when her short story "The Scarlet Anchor" was the winning entry in the daily *Seoul Shinmun* spring literary contest. Since then, she has gone on to win the Yi Sang Literary Prize, Today's Young Artist Award, and the Korean Literature Novel Award. Currently she teaches creative writing at the Seoul Institute of the Arts. Her major works include the short story collections *A Convict's Love* and *The Fruit of My Woman* and the novels *Dark Deer*, *Your Cold Hands*, and *The Vegetarian*. She has also published the essay collections *Love and All Surrounds Love* and *A Quiet, Still Song*.

Janet Hong is a writer and translator living in Toronto, Canada. She won the grand prize for her translation of Ha Seong-nan's "The Woman Next Door" in the 32nd *Korea Times* Modern Literature Translation Contest, and was the recipient of a grant from the Korea Literature Translation Institute. She is currently completing the final year of her M.F.A. in creative writing.

Minsoo Kang is an assistant professor of European history at the University of Missouri – St. Louis. He is the author of the short story collection *Of Tales and Enigmas* and co-editor of the essay anthology *Visions of the Industrial Age, 1830-1914: Modernity and the Anxiety of Representation in European Culture*. His book on the history of the automaton in the European imagination, *Sublime Dreams of Living Machines*, will be published by Harvard University Press in 2010.

Ki Hyŏng-do (1960-1989) began publishing his poems in 1985 with "Gog." Working as a reporter, he published poetry until his unexpected death due to a stroke in March 1989. *The Black Leaf in My Mouth*, his first book of poetry, prepared by the poet himself, was published two months after his death and immediately earned critical acclaim and exceptional popularity among young readers, becoming one of the best-selling books of poetry in Korea to this day. *The Complete Works of Ki Hyŏng-do* was published in 1999.

Atta Kim was born in South Korea in 1956. His solo exhibition, *AttaKim: ON-AIR*, was accepted for the Collateral Events of the 53rd International Art Exhibition La Biennale di Venezia in 2009. He also has had solo exhibitions at the

International Center of Photography, New York, in 2006; Leeum Samsung Museum of Art, Rodin Gallery, Seoul, in 2008; the Society of Contemporary Photography, Kansas, in 2001; the Nikon Salon, Tokyo, in 1993; and has participated in numerous group exhibitions, including shows at the National Museum of Contemporary Art, Gwacheon, Korea, in 2008; the Museum of Contemporary Photography, Chicago, in 2007; *Sotheby's Contemporary Art Asia: Presenting 30 Top Asian Artists,* Miami, in 2007; Gwangju Biennale in 2004; the Australian Center for Photography, Sydney, in 2002; Haus der Kulturen der Welt, Berlin, in 2002; the 25th Sao Paulo Biennale in 2002; the traveling exhibition *Translated Acts: Performance and Body Art from East Asia* in 2001; FotoFest, Houston, in 2000; and the Odens Foto Triennale, Odens, Denmark, in 2000. Atta Kim received several awards including the 6th Hachonghyun Art Award; 6th Dong-gang Photo Prize; 4th Lee Myoung Dong Photo Prize; 1st Hanam International Photo Prize, and Annual Artist's Prize of *Photography Art* magazine in 1997. His work has been collected by several institutions, including the Microsoft Art Collection; the Museum of Fine Arts, Houston; the Los Angeles County Museum of Art; the National Museum of Contemporary Art, Seoul; and the Samsung Museum of Modern Art, Seoul. The publications of Atta Kim, including *The Museum Project* from Aperture Foundation (2005), *Atta Kim: ON-AIR* from ICP and Steidl (2006), *Atta Kim- water does not soak in rain*, and *Atta Kim ON-AIR EIGHTHOURS* from Hatje Cantz (2009), are also available. (http://www.attakim.com).

Elizabeth Yeonkyung Kim did her undergraduate work in English literature and her master's studies in East Asian studies at the University of Toronto. She is a master's student in the Department of Korean Literature at Seoul National University.

Kim Hyesoon is one of the most innovative and important contemporary South Korean poets. She has received numerous prestigious poetry awards and is the first woman to receive the Kim Su-yŏng and Mi-dang literary awards. Most recently, her book,

Tangsin ŭi ch'ŏt (2008) was awarded the Daesan Literary Award. Her poems in translation are in *When the Plug Gets Unplugged* (Tinfish, 2005), *Anxiety of Words* (Zephyr, 2006), and *Mommy Must Be a Fountain of Feathers* (Action Books, 2008). Kim Hyesoon also writes literary criticism and essays about her travels in Asia. She lives in Seoul and teaches at the Seoul Institute of the Arts.

Kyung Hyun Kim is associate professor of East Asian Languages and Literatures at the University of California, Irvine. He also holds a joint appointment in the Department of Film and Media Studies. His essays and reviews have appeared in *Cinema Journal*, *Film Quarterly*, *positions: east asia cultures critique*, and *Film Comment*. He is also one of the co-producers of *Never Forever* (a feature film directed by Gina Kim and starring Vera Farmiga and Ha Jung Woo) and the author of *The Remasculinization of Korean Cinema* (Duke University Press, 2004). He has just completed a new book manuscript, tentatively titled *Virtual Cinema: Korean Cinema of the Global Era*.

Peter H. Lee is professor emeritus of Korean and Comparative Literature at the University of California, Los Angeles, and the author and editor of some twenty books.

Susanna Lim, assistant professor at Robert Donald Clark Honors College at the University of Oregon, teaches Russian literature and culture. Focusing on Russian orientalism, she has published articles in many journals, including *Intertext*, *Slavic Review*, and *Slavic and East European Journal*. She is currently working on a book-length study of Russian perceptions of China and Japan during the nineteenth and twentieth centuries.

Pyun Hye-Young was born in 1972 in Seoul. She graduated from Seoul Institute of Arts and Hanyang University where she earned a master's degree. She began publishing in 2000 and published two collections of stories, *Aoi Garden* (2005) and *To the Kennels* (2007). She was awarded the Hanguk Ilbo Literary Prize in 2007.

Chae-Pyong Song is associate professor of English at Marygrove College in Detroit, Michigan, where he has taught since 2001. He has published articles on modern fiction, as well as translations of Korean poetry and fiction. His fields of interest include 20th-century English literature, postcolonial literature, and globalization of culture.

Jane Suh is a recent graduate of the University of British Columbia with a B.A. in Speech Sciences. She has translated several works by Gong Sun Ok and has had the privilege of participating in the International Communication Foundation's translation workshop this year. She is currently working and living in a group home, sharing the joys and struggles with individuals who have developmental disabilities.

Gabriel Sylvian is a graduate student in modern Korean literature. His project seeks to internationalize the Korean GLBTIQ human rights issue through translations of same-sex works from Korea written by both identitarian and non-identitarian authors, and the production of same-sex discourses within Korean academia. He is currently translating the complete works of Ki Hyŏng-do. (http://www.myspace.com/gabsylv).

Yun Young-su was born in 1952 in Seoul. She graduated from the Department of Education at Seoul National University where she studied history education. She debuted as a creative writer in 1990 when her short story "Saengtae kwanch'al" was selected for the debut award by, and appeared in, *Hyŏndae sosŏl*. Her publications include the novels *Sarang hara hŭimang ŏpsi*, and *Ch'akhan saram Mun Sŏng-hyŏn,* for which she won the Hanguk Ilbo Literary Prize in 1997, and *Charin'gobi ui chugum ul aedo ham*. Her recent publications include a collection of her short stories in two volumes entitled *Nae yŏchach'ingu ŭi kwiyŏun yŏnae* [My girlfriend's sweet love affair] and *Nae an ŭi hwangmuji* [The wasteland in me].